Happy Hiking

TAKE 2

Happy Hiking

On the Appalachian Trail with Shortcake

TAKE 2

Emily M. Leonard

Edited by Elaine Starner, ElaineStarner.com

Cover and interior designs by Chris Berge, Bergedesign.com

Photo Editor: Ryan Leighton

Photographs by Bruce A. Leonard, Sharon Cassidy, Emily M. Leonard, and a few other anonymous hikers

Summary: *Happy Hiking Take 2* is an autobiographical account of Emily M. Leonard's second thru-hike of the Appalachian Trail and Sharon Cassidy's first long-distance hike.

ISBN 978-1-7361568-7-2 (paperback bw)
ISBN 979-8-9903939-0-5 (paperback color)
ISBN 979-8-9903939-1-2 (ebook)

Other titles written by the Author
Happy Hiking
Black Bear's Adventure
Black Bear's Adventure Companion Book
Trail Journal
As Fresh As Daisies
The 123s of the Appalachian Trail
The ABCs of the Appalachian Trail

The author can be reached through her website: EmilysEscapades.com

Some names have been changed to protect the privacy of the individuals.

Printed in the United States of America

Life was meant for
good friends
and
great adventures!

This book is dedicated to Sharon "Shortcake" Cassidy.
If it weren't for you, neither one of my
Appalachian Trail thru-hikes
would have taken place.
You are the example of
"When the dream is big enough,
the facts don't count."

Contents

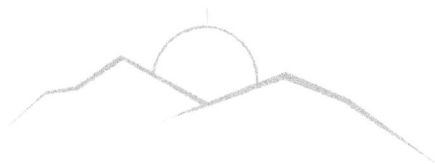

Prologue

STOP!!!

*I*f you haven't read *Happy Hiking: Falling in Love on the Appalachian Trail,* my first memoir in this series, put this book down, grab a copy of *Happy Hiking,* brew yourself a cup of coffee or tea or a shot of tequila, sit in your favorite chair, and be ready to laugh and cry your way from Springer Mountain in Georgia to the top of Katahdin in Maine. Then come back here.

Naw, just kidding, you still will crack a smile and shed a tear with *Happy Hiking Take 2.* It isn't possible to write about hike number two without the experiences of hike number one. But I do make many references back to my first hike that will enhance your enjoyment of this book if you have read *Happy Hiking: Falling in Love on the Appalachian Trail.* With that said, a reader will still thoroughly enjoy each volume solo.

Pre-hike reflections

1

And So It Begins, Again

"One and done!"

Two months into my first Appalachian Trail thru-hike, I vowed to never long-distance hike again. I hated it! I hated the cold! I hated the heat! I hated being wet, either from rain, from sweat, or both at the same time! I hated my food and always being hungry! I hated hurting! My feet raged in protest with every step I took. I was tired and I was miserable. I found no joy in being on the trail under such conditions.

I can't remember exactly when, during my 2015 hike, I began saying, "One and done," but I knew I was never going to long-distance hike again. Hiking day after day with a heavy pack was not for me. I wasn't going to quit. I am not a quitter, but one and done was good for me. I even remember saying a few times, "If I never hike a long trail again, it will be too soon." I complained so much that hikers around me wondered if I would even make it to Katahdin that year.

When I wasn't thinking about all the yuck, I absolutely loved it. I loved the way the sun warmed my skin and the birds sang in the trees. I loved the flash of a deer tail and the owls hooting at night. I liked the way the woods would change in character depending on what type of trees were growing there. I loved the people I was meeting. But at times, it was hard to remember the good in the middle of the bad.

In hindsight, I learned to embrace all the yuck. The yuck made me stronger. The yuck made me more perceptive. The yuck made me more grateful. Sometime between hating the trail and finishing the trail, I changed. My first memoir, *Happy Hiking: Falling in Love on the Appalachian Trail*, tells how the trail broke me down only to rebuild a new me. No longer did I despise the misery; rather, I respected it. The tough stuff made me appreciate the smallest of small details and taught me to enjoy the simplicity of it all and of life in general.

In 2015, I asked August, a six-time thru-hiker, why he thru-hiked the A.T. as many times as he had. He never gave a definitive answer. Instead, he replied, "Ask yourself that same question when you have been home a month." I can remember as clear as spring water my response. In no uncertain terms, I informed him there was *nothing* that could make me thru-hike again.

But three weeks post-hike, not even a month, I was begging to get back to the trail!

I couldn't handle life in the real world. I was having nightmares, panic attacks, and a host of other irrational behaviors. My diagnosis was post-trail depression. I had heard about this in my pre-hike planning but sloughed it off as though it wasn't really a *thing*, rather, just a saying. I was wrong. It is all too real among thru-hikers. So it was no surprise a year later when my friend Sharon, whose idea it was in the first place to hike the Appalachian Trail, asked me if I wanted to hike the A.T. again and I said, "YES!!!"

"Yes! Yes! Yes! I will go again! When?" And just like the that, planning for a second Appalachian Trail thru-hike began. It was only fitting the invite to go on this adventure came via a text message. since that's how my first thru-hike came to be. But this time my excitement was beyond ecstatic.

In 2013 Sharon had texted me, asking, "Do you want to hike the AT?" My initial emotions were neutral and kind of humdrum. Sure, I was happy to be asked and was intrigued, but I knew nothing about the Appalachian Trail, so I had nothing on which to base my response. A year after completing my first thru-hike and three years after her first text, I knew exactly what an affirmative answer to that question would mean and I was all in!

This would be Sharon's debut hike. While it was her idea back in 2013 to go on an AT adventure, life threw her a huge knuckleball. Her for-better-or-for-worse and happily-ever-after ended. The pain, sorrow, and dealings of a divorce kept her from hiking in 2015. But I was ready. I was too pumped up and excited not to continue with my plans, so I went without her. Fast forward to 2016, Sharon's game smoothed out, and she was ready to step up to the plate again. She didn't want to hike alone, hence, her text to me asking if I was up for take two on the A.T.

Just as before, planning started as soon as we got off the phone, but this time with much more vigor. I am easily excitable. I tend to be the type of person who gets an idea and runs with it, planning as much as I can, as fast as I can. Usually, this jumping in produces little value, but it does create excitement. Sharon, on the other hand, is more of the let-the-idea-hang-out-there kind of gal who doesn't waste good energy on the what-ifs. Her words and actions are few but mighty.

———

For most hikers, a huge part of the experience is the pre-hike planning. This time, I had the experience of a completed thru-hike to draw from, which elevated my enthusiasm even more. My mind raced as thoughts bounced around in my head.

We need to stay at Green Mountain House Hostel.
Oh, we have to remember to bring…
We can skip that place.
The River's Edge has great hamburgers.
I need a new pack.
I should check with Bruce to see if he minds if I hike again.
Hot Springs is a must!
Should we go to Trail Days this year?
Ohhh, I can't wait to eat half a gallon of ice cream again!
Oh dear! I haven't even finished my first memoir yet!

A multi-ball pinball game ping-ponged in my head, and with each ricocheting thought, I heard the bells sounding and saw the lights blinking. Stimulus overload for sure. It was like I was having a "positive" panic attack, if there is such a thing.

During my 2015 hike, I learned how to control my panic attacks. I wasn't, and I am still not, always successful, but at least now I can recognize one coming on and I possess the skills to stop them. So instead of letting the noise and lights of my thoughts run rampant in my mind, I took a deep breath (like I did when I got lost after crossing Max Patch in 2015) and stepped away from thinking about my next hike for a day or two. I couldn't stop long though; after all, we had less than six months to get ready.

Once I took that timeout, I came back with a plan, and a good plan starts with a list. Out came the notebook and those pinball thoughts bounced from my cluttered brain down the pen and onto the paper with ease and calm joy as hike number two's planning began.

Sharon no longer lived an hour from me in Maine. After her knuckleball, she packed up and moved to North Carolina, just outside of Asheville. She couldn't have chosen a more perfect place to live. Not only is Asheville a quaint, hip town and one of the hottest growing places to live in the United States, it isn't far from the Appalachian Trail. Sharon's new location was only a three-to-four-hour drive, even much closer in several spots, from most trailheads for the southern half of the trail, making it an ideal home base for my husband, Bruce, to work while he supported us. Poor Bruce still had to work.

Since distance prevented us from in-person strategizing, our planning took place via texting and a few phone calls. Sharon didn't really care too much for the planning, whereas Bruce and I loved it. In the beginning, I let my first hike overshadow this hike. So I adopted the saying, "It's not about me" to help keep the focus on Sharon. This was her hike, not mine. I was just along for the ride. While I wasn't always successful at not letting hike number one cloud hike number two, the experience from the first go-around was valuable in making certain decisions, like when to start hiking.

I don't like to be wet and cold at the same time. Usually, I can handle one or the other without too much discomfort or danger. It is inevitable that hikers will be wet or cold and, unfortunately, often both at the same time. A good start date, though, can help reduce the number of times these two conditions collide. I started in early March in 2015 and endured my fair share of cold rainy days. I really didn't want to repeat that, so we chose to start in late March, hoping for better weather.

———

Now that lists were being made, Bruce and I tackled logistical plans. No more bells and lights and excitement mayhem. We ordered *The A.T. Guide* for 2017 by David "AWOL" Miller and updated the Guthook app, co-founded by Paul Bodnar and Ryan Linn and now known as FarOut. Most successful thru-hikes begin and/or end with one or both resources. I will admit, Bruce again did most of the logistics. I threw out ideas while Bruce calculated why the idea would or would not work, then we presented it to Sharon. Sharon was all too easy to please.

But just like most plans, there were changes. *Walking Home*, a documentary about a father-son duo who hiked the Appalachian Trail together in 2015, created by independent filmmakers Ryan Leighton and Cody Mitchell, was scheduled to screen in early March. Since I had hiked with the men for a while, I wanted to see it.

We postponed our start date. Then the screening was pushed to mid-March. We again pushed out our date. The screening still didn't take place, so March 24, 2017, became our start date, and we decided we would catch the movie screening later when it finally debuted. Our hiking speed is on the sloth side, so we knew we needed to start hiking if we had any plans of making it to Katahdin in Maine, the northern terminus of the Appalachian Trail, before it closed for the season on October 15.

Even with the start date push-outs, before we knew it, it was time to put our plans into action and head south to Springer Mountain, the southern terminus for the Appalachian Trail. It was 11:29 p.m. the night before Bruce and I needed to leave, and I still had several items on my list that were not completed. But I always set high expectations. I believe in aiming for the moon. If I miss, the worst I can do is fall among the stars.

Before we knew it, Bruce and I were making the bed together without a word. It was a task we did daily together like clockwork. With less than six hours of sleep, we were surprisingly refreshed. It's amazing how much energy you have when you are chasing a goal. Any other day, we would be whining and complaining about the lack of sleep.

Just as we did in 2015, Bruce and I loaded our Outback with all our gear, pulled out of our driveway in Lowell, Maine, and headed south. We drove as far as Winchester, Virginia, the same layover we had in 2015, but this time without the pillow-surfing pooch of my 2015 hiking buddy.

The next day brought us to Sharon's place in North Carolina, where we spent one day and two nights. That gave us a chance to hit REI, a popular outfitter for outdoorsy people, just in case we had any last-minute gear changes.

———

"Day compared to night" sums up Sharon's and my qualities. I already mentioned that she is more relaxed and easygoing than I am. She doesn't really like to play out scenarios like I do. She is a brunette, the smart one, and I am blonde (gray now) and fit that stereotype. She's more of a cultured city girl and I am a hick who is rough around the edges. I was a multi-sport athlete, and she tried her skill at one.

She's quiet and reserved, and most people wish I was. We even differ politically and spiritually.

I packed and repacked my bag countless times, starting soon after Sharon asked me to hike. One would have thought I had never hiked before. I had most of the same gear. I was experienced. I had stuffed and emptied my pack over 180 times during my first AT thru-hike. I even had the same style pack now, only in a different color. I don't know why I needed to repack it another dozen times. It must have been the alternate color that threw me off.

When we arrived at Sharon's, her pack was still in the shipping box. March 24 was our start date, and as of March 22, she decided it was time to open the box. Most of her gear was brand spanking new with the tags still on. As I was reviewing my notes and photos to write this chapter, I came across a video of Sharon. After opening her pack, she decided to test her skill with a lighter. Neither one of us are smokers, so is that a skill one really needs? Probably, if you're planning a backcountry multi-month hike. She finally figured out the lighter. I had to chuckle. We are so different. She obviously is the smart one— look at all the time she saved.

It didn't matter, though, that one of us had spent hours packing and rechecking gear and the other one had just loaded her pack for the very first time, we both were about to start on a grand adventure together. With our differences set aside, we had a common goal, Katahdin! First, we wanted a good night's sleep. It would be several weeks before we slept in our own beds again.

Sharon lived a mere 182 road miles from The Lodge at Amicalola Falls State Park, the unofficial start of the Appalachian Trail for a northbound hike. It's a short three-and-a-half-hour scenic drive. We couldn't wait to get there. Sharon was anxious to start the adventure she had dreamed up four years prior, and I couldn't wait to escape reality again.

BLACK BEAR TIP

Never let the facts get in the way of reaching your goal.

Day 1 Friday March 24, 2017

Time: 8:30am – 4:00pm
Mile: 0.0 – 8.8 Approach, 0.0 – 0.2 AT
Miles hiked: 9.0
Tented at Springer Mountain Shelter
Weather: Sunny & warm

2

And We Are Off

Our gear had been checked. Well, mine was checked multiple times, and we already established Sharon's pre-hike prep. With all our gear strategically stowed, Bruce, Sharon, and I climbed into the Outback for the final drive to the southern terminus of the Appalachian Trail. I remember at some point telling Sharon that she was no longer Sharon, and it was time she became Shortcake. Also, it was time for Bruce to transform back into Batman, and myself to Black Bear.

The use of trail names is a common practice among hikers. It is a chance to be incognito out on the trail by not divulging one's real name. For me, it is just fun. Usually, hikers earn a trail name by doing something ridiculous or memorable. But it is also acceptable to choose your own trail name. I like to be in control, so I chose my own—Black Bear. There is a lot of symbolism in it for me, mostly because the black bear is my alma mater's mascot, and I can be grouchy like a bear.

Bruce earned his trail name. In 2015, I was hiking with Wye Knot, a hiking buddy who I had known for several weeks. One day we met up with a gal, Hoosier Mama, from Indiana. We were hiking along, having a grand ole time, when we crossed a road and then entered a field. I recognized landmarks mentioned in the guidebook telling us we were close to our destination for the day. I hollered up to my friends that it was time for me to call Bruce to let him know we were almost out. Before I had even finished my sentence, Wye Knot and Hoosier Mama simultaneously blurted out as if they had rehearsed it, "His trail name needs to be Batman!" They were hysterical at this. I had no clue why. Sure, I knew who Batman was, but I didn't get the connection. They reminded me that when the fictional character Batman isn't Batman, he is Bruce in the fictional real world. And since Bruce was always rescuing me, the name was perfect. He has been Batman ever since.

Sharon earned her trail name also, but pre-hike. She was like me and didn't really want to earn a trail name, fearing what it might be. So she and I thought about it and one day I offered the trail name "Shortcake." When she lived in Maine, she worked as a baker, and she is even more vertically challenged than I am. Plus, she is one of the sweetest people I know. I thought "Shortcake" was a good fit. The nice thing about trail names is that when someone gives you one, you don't have to accept it. But in this case, Sharon loved it.

As we pulled out of Sharon's driveway heading out on our adventure, we left our old selves behind and took on the characters of Batman, Shortcake, and Black Bear. Oh, what fun we all were about to have.

———

The three-and-a-half-hour drive was over in no time, and we arrived at Amicalola Falls State Park at 3:30pm. Upon arrival, we proceeded to the gift shop, where we signed in at the visitor center, claiming hiker number 1165 for Shortcake and number 1166 for myself. We also listened to other hikers who were taking advantage of the free trail information and pack shakedowns offered by Appalachian Trail volunteer staff members. When browsing was over, we drove up to the lodge for check-in and an evening filled with our own gear go-thru, making sure everything was organized.

I was just as excited about the start of this journey as I was in 2015. Sharon is more reserved than me and hard to read at times. But the night before our big day, she was a little chattier than her usual self, and the smile that sliced through her countenance was a dead giveaway that she was happy.

We were down to less than twelve hours to bingo. We finished supper at the lodge's restaurant and whatever other tasks we needed to do, then watched the sun as it sank behind waves of tree-covered mountains. As the last bands of color disappeared from the horizon, we knew it was time to snuggle into our own beds for the last night of comfort we would have for a while.

Rise and shine! It's go-time. First, we needed to eat. So I guess it wasn't quite go-time. We enjoyed a full breakfast at the lodge's restaurant. There we saw several other hikers either leaving, eating, or starting to eat as we were leaving. That wasn't surprising. It was hiker season at Springer. It's common for 20 to 30 hikers a day to be starting their northbound hike that time of year.

Experience is knowledge, and even though I really wanted to keep my 2015 hike separate, it just wasn't going to happen. In 2015, I pigged out at supper the night before hiking and then again at breakfast. Gorging on back-to-back meals before starting the hike had made the 700 steps I had to climb in the morning horrible. So this time, I still ate well, but not quite as much. If only I hadn't packed on an extra ten pounds of body weight. I knew the hike would be a challenge since I was heavier, but I really didn't worry about it because I knew I would lose the extra pounds on the trail. One of the many awesome reasons to long-distance hike—it's a proven weight-loss program.

With our tummies full, we were ready to check out of our room and start our adventure. First stop was the weigh station. Not for our bodies—I already knew mine was overloaded, and Shortcake was just a peanut. We needed to weigh our packs. It's a formality to check the weight of one's pack before a thru-hike.

According to an article written by Joe Pasteris for REI, a hiker should not carry more than twenty percent of their body weight. This is just a guide. Not everyone is built the same, yet most hikers carry nearly the same items. Differences in items packed occurs depending on how much one wants to be a minimalist, one's budget for high-tech lighter gear, how far one is hiking, and the weather. So pack weight to body weight ratio will vary from hiker to hiker.

My pack weighed 37 pounds; Batman's and Shortcake's both weighed 32 pounds. As much as I want to carry less, luxury items always seemed to find their way onto my shoulders. I was heavy in the electronic and food departments. I carried an SOS device, extra battery power sources, special foods, and even a frying pan. Also carefully protected in a cloth pouch was a special stone with the word *Gratitude* written on it. I called it my spirit stone, and I was carrying it in honor of The Summit Project, an organization in Maine that is a living memorial to post-911 Maine fallen heroes.

Once we had strapped on our packs, the three of us looked like ninja turtles without the cool face masks. Not so much Batman, since he is tall, but Shortcake and I were dwarfed next to our packs. And just like turtles, we would be carrying our homes on our backs for the next several months.

Under the arch over the approach trail, we posed for the iconic start-of-the-hike photos. It was a chilly, cloudy morning. The mountain air was nippy. We all wore long sleeves and long pants, and Shortcake even had on a coat and topped her coiffure with a custom-made cupcake hat that would become her signature.

The Approach Trail is an 8.8-mile blue-blazed trail from Amicalola State Park to the top of Springer Mountain where the first white blaze of the southern terminus of the Appalachian Trail is. The other way to start a northbound AT thru-hike is to drive to Big Stamp Gap using USFS-42 and park. Then hike one mile south on the A.T. to the top of Springer Mountain, turn around retrace your steps back to the parking lot, and continue north following the white blazes. This option cuts out the 8.8-mile approach trail and 700 steps.

We chose the former route. The stairs carry hikers along the beautiful Amicalola Falls, the highest waterfall east of the Mississippi. It is no easy task for beginner hikers, but the reward is worth the work. Our climb was slow and methodical. Part way through, I was already rethinking my decision not to care about my extra weight. The stairs kicked my butt. I was really having a great time, but looking back on the photos of just the beginning stairs, my face sure told a different story.

Shortcake seemed to breeze through the day. She was finally on her adventure. It had been her idea in 2013. She took her knuckleball of life like a champ and kept on swinging until she made it around the bases to 2017. Nothing was going to stop her.

———

We started hiking at 8:30am on March 24 and reached Springer Mountain at 3:30pm. At the summit, a bronze plaque, weathered green, marks the start or end of a thru-hiker's journey. An image of a hiker, who in some ways resembles a soldier when you first look at it, is centered on the plaque with the words,

APPALACHIAN TRAIL
GEORGIA TO MAINE
A Footpath for Those who
seek Fellowship with
the Wilderness
The GEORGIA APPALACHIAN TRAIL CLUB

We posed for more pictures, then took our first steps on the Appalachian Trail, guided by white blazes two inches wide by six inches long. After leaving the summit, we traveled north on the trail 0.2 mile, arriving at Springer Mountain Shelter by 4:00pm, ending our first day.

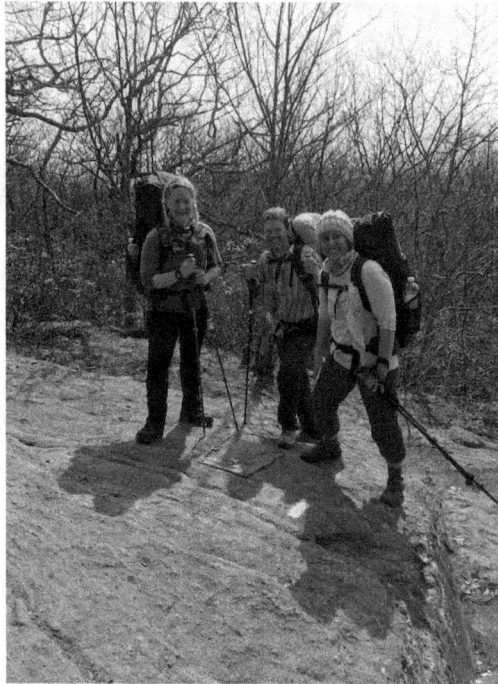

We weren't setting any records, nor were we trying to. We may have looked like ninja turtles, but our speed was more that of slow and steady box turtles. The stairs really did us all in, and we were happy to be at the shelter. The work didn't stop, though, once we reached our day's destination. Camp chores were next. Setting up camp, collecting water for supper and the next day, and eating are all things that need to be done before bed.

It may have been my second go-around, but anyone watching would have thought I was a novice. My skills were rusty; it took me three-and-a-half hours to do all that needed to be done. I had no time to roll my feet, no time to write a web post, and no time to journal well.

Five years later, many details escape my memory (and a lack of good note taking), but one thing that I will not forget—and neither will Shortcake—is that her stove failed to work. Since she wasn't too good at using a lighter, she had bought a Jetboil backpacking stove with an igniter. But it didn't work. She tried it, I tried it, and Batman attempted to get it to work. We were all unsuccessful.

Sometime during the trial and error, I asked, "Did it work at home?" Shortcake tilted her head sheepishly upward from the picnic table where she was still trying to light the stove. As she looked at us, tuffs of dark curls spilled from under her cupcake hat framing her face. Then she shrugged her shoulders and said, "I didn't test it."

I am laughing now as I write this. I cooked several meals with my stove before my first hike, then did some more testing before this second hike since I had a new frying pan. But not Shortcake. *It's new; it should work.* That's how she rolls. We were so different. It was going to be a wild ride.

The great thing about having a hiking buddy is that when you need something, the other person can help. Batman and Shortcake swapped stoves, since he was only joining us for the night.

Exhaustion finally won. Shortcake headed to her tent, and Batman and I went to ours. Unlike 2015 when we couldn't sleep the first night, we had no issue catching shut-eye. Before I drifted off, I could hear Shortcake rustling in her tent. I am sure she was just like I had been two years earlier, eager to be out there, maybe even a little scared, but mostly, having her mind racing with uncontrollable thoughts and feelings.

BLACK BEAR TIP

Test your gear before using it in a live situation.

Day 2 Saturday March 25
Time: 9:20am – 4:20pm
Mile: 0.2 – 9.0
Miles hiked: 8.8
Stealth camped
Weather: Cloudy start, then sunny
Torrential downpour & windy at night

Day 3 Sunday March 26
Time: 9:00am – 3:00pm
Mile: 9 – 15.8
Miles hiked: 6.8
Tented at Gooch Mountain Shelter
Weather: Wet misty start; some cold, then sunny

Day 4 Monday March 27
Time: 8:50am – 5:15pm
Mile: 15.8 – 26.4
Miles hiked: 10.6
Tented at Jarrard Gap Shelter
Weather: Pleasant, cloudy, rained a little
Thunderstorm at night

Day 5 Tuesday March 28
Time: 8:50am – 5:45pm
Mile: 26.4 – 35.7
Miles hiked: 9.3
Tented just past Wolf Laurel Top
Weather: Cloudy start, then partly cloudy & hot

3

One Milestone at a Time

It was a fabulous first evening in a tent for Shortcake. It's always nice to start a new adventure with a positive experience. The temps were cool, but once we were all in our sleeping bags it was cozy. But I did have Batman to snuggle with and Shortcake was alone. Even still, I remember her saying she had a nice sleep. Which was great, because she does love her comforts of home.

Not wanting to lallygag, we packed up quickly. We tend to be slow hikers, and not yet knowing each other's hiking pace, we wanted to make sure we made it to our destination before dark. I prefer to use the phrase *meticulous hikers*. Add the facts that this adventure would be Shortcake's first time carrying a full pack for any distance and I had put on extra weight since my last hike. We expected a slower than normal pace.

Batman, Shortcake, and I slung our packs onto our shoulders and headed down Springer Mountain. The trail wasn't hard, but there were several odd-shaped rocks in the path, making it challenging to place our feet at times. It was nothing compared to most trails in Maine where I had trained, but for some reason, that day I found it difficult—or I just wasn't being as meticulous as usual.

We hadn't even hiked a quarter of a mile and I felt my ankle give. Grimacing in pain and stifling a moan, I caught myself with my poles, hoping Batman, who was behind me, didn't notice. He didn't speak out, and my moan must have stayed in my throat because neither he nor Shortcake said anything.

Oh, no! Had I just ruined our hike before it even got started? It reminded me of the time Batman and I and our two sons went on a family bike ride from the top of Maine to Maine's southern border with New Hampshire. On that trip, just a few miles into the adventure, Bruce and Patch, our youngest son, dumped their bikes when we crossed railroad tracks. Luckily, just a few bumps, scrapes, a broken speedometer, and bruised egos were all that happened.

Using my pole to take some of the weight off my ankle, I walked it off. I still had pain, but I felt it was just a little tweak and all would be fine. Thank goodness! A huge reminder that things can go from great to horrible in a flash…

––––––

Big Stamp Gap parking is only one mile from the top of Springer Mountain. Hikers who do not want to do an extra 8.8 miles and want to skip the 700 steps can drive to this backwoods trailhead to reach Springer Mountain. Batman's plans were to turn around at this spot. It was also the place I had lost my first item in 2015 when I stopped to take a picture and didn't know my hat came unclipped from my pack.

We said good-bye to Batman, who would hike back up Springer and then back down the approach trail. He would return to Shortcake's house to use it as a base camp for work when he wasn't helping us on the weekends. Shortcake and I did a look-see to make sure we didn't leave behind any items this time. Then off we went into woods.

The day was cloudy, and the air had a brisk feel to it. I was comfortable with just my lightweight long-sleeved merino wool shirt and capri leggings. But Shortcake sported several layers. Another way we were opposites. She runs cool, and I overheat. If you ask hubby, he will say I am never comfortable. Which is kind of true; my temperature comfort window is very narrow.

We hiked leisurely, as though we had a lifetime to get to Katahdin. It was only Day 2, and we were not about to start rushing. Everything caught our eye, from an iconic tree with a giant hole in it to manmade structures such as footbridges that carried us across lazy little streams. We took it all in while we were adjusting to our new way of life. The highlight of the day was lunch at a waterfall, where I took the time to pull out my stove and cooked a lunch, something I rarely did in 2015. I made cheese quesadillas.

Our plan was to hike to Hawk Mountain Shelter at mile 8.1. But we felt great, even with the huge monkey each of us was carrying on our backs, so we continued past the shelter and camped at about mile 9, according to my Guthook app. At nine miles in seven hours, we weren't breaking any speed records, but we were enjoying the day. I loved our slow, meaningful hike. It was a great warm-up for our bodies and easy on the legs, back, and spirit. We weren't bothered by the hordes of thru-hikers and day hikers that passed us. We even had a theme song already: "One Foot in Front of the Other" from the movie *Santa Claus is Comin to Town.*

Camp for the night was at 3,140 feet. We were somewhere between Hightower Gap and Horse Gap. The trail crested a peak that provided a flat-ish area with plenty of room to spread out. It wasn't a designated campsite in the guidebook, but it was obviously used by previous hikers, so we felt confident we weren't breaking any Leave No Trace principles (LNT), as we only used the areas already flattened by others.

By the time we had set up camp and eaten, it was getting late in "hiker time," and we were confident we wouldn't see any other hikers. We took the liberty of stripping down naked and letting the cool mountain air freshen up our parts that don't usually see the sunshine. It was fantastic and felt oh so good. We didn't run around in our birthday suits long; the temperature was dropping faster than the sun, and we didn't want to risk being caught.

It was also time to hang our food bags. That is a necessary task for backcountry living to keep humans and animals safe. Bear encounters are rare, but if you ask the victim of one such event, they will tell you that encounters aren't rare enough. One encounter is too many.

Hanging a bear line is tough. You must find the right tree limb, and when all is said and done, the rule of thumb is that your food bag should be fifteen feet off the ground and six feet from the bottom of the limb and six feet away from the tree trunk. To make matters worse, bears are becoming increasingly clever and can finagle bear lines to gain access to the goods inside.

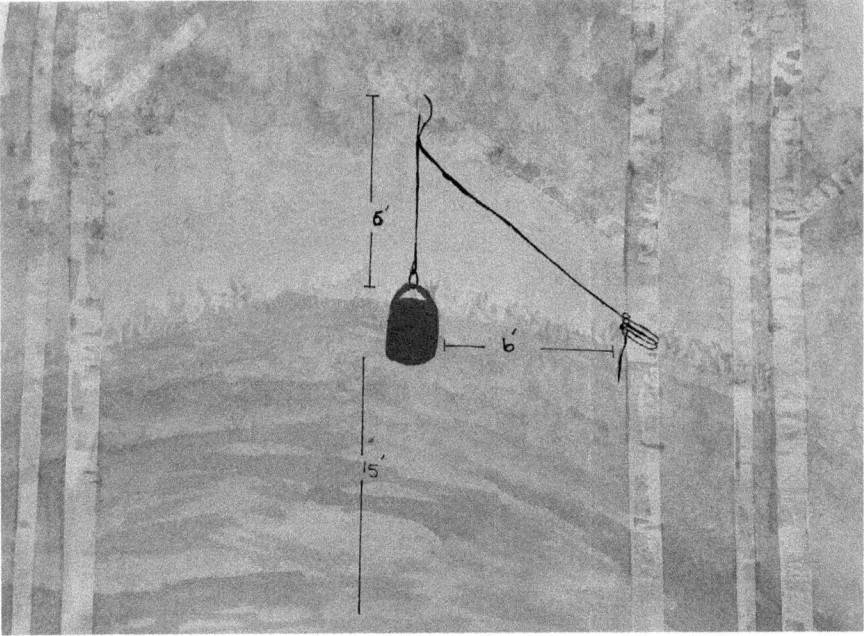

With our chores done for the evening, we sat on our ground cloths under a semi-clear sky and watched the vibrant setting sun illuminate the barren trees. Before the sun disappeared completely, we climbed into my tent. Shortcake had her own tent back at Springer Mountain. It was my spare tent. But it had gone back down the mountain with Batman. Shortcake and I decided to share a tent until she became strong enough physically as well as confident mentally to carry and sleep in her own tent—or until I kicked her out, whichever was to come first.

––––––

We went to bed with favorable weather and without a care in the world. That peace was blown away as the wind kicked up soon after we went to bed. I was glad I had staked down the tent. In 2015, I had learned to do that no matter how favorable Mother Nature was when she tucked me in at night. Then came the rain; heavy, torrential rain.

We stayed dry in my MSR Hubba Hubba™ two-person tent, but the outside of it was a mess. The ground was soft, with a thin layer of decaying leaves from the previous fall. The heavy rain pureed the crumbly leaf litter and the dirt, and the force of the downpour splashed the puree onto the lower two feet of all four sides of the rain fly as well as the tent underneath the fly. I had never seen such a mess, and I had to put it into my pack.

As I write this, I remember thinking that next morning that the modern conveniences of home would have been nice to have at the time. Then I remembered something my friend had sent me days before. Dave is always sending me funny pictures, memes, quotes, and an inbox full of other things to make me laugh. I received an email full of various one-liners. He is one of my biggest fans, even though he thinks I am totally nuts to go off into the woods for extended periods of time. This quote was in the email: "Camping: where you spend a small fortune to live like a homeless person." Just substitute camping for backpacking, and that pretty much sums it up.

I brushed off the tent the best I could, placed it into its own dry sack to prevent it from wetting all my gear, and shoved it into the bottom of my pack to deal with later.

The rain didn't dampen our moods; after all, we were in the honeymoon stage of our hike. The beginning of anything is always so exciting. A new job, a new hobby, a move to a new city, new friends, a new puppy or kitten, a new baby, getting married—it's all fun when just starting out. Then reality sinks in, and sometimes you wonder why you did the "new" thing. (Hopefully not the new baby, spouse, or pets—those should be keepers.)

So a little dreary weather was just part of the adventure. It made for an interesting hike our third day on the trail. The mountain was covered in a thick cloud, making everything seem mystical and eerie. We walked through a canvas of white with silhouettes of stark brown columns formed by the trees. At any moment a member from Robin Hood's gang could jump out from behind one of them to rob us of our treasures.

We had nothing to fear. Only snails who were also carrying their "packs" and centipedes accompanied us on the trail. We didn't see any other hikers until we arrived at camp that evening.

There were 29 hikers at Gooch Mountain Shelter. Our start date put us in a huge bubble. Safety in numbers is a great thing, but as we would soon find out, that many hikers on the trail at the same time can make finding a place to sleep at night difficult.

We made it to the shelter by 3:00pm. Thankfully, the sun decided to make an appearance. With an early arrival time and the warmth of the sun, we were able to dry things out. Everyone else had the same idea. With that many hikers converged in one area, it really did look like a homeless encampment with everyone's gear strewn around on whatever structure, branch, rock, or clean dry surface was available.

We only did 6.8 miles. We still weren't in any hurry. We were allowing our bodies to adjust to trail life. Shortcake had never done anything like this before, and even though I had completed a thru-hike a year and a half ago, I was now fifty-one and slightly overweight.

I have struggled with my weight all my life. Even though I have been active since I was a toddler, when my nickname was Monkey, I have always put weight on very easily. If I am not moving at Mach 5, just thinking about food adds layers to my thunder thighs. It doesn't help that I love to cook and eat. Thru-hiking helped me get into the best shape of my life, and I could eat all day and still be fit. The only problem was when the hike was over in 2015, the hiker hunger was still real. I was still taking in calories galore, but I wasn't hiking 10 to 12 hours a day carrying a 30-pound pack. So by the time 2017 rolled around, I had rolls around the mid-section as well.

Back on the trail, I didn't have to worry about what I ate, so I made another calorie-rich, delicious supper consisting of macaroni and cheese (gluten-free) with chopped-up beef stick, fresh veggies I packed out, and lots of cheese. Shortcake was sticking to the simple, more traditional hiker meals, some sort of dehydrated concoction.

Another day ended as we completed our camp chores. Our tent and belongings had completely dried so getting ready for bed was easy. It would have been dreadful to squeeze two bodies into a slimy, muddy tent. Thank God for little blessings.

Slept through a thunderstorm. A more accurate statement would be, "tried to sleep through a thunderstorm." We were hoping the sun that had appeared late the previous afternoon would have burned away any cloud cover for the night, but no such luck. At least, by the time morning came, the sun graced us with her presence to start the day.

We were headed for Lance Creek, a designated campsite. Our starts were not as early as I would have liked them to be, but again, I was really trying to let this hike be Shortcake's hike, so I didn't push the issue. . . yet. On our fourth day on the trail, we had boots on the ground by 8:50am.

Our day was filled with lots of uphills and some rain. Not too much rain; just enough to keep the woods clouded in that white mysterious fog and dampen the trail. But with those showers providing hydration for the soil, little flowers were beginning to dot the forest floor along the trail, a true sign that spring was soon to follow and, hopefully, more consistently good weather. One could hope, anyway.

I noticed something else in abundance, but not as pleasing to see as the wildflowers—lots of little pieces of trash, the kind from snacks and drink mixes, the little corner you tear off to access the tasty treats. I know it can be unintentional to accidentally drop that small section when enjoying one's snack on the move, but this looked like an epidemic of carelessness spreading throughout the hiking community. Sure, maybe one or two of these landing by accident in the wilderness wasn't going to ruin one's outdoor experience or contaminate the wilderness for generations to come, but it was still bothersome nonetheless. I picked up as many as I could until it became a chore.

Shortcake and I were already becoming trail famous. She was being recognized for the cupcake hat adorning the top of her head, and a couple hikers had recognized me from the documentary by Ryan Leighton and Cody Mitchell, *Walking Home*. It was fun to be recognized.

When we reached Lance Creek, we felt strong, so we pushed on another couple miles and camped at Jarrard Gap, by ourselves again. In 2015 I seldom camped alone, but having a hiking buddy gave us the courage to venture out on our own, which gave us solitude from the large bubble we were in.

The day ended with a magnificent sunset. A blaze-orange fireball nestled above the distant mountains on the horizon. An outer glow of the same hue produced a translucent ring that hugged the main fireball like Saturn's rings. As the radiant light dropped lower and lower, we knew another day was almost over. We would soon crawl into our sleeping bags and try to grab what comfort we could while crammed into our tent for two, where there was really only room for one.

Neel Gap here we come. The first of many milestones wannabe thru-hikers reach on a northbound thru-hike is Neel Gap, 31.4 miles from Springer Mountain or 40.2 miles for those who have tackled the approach trail, as we had. But first, we had 9.3 miles to trek. After another thunderstorm, we packed up and began our day.

Between us and Neel Gap was Blood Mountain at 4,457 feet elevation, the tallest mountain that the A.T. summits in Georgia. Many hikers cringe at this climb, especially those not used to hiking on such terrain. But when you come from Maine, a 1,207-foot climb over two and a half miles isn't so bad. It isn't easy by any means, but it wasn't straight up either. If you looked at a map with the elevation profile from Jarrard Gap where we had camped to Blood Mountain, it would resemble a serrated knife with each little up slightly higher than the previous one. The low spots, never dipping below the one before, gave a little reprieve before climbing up the next tooth. Then a slightly steeper incline for the last mile brings you to Blood Mountain Shelter.

It was another cloudy day on the Appalachian Trail. When we reached the summit, no view could be seen. The sun may have been hidden for most of the day, but it was hot. We rested briefly in the old stone four-sided shelter with paneless windows and absent door. I didn't like it in 2015, and it didn't give me any warm fuzzies this time around either, but we did enjoy its damp coolness before we headed down the other side of the mountain.

The up may not have been so terrible but the descent was a whole other chapter. It could be its own book. I was a little apprehensive about the climb down. In 2015, I barely made it; my knees had cried out in pain with every step. We took it slow and steady this time, and all was well. Any pain that did creep in on the rocky descent was soon forgotten once I saw Batman. He had hiked south from Mountain Crossings to meet us. I don't know who was more excited—Batman, to be outside for a few hours away from work, or me, getting to see my hubby.

The climate at Neel Gap, at the base of Blood Mountain, was completely opposite from the weather at the summit. It was still warm, but the sun managed to burn a few holes in the white cloud that shrouded the top of the mountain, and everyone's spirits brightened after the thunderstorm the previous night and a dreary day of hiking.

The Appalachian Trail goes right through the buildings of Mountain Crossings, an outfitter located at Neel Gap. The Civilian Conservation Corps built the structure in 1930 as an inn and dining hall. In the early 1980s, it was purchased and became an outfitter catering to hikers and visitors. Besides offering gifts, food, a hostel, showers, and gear for patrons, the most iconic aspect of Mountain Crossings is the boot tree that stands at the center of attention in front of the store. In one way it resembles the Tree of Life at Disney's Animal Kingdom. But it doesn't really represent life. With hundreds of worn-out pairs of footwear dangling from its limbs, it has become the place where hiking shoes go to die.

Boots aren't the only thing that die at Mountain Crossings. Many hikers' dreams of thru-hiking the entire Appalachian Trail also meet their fate at Neel Gap. For whatever reason, this is a place where hikers quit. There isn't firm recordkeeping stating the fact, but rumor has it that 25 percent of thru-hikers who start in Georgia quit when they reach Neel Gap.

Shortcake and I were not giving up, nor were we even thinking about it, but we were stopping for a respite along with many other hikers. Gear littered the premises as we all took advantage of the sun's warmth and dried our belongings on any available surface.

Two and a half hours later, we followed the white blazes through the stone building's structure and continued north. We were accompanied by Batman for a little while. Our spirits were high when we said good-bye to him. Not because he had to hike back out and go to work, but because we were proud of ourselves for making it to the first milestone.

We moseyed along without a care in the world. Our gear was dry, we had resupplied from our boxes Batman brought us, we were fed, and the day was gorgeous. We hiked a mere 4.3 miles after leaving Neel Gap, making our total for the day just under 10 miles. We decide to call it quits after Wolf Laurel Top. The shelter was another 2.4 miles, and it was already 5:45pm. Fast was not in our MO.

We had the camping area to ourselves again. Our non-traditional itinerary resulted in our desired mileage ending in between shelters. We didn't mind. It was a warm, sunny evening, and we had the whole place to ourselves.

Or so we thought.

It was a good thing we kept our clothes on this time. As we were setting up camp, this guy comes strolling up over the ridge from west of the trail. The hairs on the back of my neck instantly rose, and my fight or flight instincts switched to alarm. There was something off about this guy.

On previous hikes in the woods alone, I easily became paranoid. It bothered me that I couldn't be alone without always fearing some perceived danger. The more experience I gained being independent, the less often I freaked out in scary situations. I still listen to that sixth sense I seem to possess—most women do, I think—but I now react with a more level head.

The mystery guy was wearing a graphic t-shirt and town shorts with canvas sneakers—not your ordinary hiking attire. Sure, maybe if we were near a town or tourist trap, but we were a few miles from civilization. He definitely was not a thru-hiker, or even a section hiker. Heck, at that time of evening and dressed the way he was dressed, he wouldn't even qualify as a day hiker.

I gave a friendly hello as he crossed the Appalachian Trail, meandering through the campsite only yards from our tents. He looked at me but made no acknowledgment of my greeting. Hopefully without being obvious, I kept my eye on him while I continued to set up camp. Then he disappeared down into the ravine just as fast as he had appeared.

Shortcake and I looked at each other, and I said something on the lines of, "Did that just happen?" We both were a little bothered by the situation. We investigated the area, searching for another trail the hiker could have used. There was nothing there, no trail, no flagging, nothing at all that might even suggest a path. We had heard and read about paranormal sightings on the trail, but you never really think it is going to happen to you until it does, or until something weird like that happens and you just can't explain it. Whatever or whomever it was, I slept with one eye open and both ears on extra sensitive.

At 5:30am, a loud crashing with snapping of branches brought all my senses to full-on terrified mode as I envisioned a flannel-clad, toothless man with a chainsaw ready to shred my tent and me in half. Once I cleared my delusional brain, I woke up Shortcake so we both could be ready for whatever was outside our tent.

We didn't see or hear anything else. At that point though, sleeping was over.

BLACK BEAR TIP

After a rest stop, take a few steps away from where you were resting, and look back for a look-see to make sure you haven't forgotten anything.

Day 6 Wednesday March 29
Time: 8:57am – 5:15pm
Mile: 35.7 – 47.9
Miles hiked: 12.2
Tented at Chattahoochee Gap
Weather: Sunny & hot

Day 7 Thursday March 30
Time: 8:13am – 4:45pm
Mile: 47.9 – 58.3
Miles hiked: 10.4
Tented at Trey Mountain Shelter
Weather: Cloudy & warm

Day 8 Friday March 31
Time: 8:33am – 3:30pm
Mile: 58.3 – 69.3
Miles hiked: 11.0
Stayed at Top of Georgia Hostel
Weather: Sunny & mild

Day 9 Saturday April 1
Time: 10:38am – 2:00pm
Mile: 69.3 – 73.8
Miles hiked: 4.5
Tented at Plumorchard Gap Shelter
Weather: Warm

Day 10 Sunday April 2
Time: 8:30am – 5:45pm
Mile: 73.8 – 86.0
Miles hiked: 12.2 miles
Tented at Standing Indian Shelter
Weather: Warm
Entered North Carolina

4

Settling In

Our strange visitor and sleepless night were enough excitement for a while, and we were glad the 12.2-mile hike to Chattahoochee Gap was uneventful. I know I was exhausted from sleep deprivation brought on by an over-active imagination. I can't speak for Shortcake.

It was our first morning of waking up to sunshine. Most other days were either rainy or at least cloudy. We are never happy, though. With the sunshine came the heat, and this northern girl was hot. I'm either too hot or too cold, never just right. My name should be Goldilocks instead of Black Bear.

Goldilocks may have been a fitting moniker a few years ago before I stopped visiting my hairdresser, but as a fellow hiker asked, "Why Black Bear for a trail name with all that white hair?" Even being north of 50 years old, I still feel so young inside, and the only time reality sets in is when I look in the mirror—which I try not to do—or when someone points it out to me as that brash hiker did. I was speechless. I couldn't even offer a rebuttal with one of my quick off-the-cuff sarcastic responses. I guess the truth hurts at times.

The rest of the day we sauntered through the wilderness with Shortcake in the lead. That was our usual order of hiking. Since it was her debut hike, I wanted to give her the best view. Plus, she made a pretty good web-walker. One never wants to be in front in the mornings. Whoever hikes out first is burdened with the task of clearing the spider webs that have been strung across the trail the previous night by our lustrous arachnids.

She didn't get them all. I am not too tall, but I have several inches on Shortcake. She missed the ones that would catch me right across my eyes or tickle my nose. Out of the hundreds of thread-like silk lines I walked through, never did I have the misfortune of having its spinner be in one. Not sure I could have handled that.

While Shortcake cleared the webs and had the first sightings of whatever the day had to offer, my view consisted mostly of a black backpack. But what was so adorable was Shortcake's signature hat.

Since she was not even five feet tall and her fully loaded pack measured at least twenty-four inches, that left little distance for a head and legs to be visible from above or below the pack. Just peeking topside of her pack was the crest of a white handknit cupcake hat with multi-colored sprinkles and even a cherry to top it off. It's no wonder I always wanted ice cream whenever we came to a town.

On Day 7, we summited three different mountains, all over 4,000 feet in elevation: Blue Mountain, Rocky Mountain, and Tray Mountain. We didn't have the sun to roast us, but that meant we didn't have any views either since the summits were clogged in fog.

One and a half miles after descending our first climb, we came to Unicoi Gap. I happened to be hiking in front this time, and I could smell the grill while we were still up on the ridge. I stopped to wait for Shortcake. This would be our first trail magic. Trail magic is the generosity of strangers providing something to hikers. It can be anything from a ride to town, a place to stay for free, provision of items needed, and sometimes, just a hug or kind word.

After we descended the mountain, we were greeted by a church group feeding hungry hikers. Under two tents were a grill, cooks, greeters, and feasting hikers. The overcooked burger never tasted so good. There is something about trail magic that makes it so wonderful, even if the beef patty was as tough as the leather on my boots. It's not necessarily the quality of the food that is satisfying; rather, it's the love and kindness that are the secret ingredients feeding the soul as the "trail angels" feed the stomach. Put together, it's a perfect combination to rejuvenate a tired hiker.

Our trek from Chattahoochee Gap to Tray Mountain Shelter was slightly lonely. We saw hardly anyone from our bubble. A "bubble" is the hikers one hikes around for days or weeks at a time. We met a few hikers at the trail magic, one being a nice German man who spoke very little English and his yellow lab.

Besides the free food at Unicoi, the only other highlight of that day was a field mouse, or should I say, a "forest mouse." She was doing her darndest to cross the trail, but she kept stumbling and falling. The smallest of rocks, leaves and sticks got in her way. I don't think she was sick. I believe her problem was the load she was carrying in her belly. She was one fat rodent. She looked like she was ready to pop with little babies.

I felt for her. I bet most hikers at the beginning of a thru-hike, as they are adjusting to the weight of their pack and the terrain as both Shortcake and I were, could relate to her plight. I didn't pick her up and move her, but I did clear an easier path for her to navigate the width of the trail. She didn't know how lucky she was. Back home, if I would have found her in my house, I won't say what I would have done, in fear you will stop reading and demand a refund. But I was in her home, and I tried to show her my gratitude.

After our long day of mountain summits, we made it to the shelter early, even with all the climbs and a stop for trail magic. I had time to make a gourmet meal. Bacon quesadillas were on the menu. I love pulling out my backcountry kitchen skills. I was being a little turd though. Instead of cooking discreetly, I boldly prepared my cuisine in sight of the shelter that was now packed with hikers, not just in the shelter but around it also. The smell of corn tortillas wafted through the area. I could tell eyes and noses were on me.

It's always amazing how one will see so few hikers throughout the day but at the shelter it seems like everyone has been airlifted in at the exact spot where you want to rest. That was the case at Tray Mountain Shelter. Thankfully, there were plenty of tent spaces for us all to spread out.

I love being in the woods. You appreciate the simple things of life all that much more, like running water and not having to squat to do a "Chapter-5." I learned this term after reading Bob and Matt Hunt's book *They Call Me Panda,* about a father and son who hiked the Appalachian Trail in 2003. They devoted a complete chapter to the different ways to go poop in the wilderness. It's hilarious.

Basic amenities like a bed and a table to eat at are also very much appreciated, and that's what we were going to get when we reached Dick's Creek Gap. We would also see Batman for the weekend—the best part. But first we needed to reach the road before the last shuttle to the hostel. Then we needed to quickly check in to catch the last ride to town for an AYCE buffet. An AYCE is a hiker's lottery. It is all the food you can eat.

Included with the hostel fee is individual laundry service, and they even provide hospital scrubs for you while your clothes are being washed so you don't have to wear your rain gear. It isn't the most comfortable thing to wear non-breathable fabric and then sit around in the heat and/or sun. It would be fine if one was trying to make weight for a wrestling tournament. But we weren't. Hospital scrubs, another simple thing to appreciate.

A shower is usually the first of many duties for hikers when they come out of the woods, but we had to make a choice: shower and miss the last shuttle to the AYCE, or skip the shower and go eat. Well, we were thru-hikers, and that means food that isn't dehydrated is always choice number one. The most courteous thing to do is to wash away the wilderness yuck that has enveloped one for the past few days, but we didn't have time. A quick change into our infirmary attire and we were off.

Batman joined us in the evening. He would be out with us for the weekend, hiking and resupplying.

The next two days were humdrum in our hiking world. Sometimes that is good. We were only on Day 9. I remember in 2015, I was ready to take off, but my hiking buddy at the time preferred a more leisurely pace. This time, I welcomed the slower start, for the time being.

Our nero day—a day with fewer miles than you are used to doing—was only 4.5 miles. But a little can mean a lot. What we didn't gain in mileage, we benefited from rest. We didn't need a zero day—a day without hiking—but we did need a little R&R. Our late start and early finish allowed our tired legs to recover.

Our destination was Plumorchard Shelter, a three-level structure, and I was excited to introduce Shortcake to shelter life. With our tortoise pace, we usually arrived too late at shelters to be able to stay in them. I don't usually like to stay in a shelter for a host of reasons, although it is nice to at least have the option. But that day we arrived early enough to claim a spot.

Before I reached the shelter, Batman, who had hiked in from the north, was already there. He informed me the man already set up in the shelter was the same hiker who, back at the hostel, had rattled the shingles off the roof with his snoring. Shelter life would have to wait, and we set up our tents.

Our early arrival gave us down time and a chance to chat with all the other hikers around the fire, one of those simple joys. Shortcake was tired though, and she retired early. I was a little concerned for my friend. She had been extra quiet that day and more exhausted than normal.

The next day the tables were flipped. I was tired and Shortcake was the one who encouraged us to go just a tad farther to make it to the shelter instead of camping prematurely. Before the end of our day, we said good-bye to Georgia and entered North Carolina, Shortcake's home state.

We also said good-bye to Batman. The weekend was over, and he needed to head back to his base camp. But, like Batman does best, he hiked south to meet us one last time for the weekend. We hiked back out to the car to resupply, and at the parking area of Deep Gap there was trail magic. Ah! A wonderful way to end the weekend.

It was here I wanted to set up our tent in the woods and call it quits, but Shortcake told me to suck it up. So we hiked the mere 0.9 mile to the shelter and tented there.

BLACK BEAR TIP

A large blob of hand sanitizer lathered under the arm pits and other smelly parts does wonders to diminish hiker stench.

Day 11 Monday April 3
Time: 7:55am – 12:10pm
Mile: 86 – 93.6
Miles hiked: 7.6
Tented Carter Gap Shelter
Weather: Rain, windy, cold, miserable

Day 12 Tuesday April 4
Time: 8:55am – 4:58pm
Mile: 96.3 – 105.7
Miles Hiked: 9.4
Tented at Rock Gap Shelter
Weather: Beautiful sunny day

Day 13 Wednesday April 5
Time: 7:11am – 3:15pm
Mile: 105.7 – 115.4
Miles hiked: 9.7
Went to Shortcake's in Weaverville, NC
Weather: Rainy & cold

Day 14 Thursday April 6
Zero Day

Day 15 Friday April 7
Zero Day

Day 16 Saturday April 8
Time: 9:02am – 5:05pm
Mile: 115.4 – 125.3
Miles hiked: 9.9
Tented at Cold Spring Shelter
Weather: Sunny, but snow on ground

Day 17 Sunday April 9
Time: 7:45am – 4:30pm
Mile: 125.3 -137.1
Miles hiked: 11.8
Stayed at the NOC
Weather: Sunny, brisk morning,
then hot

5

Tuna, Rain, Snow, and Poop

Beautiful weather had graced us on April 2, Day 10. But just like flipping a switch, Day 11 brought misery. A pleasant mist greeted us as we made our way into the morning hike; but with every footstep, the mist thickened, collecting into drops that fell faster and faster until it couldn't rain any harder.

It's one thing to hike in the mountains during the rain. It's a whole different experience when precipitation is joined with a choreographed light and sound show. Shortcake confessed her fear of thunderstorms early on. She handled two other ominous nights tucked away in her sleeping bag like a champ. But hiking in it was a different challenge. When the first flash of lightning and percussion rumbled overhead, Shortcake took off up the trail at a pace I hadn't seen her do yet. If it hadn't been so dangerous, it would have been comical.

I had just glanced at the GPS and knew we were headed up. Not a good direction, with the electricity flying around, but Shortcake was on a mission to get to the shelter, and I was not going to stop her. At one point, I did suggest we put our poles away. A while later we reached the perceived safety of the shelter unharmed. To our disappointment, it was already packed with stranded hikers.

If the trail lacks anything, it's not people. There are so many hikers on the path it's hard to find peace and quiet. It's good for some safety in numbers, but it's bad when thirty people try to fit into a space designed for eight.

The shelter was filled with thru-hikers, section hikers, and a group of nine Boy Scouts and their leaders. I know we are all out there in the wilderness voluntarily and no one has priority over another, but I was a little disappointed that it took the pack leader two hours to ask his Scouts to give their seats to the hikers who were wet, shivering, and standing in the windy rain, while the rest of us played musical chairs the best we could, giving reprieve to ones closest to the elements.

Hypothermia was seeping into a young, thin hiker we named Jersey Boy 1. Shortcake and I sandwiched him between us to conserve what heat he did have. It wasn't working. Then one of the Scouts produced an emergency blanket. Shortcake and I took turns snuggling in it with the young man until he warmed up. That flimsy piece of gear about the size of a deck of cards and weighing less than an ounce probably saved that young man's life that cold day in the mountains. I always carry one in my pack now, even on the hottest of days. Because in the wilderness, the weather can change so quickly. It's better to be prepared than to have regrets later.

An emergency blanket wasn't the only gift the Scouts gave us, but I didn't realize I was the recipient until much later. The shelter, meant for many fewer hikers than the mass crammed into it, felt like a sardine can. After seeing that some other hikers were close to hypothermia, the Scouts eventually shared the more desirable space away from the elements. We played musical space every few minutes as we all shuffled around so those toward the outside could have a reprieve from the pouring rain.

It was a pleasant environment with wet, soggy, smelly hikers smushed together. Being cuddled up with odorous strangers was better than being exposed to the harsh elements. The hiker stench that filled the space masked the scent that soaked my clothing. It wasn't until the weather improved and almost everyone hiked out and the body odors went with them that the remaining scent previously unnoticed filled the shelter—tuna fish.

I was covered in it. Apparently during our shuffling, I had scooted into tuna juice spilled from one of the Scout's snacks. Since I was already wet and the air was foul from hikers, I hadn't noticed it. The juice not only wet the surface of my clothing but had soaked in and taken up residence as I sat in it until it was time to shuffle again.

I couldn't change—I only possessed one pair of hiking clothes. So not only did we feel like sardines, I also smelled like one. It was a gift I could not give back and a gift I was stuck with for the next two days of hiking.

The weather continued to be bipolar, but this time Mother Nature was in a better mood. It wasn't only feast or famine for our guts while out in the wilderness since we could only carry so much food and had to calorie load when we were in town. It was the same with the weather. We were either drenched in rain from challenging elements or drenched in sweat from beautiful weather. The sweat was usually also accompanied by sunburns for this tender, pasty-white Mainer. Either way, conditions on the trail existed at the extremes.

Sunshine led the way as we passed our first major milestone—100 miles of white blazes on the Appalachian Trail. I'll take the sunburn for now. After several days of summer, I would change my mind and welcomed the rain.

Albert Mountain Fire Tower is the unofficial 100-mile mark. To say the 360-degree view was stunning doesn't give it justice, especially under a bluebird sky dotted with only a few fluffy puffs of white. A high place—a tower—on top of an even higher place—a mountain—is not one of my favorite places to be. But my first hike helped to calm my acrophobia. It didn't cure it completely, but I am so much better. In fact, that day, I scaled the near-50-foot metal structure on top of a 5,200-foot mountain because I couldn't get enough of the Blue Ridge Mountains sprawled out below.

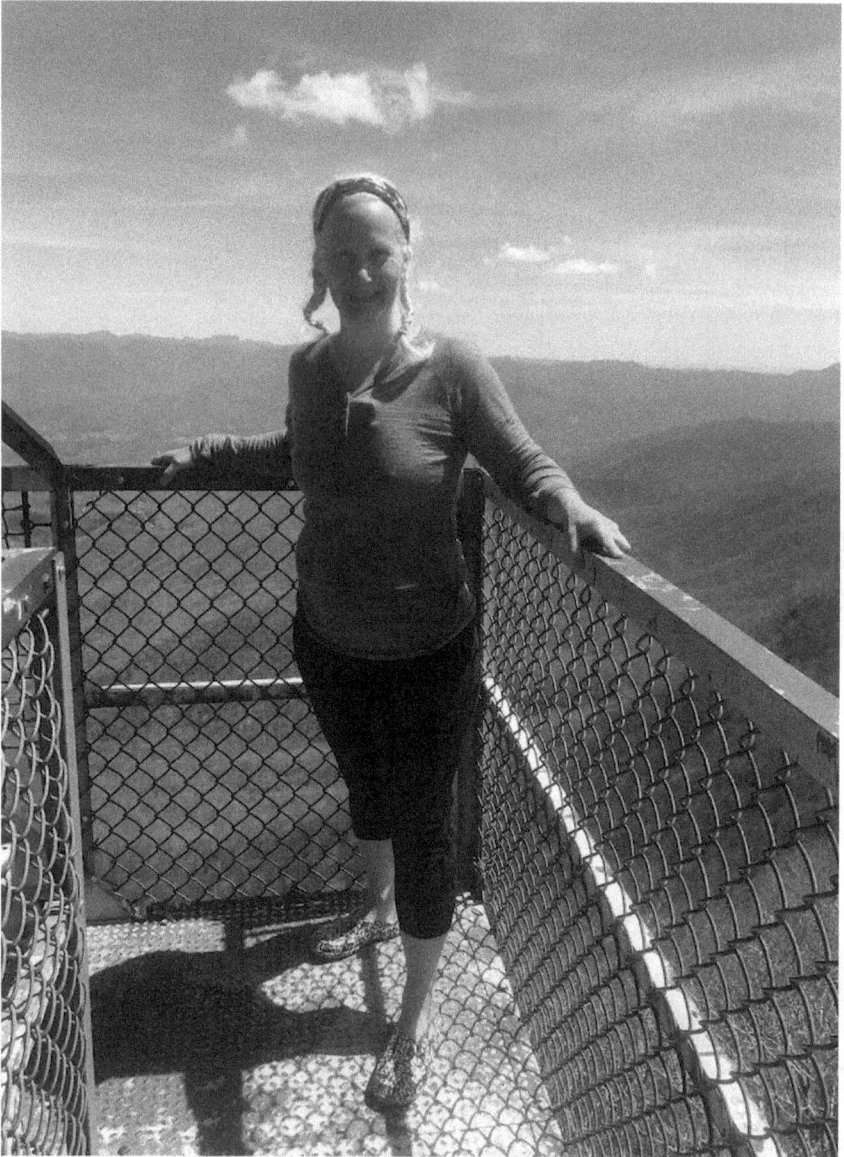

Our scorching sun wasn't going to be around long; we snagged a weather report while there was cell service and discovered a mood swing was going to rage on the mountains. We decided to push on, knowing the Nantahala Outdoor Center would only be two to three days away if we pushed. But I wouldn't call a 7.6-mile day pushing too hard.

Tuesday, Day 12, started about 9:00am and ended minutes before 5:00pm. A long day with few miles. While I relished our slow start to let our bodies acclimate to our new way of life, hiking eight hours and not really going too far was taking a toll on my metatarsals. We didn't take many breaks; it was the slow pace that hurt. For the most part, we were moving constantly. My feet still pained me. It was the same terribly agonizing issue I had in 2015. I needed to hike a little faster—by no means *fast*, just faster than what we were doing. Then rest more often. Being on my feet for long stretches of time didn't allow them to recover so I could continue pain-free a while longer before the cycle would start again. I kept my mouth shut. I didn't want Shortcake to feel bad about our sloth-like speed. It isn't just speed that wins a thru-hike. Everyone who stands on that iconic brown sign on top of Katahdin is a winner.

Stopping after 9.4 miles brought us to Rock Gap Shelter. It was early in the evening, and we went to work doing camp chores. I set up the tent. We cooked our own dinners, and when it was time to secure our food for the night, we went off to find that perfect limb on which to hang our bag. I may have been an athlete, but throwing was not my strength. Thank goodness I was a lefty. It made for an easy choice for my softball coach—he parked my butt on first base, where I didn't have to throw the ball very often. I could catch anything thrown at me, but my delivering it accurately to another player was always nerve racking for everyone. So when Shortcake let the bear line accidentally slip through her hands after I had landed a perfect shot over the limb, all we could do was laugh as we both tried desperately to restring our hang.

Years ago, I may have been mad at that. But with age comes wisdom. More importantly, as my faith has grown by leaps and bounds over the past few years, I look at mishaps as a chance to laugh at life's blunders. It did take several minutes to get another hang, time spent still on my feet. But instead of being irritated, we were two friends out on an adventure developing new skills; and to be honest, I don't even remember my feet hurting while we were doing that.

With my spiritual life deepening, I have found that lesson to work in all areas of life. When something happens at work, or with family, friends, or strangers, the more I dwell on the issue the worse it gets. But if I can use that challenge as a comic relief, if appropriate, or at the least, a lesson to be learned, then I am better able to resolve the situation with less pain or aggravation.

We woke early and were hiking by 7:11am, hoping to beat the rain and cold. The mood swings in weather were already wearing on our patience, and we weren't finding anything comical about it. After all, we started later in hopes of jumping right into spring. But no, Mother Nature does what she does best—like any great woman, she's unpredictable.

We thought if we could crank out fifteen miles, we would be within reach of the NOC the next day. We reasoned that we could tough out the wet and cold, knowing we would be under a roof the next night. But we were wrong. We arrived at the first shelter by 11:45am and took refuge under the small three-sided structure built for five. With the bleak forecast, we decided to just crash there for the day instead of hiking on.

Several other hikers also decided Siler Bald Shelter was a great place to call it quits for the day. Their behaviors were less than desirable. I can tolerate and even enjoy personality differences; it would be a boring place if everyone was like me. It would be a wonderful place, but boring. Differences are what make the world interesting. But when it comes to pot smoking and cigarette smoking within tight quarters, I have my limits.

The weather was worsening, and the forecast for the next two days wasn't much better. We decided to pack up and leave. Before we relinquished our corner in the tight shelter designed for five but holding fifteen, we first needed to give a shout-out to Batman for an extraction from the woods.

The sky cleared, making for a leisurely 1.5-mile hike to Wayah Gap where Batman came to the rescue. We were in the vehicle a few short minutes and the sky opened. Timing is everything.

This rescue was nothing like my demanding Batman rescue of 2015 that is detailed in Chapter 7 of *Happy Hiking: Falling in Love on the Appalachian Trail.* This time, Batman only needed to leave work early and go for a short afternoon drive to retrieve us from the soggy woods.

We so wanted to push on to the NOC. We had been feeling strong, our attitudes were great, and we were enjoying our adventure. But we let our brains win. The weather was going to be very cold and wet for the next two days, so we decided it was best to get out of the woods and take the next two days off to rest up and strategize for the next couple of weeks. So back to base camp we went, where we spent back-to-back zero days in the comforts of Shortcake's home.

Two days of comforts resulted in clean clothes, clean bodies, and a clean slate—only to be battered by the trail for another round in the wilderness. Two days off, two days on, then back to civilization at the

Nantahala Outdoor Center (NOC) in North Carolina, where mega burgers would be waiting for us.

First, we needed to get through the sluggish morning of post-double zero days. As much as I enjoyed the wilds of the woods and its simple life, it was difficult heading back to the trail after such a relaxing time. Town days messed with my trail mojo. The trail was where I wanted to be. Life was easy. All I had to do was get up, pack up, eat, hike, rest, eat, hike, rest, eat, set up camp, sleep, repeat. That may sound boring, but in between all that humdrum, beauty surrounded me. My soul rested. I felt closer to my Creator, and I learned what really matters in life. When I went into the real world, or the "synthetic world," as Triple Crowner, adventurer, and vlogger Jessica "Dixie" of Homemade Wanderlust said in an interview on *Mighty Blue on the Appalachian Trail*'s podcast, the conveniences of modern living made me soft and weak.

It's through struggles that we learn and become strong. When we are confronted with obstacles, we must overcome them if we want to survive, because crashing right through them seldom works. If a downed tree blocks the road, common sense would tell any driver not to proceed and find an alternate route. Continuing on the same path would surely end in injury or death. To gain muscle and strength, a person must get off the couch and start some sort of fitness program. Doing such a thing will result in a certain amount of pain depending on how long they have been enjoying the comforts of the couch. But with time, the muscles will grow and adapt to their new way of life and the pain will cease. No muscles or strength will increase without the struggle. Even a baby chick must break through its own egg in order to survive. If someone removes the shell for it, the little chick will be too weak to live and will die from lack of strength. It's the hatching process that gives the little bird strength to live.

If we don't use our brains, they will slowly die. Daily brain games, reading, writing, doing complicated tasks, and such will help to keep our cerebrum healthy and at peak performance. Sometimes I think using my brain hurts more than climbing mountains. But like the saying goes, "Use it or lose it."

The same is true for just about anything; if we don't use a particular skill, we will slowly lose the ability to do that skill. It doesn't matter if it is a physical, mental, emotional, social, or spiritual skill, if we don't use it, we will lose it.

———

Consecutive town days of comfort had made me a little soft, and those first several miles back on trail with the dirt under my boots, it took me a while to get my rhythm back. A glacier advanced faster than we did that day. But we still managed to make it to our scheduled destination, even with two unplanned stops for trail magic.

Lunch and supper were provided by strangers—former thru-hikers giving back. With the sun bright in the sky and hidden only at moments throughout the day as puffy clouds blocked its full radiance, we moved up the trail. Occasionally we were joined by Batman, who would hike in at crossings to meet us, then hike back out, then jump ahead in the car and repeat.

We even saw the remains of snow produced from the unfavorable weather conditions we had avoided by getting off the trail for two days. Struggles make us stronger, but we didn't want to improve our cold-weather backcountry skill set just yet. Truth be told, I don't care if I ever develop that skill set. Time will tell.

———

The next day started much better than it had ended the previous night. Batman was joining us, which meant Shortcake had the spare tent while Batman and I shared mine.

Just before crawling into the tent with Batman, I stepped in a pile of human poop. That's got to be one of the most disgusting things one can do. I was livid! I wanted to find the owner and rub their face in it. Yes, I do have a mean side that I try to hide. I am not perfect.

I was wearing my camp shoes, the rubber kind with holes around them for ventilation. I was just so glad that the poop did not ooze between openings, because I was also sockless. I managed to scrape most of the crap off onto a rock then hung my Croc™ in a tree for the night, to deal with the next day.

If you read *Happy Hiking: Falling in Love on the Appalachian Trail*, you already know my hubby, Batman, is a wonderful guy. If you haven't, you are about to learn. Since at the end of the next day we would be at the NOC, Batman told me not to worry about my shoe. He would hike it out, clean it, then return it to me when we reunited. I am so blessed.

Human pooh is so gross and there is so much of it out on the trail. There is a problem concerning this issue. For some reason, too many hikers do not care to follow proper waste protocol. According to Leave No Trace, the proper way to perform a Chapter-5 is to first walk 200 feet from water, trails, and camps. Dig a six-to-eight-inch cathole. No, not to bury a cat; but as a cat digs a hole to poop in, so should a hiker. The hole should be four inches to six inches at the deepest part. Poop in the hole and then cover and camouflage it. Lastly, pack out your T-paper.

The only thing the pooper did correctly was hide it. They buried it in leaves right next to the tenting area. Why? Why? Why?

Spring seemed to be taking hold as bouts of sun outnumbered the cloudy ones. Critters sunbathed on warm rocks in the sun. Flowers were blooming here and there. The way flora will grow in the most unusual of places always fascinates me.

For five miles we hiked through a section recently torched by a forest fire. We had been walking through such burned areas since we left Top of Georgia, but the day before and this day were the worst. At times, it felt like the trail was going to crumble under our feet. Mother Nature has a way of surviving though, even after disasters. While the area presently looked devastated, new growth was happening every-where. Another example of how struggles make things better.

Flowers growing where it didn't seem possible prompted me to write a devotion called, "Grow Where You Are Planted." Below is an excerpt from my devotional book, *As Fresh as Daisies: 40 Days of Nature Inspired Devotions*, published in 2022.

GROW WHERE YOU ARE PLANTED

Why do weeds grow right in the middle of your new garden? They seem to pop up faster and more abundantly than the seeds you sowed in that very same spot. And how do those dandelions spring up in what seem like mere hours after you mowed the lawn?

When hikers start a thru-hike of the A.T. in early March, the forest is void of plant life other than barren trees. Slowly over the weeks, little flowers and tufts of grass begin to announce the arrival of spring. They will grow in the darndest of places, places that you wouldn't think anything could grow.

I have seen large trees growing in a thin bed of sod on top of boulders. One time I saw a tree growing horizontally out of a ledge. Flowers grow everywhere from lush earth patches to rock fields with very little soil, even growing in the middle of a trodden dirt path. The one thing they all had in common is that they grew where they were planted. Sounds obvious enough.

But we humans tend to complain when our environment isn't ideal for growth. I know I am always complaining about something even though I try to be positive. It's too hot. It's too cold. I don't like this or that. Work is too hard. I don't feel well. Sure, life doesn't always fertilize us the way we want, and at times, it even poisons us. But it's those times we must send our roots down deep and still grow where we are planted. Just as the tree that grows in a windy area is stronger than one that doesn't, we too grow stronger as we grow through life's obstacles.

But God doesn't just throw us out there and hope for the best. He is there for us. Paul the Apostle in Philippians 4:11-13 tells us to be content in whatever circumstance we are in because we *can do all things through Him who strengthens me.*

I enjoy fluffy pillows, fleece throws, hot and cold running water. Nothing beats a toilet to potty on or cooking a gourmet meal in a well-stocked kitchen. When the sun goes down, flicking a light switch instead of strapping on my headlamp sure is easier, but it's out in the wilderness when I am at my best. I learn who I am and, more importantly, who I want to be. I enjoy being out in the woods, even with the pain and struggle. It's those times that make me appreciate the little things life has to offer, like a view through the canopy, a lizard on a log, and a giant burger at the end of a two-day hike. River's Edge Restaurant, here we come.

BLACK BEAR TIP

Keep a pocket-sized emergency blanket in your survival kit.
It may one day save your life or someone else's.
I even keep one in my vehicle.

Day 18 Monday April 10
Time: 8:30am – 5:15pm
Mile: 137.1 – 147.4
Miles hiked: 10.3
Tented at Locust Cove Gap
Weather: Incredibly hot

Day 19 Tuesday April 11
Time: 7:54am – 4:30pm
Mile: 147.4 – 158.9
Miles hiked: 11.5
Tented at Cable Gap Shelter
Weather: Beautiful sunny day

Day 20 Wednesday April 12
Time: 7:37am – 12:20pm
Mile: 158.9 – 166.0
Miles hiked: 7.1
Stayed at Fontana Lodge
Weather: Hot & sunny

6

Knocking on the Great Smoky Mountains' Door

he Nantahala Outdoor Center in Bryson City, North Carolina, is
a little piece of heaven in the middle of nowhere. Whether you
choose to drive there or hike in, it is no easy excursion. Drivers are
challenged with curvy, narrow, hilly roads making for a white-knuckle
drive, and every hiker's fortitude is tested by the descent into the gap as
well as the climb out of the gap. For those who favor a more leisurely
adventure, a train offers a relaxing option for visiting this famous but
tucked-away tourist destination.

Adventurers can stay for just a meal at the River's Edge Restaurant or bar, or they can spend a day or longer partaking in any of
the NOC's many activities: hiking, biking, rafting, kayaking, zip-lin-
ing, and more. Visitors also have a choice of lodging accommodations
from rustic four-person bunkrooms to fully stocked cabins. Shortcake
and I chose an in-between option of the female-only bunkhouse. It
was clean, comfortable, and convenient since we would only be there
for one quick night.

It wasn't too quick—we did stick around for breakfast, but that was
it. We said good-bye to Batman and headed north once again. That
seemed to be the cycle we were falling into. We hiked, Batman met us

at a predetermined future date and place, usually hiking in to meet us then back out with us. He often resupplied us and spent the night, saw us off the next morning. . . and repeat.

We were headed straight up. The only warm-up we would have would be the jaunt across the campus's driveway back to the trail. From there, we had a 2,620-foot climb to Sassafras Gap Shelter, our destination for the first day out of the NOC. It would be a short 6.6 miles.

I was feeling ill that day. I'm not sure if it was something I ate or if it was the heat, but an upset stomach and the heat made the climb less enjoyable. I do like a challenge. I may complain the whole way, when deep down, I relish the pain and agony of pushing my body. It feels invigorating. But that day, I wondered why we pushed on.

6.6 miles was not very many miles hiked, especially after double zero days a couple days prior. I am sure that had something to do with our decision to push on past the shelter to Locust Cove Gap. That meant we had to climb another 671 feet over Cheoah Bald at 5,062 feet and then descend 1,420 feet.

It was a difficult day of up, up, and up. I was enjoying this hike, but for some reason it seemed so much harder than my 2015 hike. I was only two years older. I had gained a few extra pounds but nothing that I couldn't handle. It was a mystery to me. I didn't acknowledge my plight to Shortcake or Batman. I just suffered in silence.

Looking back at my blog on EmilysEscapades.com, I see that I made more typos and grammatical errors than normal in that day's post. Post hike, I thought about editing my previous trail posts but decided to leave everything as is. The errors somehow add to the essence of the hike. Maybe one day I will revisit the blog and correct all the mistakes, but for now, they are a reminder of my state of being at that time. It was a rough day on the trail, and my writing was in perfect harmony with it.

Despite the day's woes of a challenging climb, heat, sickness, and wondering why it was so much harder, the day was marvelous. We leapfrogged with a cast of characters who ranged from pure annoyance to pure joy to be around. It was like a game of trick or treat.

Would we see the stoners taking a break at the view or would it be the youthful kids chilling at a shelter for lunch?

Don't get me wrong, some of my best friends love their wacky-weed. I don't, never have, never will. I don't care and am not judgmental. I just can't be around it because my lungs can't handle it. Most people I know who enjoy marijuana, cigarettes, alcohol, or whatever mind-altering drug they choose are considerate of their surroundings and of others. That day though, there was one couple who didn't care whose face they were blowing secondhand smoke into. They did what they wanted, even if it was bothering others.

"Hike your own hike" has become synonymous with "Make your own rules." I understand that on the trail there is an unwritten rule that there are no rules. But that is a little extreme, wouldn't you think? Of course there are rules. Common courtesy never goes on strike.

I am all for hiking your own hike and setting your own bar. In fact, just this season I helped a handful of young hikers slackpack the 100-Mile Wilderness. The second day of assisting them, three of them arrived much earlier than expected. They told me they had blue-blazed and then road walked. Being the purist of white-blazers, I was secretly horrified I had helped thru-hikers blue-blaze. As I discussed this decision with one of them, my eyes were opened. Buff, a young college athlete/graduate explained to me that all her life up to this point she had been told what to do, when to do it, what to eat, what not to eat, when to eat, who she could and could not hang out with, where she could and could not go, and so on. She didn't want to be controlled by unwritten rules of a thru-hike. If her curiosity fancied the path of a blue-blazed trail, then she was on it. Then if that meant she had to road walk to pick the trail back up, she wasn't going to let that stop her.

That's the true spirit of "Hike your own hike." Unlike what some hikers think, this well-known slogan does not mean to do whatever you want with disrespect to others. The trail may be an escape from the synthetic world, but all the same issues are still there, just fewer in number.

The highlight of the day was seeing Frosty the Snowman. It was odd to see this misshapen figure in the middle of the dirt path. Someone had fashioned a miniature sculpture from the snow that had fallen on the mountains days earlier. We were off trail for that weather event. The only thing that remained of Frosty was a tiny body about a foot tall with two twig arms. It resembled an alien more than a rotund snowman. No other snow existed anywhere else in the forest except this tiny little snowman slowly losing its figure in the heat of spring.

While spring was in full swing and the temps were rising daily, the little snowman was a reminder of why I still needed to carry my winter gear.

My pack was heavy because of it, but unlike last time, I was not going to switch out my cold gear for summer gear too early. We were knocking on the door of the Great Smoky Mountains, only two days away from entering the national park. It may have been April, but weather in the mountains is about as predictable as a two-year old's taste buds and just as ornery.

———

Mother Nature continued to be in a good mood. This made waking up at 6:00am to the sweet pungent smell of pot more tolerable. I was eager to get out of camp as soon as possible. I avoid shelters so as to not be a party-pooper for others since I have such a low tolerance for cigarettes and pot. I found it so annoying to be outside in the fresh air yet still have to gasp for breaths. While I didn't like to hinder others' experiences, the gesture wasn't always reciprocated. It didn't seem to matter, I always ended up downwind of the lung-choking smoke, even when I tented in the open air.

The warm weather invited us to hit the trail as soon as we could. We had boots on the trail before 8:00am. I love early starts. Skipping the water source helped our earlier than normal beginning. The spring was farther away than I preferred, and the guidebook showed water only a few miles into the hike. I seldom strayed from my habit of carrying too much water. But as already stated, my pack was extra heavy, so I took a chance and didn't fill up.

That's exactly why I have no desire to go to Vegas, bet on horses, or have stakes when playing any game—I tend to lose more often than win. And so it was that day. I couldn't find the so-called water source noted in the guidebook. I am usually pretty good at directions and reading a map. But not so that day. I was thirsty and about to take on Jacob's Ladder—a 600-foot climb in 0.6 mile. And it was hot. To make the situation even more worrisome, I had less than eight ounces of water.

Miraculously, I didn't panic. The book of lies (what I called the guidebook) showed several other water sources up ahead. One of them had to have something. I knew as long as I didn't push it—something I rarely did anyway—I'd be fine. I'd just have to go even slower than our already snail pace and take more rests.

7

The Smoky Mountains

I was a little apprehensive about heading off into the Smokies. Maybe next time I venture off into this famous park, I won't be so worried. This was my second time being nervous about trekking through this beautiful landscape. In 2015, Andrew went home, leaving me to my own devices as I entered the national park. This time, I was worried about Dad.

Someone wise once told me that worry is a tool of the devil. And that we shouldn't give him that much power over us. The Bible tells us repeatedly not to worry and not to be afraid. All worry does is rob us of our present joy. Most of the time, 80 percent of what we worry about never comes to fruition, and usually the other twenty percent isn't nearly as bad as we imagine it will be.

My family assured me there was no need to come home just yet. With that confidence and with the courage to put my worries into God's hands, Shortcake and I headed out to continue our trek north.

At 8:30am, the shuttle returned us to the Fontana Dam Visitor Center where Batman had retrieved us the day before. We walked across the dam as the morning sun glistened on the water's surface. Fontana Dam is located less than a mile south of the Great Smoky

We were at Stecoah Gap on NC Route 143, a heavily trafficked road. The trailhead is a popular pick-up and drop-off point for hikers. In the short time we were there, several vehicles stopped by, delivering hikers back to the trail to continue their journey. We were just passing through and ready to cross the road when one truck stopped and a jolly fella jumped out. No, not Santa. Santa wouldn't have been so cruel. More about this later. He offered trail magic, and I gladly accepted three bottles of water. The trail always provides. I didn't even have to carry the empties; he waited for me to fill my bottles and took the trash.

Before "Mr. Jolly" departed, he informed us there would be awesome trail magic at Cable Gap Shelter. That was almost three miles farther than our planned mileage for the day. We knew we had a tough but short climb ahead, and the heat zapped me, so we made no promises to the trail angel or to each other.

––––––

Jacob's Ladder took us 55 minutes. It may have been short in distance, but it was long on time. We'd walk a few feet, then rest and repeat. At times it felt like the trail was right in front of our faces. There wasn't any rock scrambling like we have in Maine, but the incline was steep and unforgiving. With no real place to rest, we would assume the hiker pose when we couldn't sit.

Poles are used for many different things and resting on them is just one. A common stature for a tired hiker tackling a steep ascent is to face the incline with feet a little more than shoulder-width apart, hold onto the poles, then lean forward, resting the nook of your armpit on your hands and putting as much weight as you can onto the poles with your head hanging low.

Jacob's Ladder wasn't the only tough climb we had that day. Maybe the second climb wouldn't have been so hard if we hadn't done the first one. Either way, we were getting worn out on this low-mileage day. I had hiked a little bit ahead. Climbing is easier for me when I can use my natural gait going uphill. So on the tougher sections, I went ahead to allow my body to do its own thing.

I wasn't far ahead, but just enough that I had a chance to sit on a log seat. Shortly after I sat, I saw Shortcake trudging up the hill. She started to say something, and what came out of her mouth caught us both off guard. It sounded like the Holy Spirit had her caught up in rapture and she was prophesizing the future. There was a loud sound escaping from her vocal cords, but it was some other language neither one of us could comprehend.

Our eyes locked briefly, then we both laughed hysterically. What had just happened? Shortcake tried to talk but she was so daunted by the exertion of the climb her brain could not produce discernable words. That was just what we both needed, some comic relief. The trail really does provide what you need when you need it.

I know "The trail will provide" is a common saying on any long trail, but my heart knows that it isn't the trail that does the providing. It is our heavenly Father who sends us such gifts. It may come in the form of sunshine, or even rain. It may be bottles of water from a stranger. It could be a beautiful view when your mood is low. It is often the smile from another hiker when you need a friend. And sometimes, it's just an incident that makes you laugh so hard that you forget about the pain you are currently enduring.

Some see these things merely as coincidences. I don't believe it is that simple. My first thru-hike taught me to enjoy the little things. I would go out of my way to see the smallest of details and take joy in them. It wasn't long before I was seeing goodness all around and I didn't need to search for it. God works like that too. He is all around. All we have to do is be open to His presence and realize the little things that take place all day and every day are His little ways of providing what we need when we need it.

Our bout of laughter and the prospect of mega trail magic at the shelter gave us an energy boost to go the extra distance to make it to Cable Gap Shelter. We arrived by 4:30pm, plenty of time to set up camp, do camp chores, and wait for the magic to happen.

And we waited. And we waited. And we waited some more, until finally, at 7:30pm we gave up all hope of being treated.

My mind briefly thought how cruel it was of Mr. Jolly to tease us with such expectations. That was a fleeting thought, and then my disappointment turned into concern. We worried that something had happened to our happy trail angel and hoped he was okay. Maybe his gifts weren't meant for us that day and someone else needed his services. Even without the trail magic, our push to move on had set us up for an easy stroll into Fontana the next day.

It seemed like a short seven miles to Fontana. But before we reached the end of the day's hike, I received a satellite message from Batman on my inReach. For being a positive person, my mind always goes to the worst possible scenario when unexpected things occur. Just like I worried about the trail angel not showing up the previous night, I couldn't help but think there was something wrong; that's why Batman was contacting me. He didn't usually communicate with the inReach unless I initiated first contact.

My worries usually pan out to be nothing. I wished it was so this time. I looked at the text from Batman. My heart sank. My dad had a heart attack, and I had no service to reach out to him or my family back home to find out how he was doing.

Pre-hike in 2015, I had a chat with Dad discussing what I would do in the event something happened to him while I was on the trail. It was mutual that neither one of us wanted me to come home. We knew it was a once-in-a-lifetime journey, one Dad himself wished he could have gone on. He did not want to be the reason for me not finishing. We both knew I probably would not go back to the trail after such an event. So he and I had a pact that if something happened, I would remain on the trail, even if that something was his death. We knew the family would be furious if that did happen, but he wanted me to finish.

Fast forward to 2017. My once-in-a-lifetime event was on take two, and I was facing a tragic event—Dad's heart attack. I did not have the same conviction about staying on the trail. Shortcake and I were three weeks into our journey, and I wondered if I needed to go home. Ironically, it was at the same point where Andrew, my very first hiking buddy in 2015, had made his decision to leave the trail and go home.

———

The day was easy. We made it to the Fontana marina just before noon and freshened up briefly in the restrooms before continuing the short jaunt high above the shore of Fontana Lake, stopping at Fontana Dam Shelter, nicknamed Fontana Hilton. This wooden, four-sided, double-terraced shelter sits overlooking the lake, with picnic tables, charging station, and a fire pit. The shelter is spacious, with two levels of sleeping areas on each side of the entrance. For those who prefer solitude, tent pads are strategically placed to give adequate room for tents and hammocks. If that wasn't enough luxury for a shelter, bathrooms with showers were located mere yards away. And there were trash receptacles.

As nice as it would have been to stay in this shelter, we only stopped long enough for lunch. We were going for a little extra comfort before entering the Great Smoky Mountain National Park the next day. After lunch, we continued north 0.4 mile to the Fontana Dam Visitor Center, where Batman whisked us away to Fontana Lodge.

At the Lodge, we dried our stuff, hand-washed a few items, resupplied from Batman, and ate at the Wildwood Grill. I had my usual burger and fries. I never thought the day would come when I would be sick of burgers and fries, but it eventually happened. My choice of menu options was limited due to my intolerance of gluten, corn, and vinegar. I was only three weeks into my hike and already getting bored with food.

Batman only joined us for the afternoon. He headed back to base camp and left Shortcake and me to ponder the next several days of our journey as we geared up and mentally prepared for our trek through the Smokies.

Before heading to bed, I was able to contact family to ease my worried brain and heart. My dad was stable and expected to make a full recovery, but the term "full" was an overstatement. His health was not good to begin with, and this only weakened his state.

My dad was my rock. He was far from perfect, but he was perfect for me. We argued and butted heads more than most, but we were always each other's cheerleaders in life. He narrowly escaped this brush with fate. I talked with my brother and sister, and they didn't see any need for me to come home just yet. So I stayed on the trail to continue into the Great Smoky Mountains the next day.

BLACK BEAR TIP

Set goals and expectations but also be flexible.
The trail will guide you to where you need to be.

Day 21 Thursday April 13
Time: 8:45am – 4:50pm
Mile: 166.0 – 177.0
Miles hiked: 11
Mollies Ridge Shelter
Weather: Hot & sunny

Day 22 Friday April 14
Time: 7:30am – 5:00pm
Mile: 177.0 – 189.0
Miles hiked: 12
Tented at Derrick Knob Shelter
Weather: Hot & sunny

Day 23 Saturday April 15
Time: 7:15am – 6:00pm
Mile: 189.0 – 202.5
Miles hiked: 13.5
Tented at Mt. Collins Shelter
Weather: Hot & sunny, cloudy cool
evening

Day 24 Sunday April 16
Time: 7:18am – 10:50am
Mile: 202.5 – 206.8
Miles hiked: 4.3
Went to Shortcake's house
Weather: Cold morning

Day 25 Monday April 17
Zero Day

Day 26 Tuesday April 18
Time: 9:28am – 7:30pm
Mile: 206.8 – 221.9
Miles hiked: 15.1
Tented at TriCorner Knob Shelter
Weather: Rain

Day 27 Wednesday April 19
Time: 8:04am – 12:30pm
Mile: 221.9 – 229.6
Miles hiked: 7.7
Cosby Knob Shelter
Weather: Cloudy

Day 28 Thursday April 20
Time: 7:53am – 6.55pm
Mile: 229.6 – 245.4
Miles hiked: 15.8
Tented near mile 245.4
Weather: Cloudy

Mountains National Park (GSMNP) entrance in North Carolina. It is the tallest concrete dam east of the Rockies. The dam was built to support the war efforts of WWII.

The day started at 1,700 feet elevation. It didn't stay there long.

After crossing the dam, the trail progressed along a road for half a mile until turning back into the woods, the entry for The GSMNP. Our level ground soon became a steep incline. We were headed for an elevation over 4,500 feet. But it wasn't all up. There were several PUDS (pointless ups and downs) between us and our destination.

Four and a half miles into the hike, we came to a blue-blazed trail leading to Shuckshack fire tower at 3,889 feet elevation. We dropped our packs at the trail junction and proceeded with our poles up the steep incline to check out the tower.

So far, the score is Shuckshack Fire Tower - 2, me - 0. In 2015, I was only able to climb to the first platform. This year, I was sure I could handle the exposed structure with no problem. I confidently ran up to the base and took one step up—and my stomach fell. There was no right-side railing for the first flight. *No worries,* I cheered myself on. When I reached the first platform and tried to round the corner, I was unable to continue. I slowly did an about face and retreated to the safety of the ground.

Shortcake was able to claim ownership to the second level. As she did, the competitiveness awoke inside me. When she was down, I went back to the base step and made a motion to go back up, then quickly changed my mind and silently said, "Nah, it's not worth it!"

Back at the trail junction, we sat enjoying a snack. As we did, a hiker in his 70s approached and joined us. Soon, a second hiker appeared. As he got closer, Shortcake said to him, "What trail are you coming from?"

I looked at him, he looked at me, and, dumbfounded by her question, we both looked at Shortcake.

Puzzled, he replied, "The A.T."

Shortcake soon realized her error. She was a little disoriented from our jaunt up to the tower, and when she saw the two hikers coming, she thought they were on a different trail. We all laughed and got lots of enjoyment from that, at her expense.

Later that evening, it was my turn to have the brain fart. At the shelter as we were chitchatting with other hikers, someone asked if I had started from Fontana Dam that morning. I quickly replied, "No! The visitor center." Well, the visitor center is at the dam. I'd like to record all brain-dead conversations we hikers have. You'd think all the fresh air and exercise would improve our mental awareness, but on the contrary, we are all flatlining in the EEG department.

Our second day in the Smokies scored low in the spectacular department. There were few jaw-dropping vistas or heart-pounding experiences. But to say the Smoky Mountains were less than entertaining is really an oxymoron. Just being out there in the vast wilderness is incredible. I learned in 2015 that things don't have to be intense 24/7 to be awesome. I always made sure to find joy in the little things, and Day 2 in the Smokies had many little things adding up to greatness.

For starters, just a few yards after we left camp we were greeted by a young deer. I thought it was a doe, but five years later as I zoomed in on the photo I took of "her," I can see the nubs of antlers. Deer shed their headwear in the winter and grow new ones in the spring and throughout the summer. Since it was early spring, the little fella we said good morning to looked more like a young lassie than the fearless buck he soon would become.

Soon after we entered the Smoky Mountains, the dull, dry, lifeless forest we had been hiking through since we left Georgia was morphing into what seemed like a place from once upon a time. Sure, random flowers were beginning to awaken everywhere, but here in the national park it was lush, green, and blanketed with tiny forest flowers.

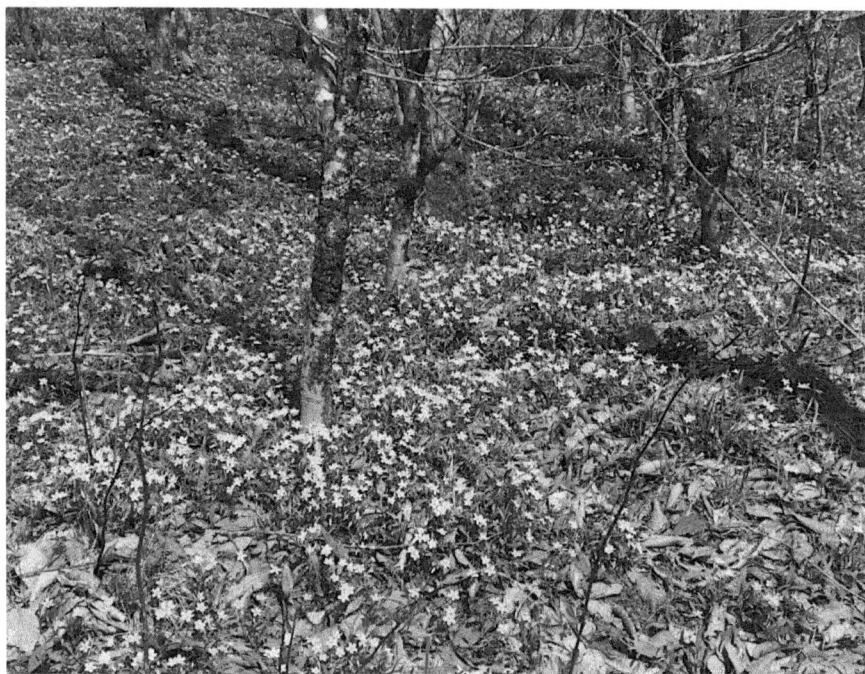

The higher elevations of this area receive on average 85 inches of rain a year, qualifying it to be a rainforest. That was a neat fact I learned while on my hike. I thought rainforests were only in the Amazon and the Pacific islands, not on the east coast of the United States. Lucky for us on Day 2 through the park we did not get any of that "average" precipitation. It was hot and sunny for our travels.

At northbound mile 184.1, we summited Rocky Top at an elevation of 5,440 feet. This view was spectacular and yes, the top was rocky, but easily navigable. We could see waves of mountain ranges, each layer rising higher than the one in front of it until the most distance peaks kissed the sky. The sunny blue sky was filling with fluffy dense clouds that were darkening in the center.

Even with the thickening clouds our eyes still strained against the sun, and we hoped the clouds would hold their weight until we were off the highest parts of the trail for the day. But we weren't done climbing; we still had another hundred feet to climb in half a mile before starting our descent to the Derrick Knob Shelter at 4,882. It wouldn't be straight down either. Remember, we were on the A.T. Point A to Point B is seldom a straight line, and it is never just up or just down.

The day may have been low on grandeur but it was a hard hike. By the time we reached the shelter, we were ready to call it a day. We tented. The rule in the Smokies is that hikers must use the shelter unless it is full.

The shelters are nice in that they are large, usually with two levels of sleeping areas, and most of them are tarped in front to keep out the driving rain and hurricane-force winds that are so common at higher elevations. Some of them even have a fireplace.

Since the shelter was full, I set up our tent. My once-Taj Mahal of a tent for one was slowly beginning to feel like a sardine can. Shortcake and I were still sharing my Hubba Hubba 2-person tent. It was super fun at first, being snug in it together. I felt like we were little kids at a slumber party. But lately, to be honest, it was miserable.

I never complained, or at least I don't think I did, and Shortcake never did. But it was hard for me. I don't sleep well on a good night. Sharing tight quarters with someone who has different sleep habits is all that more difficult. It didn't matter how long I stayed up; she would always stay up that much longer. Then if I did happen to fall asleep, when Shortcake finally finished her nighttime routine and settled down in her sleeping bag, that would wake me up. It would take forever for me to fall back to sleep. I also sleep like a rotisserie chicken, turning a quarter turn every so often just to keep comfy; but now, so I wouldn't bother her, I was prolonging my flips till I absolutely needed to shift positions. It was horrible. I wasn't getting rest, but it was my own fault because I didn't communicate my discomfort.

The clouds from the day before held their water and we had another hot and sunny day as we continued our trek north through the Smoky Mountains. We had 13.5 miles planned for the day, with a stop at Clingman's Dome ten miles into the day.

Clingman's Dome is the highest point on the Appalachian Trail at 6,643 feet elevation. It is a tourist trap like Mt. Washington, New Hampshire. View seekers can drive up the mountain then hike the paved quarter-mile to the top from the parking lot. The ramped, round observation tower is easily walked by anyone who desires to put one foot in front of the other and allows anyone with physical challenges access to see the grand panorama as well.

Our third day in the park was a Saturday, which automatically meant the place would be busy. Combine that with Easter weekend, and the numbers were staggering. Shortcake and I cruised to the top of the observation deck, snagged a few selfies and pics, then headed back down to the base.

At one point as I stood among the tourists trying to capture the perfect photo, I felt a panic attack rising in my chest. I don't do well in crowds, and after spending three weeks in the woods, that trait only worsened.

Back at the base, Shortcake and I snacked and rested on the rock wall. As we were doing so, a middle school-aged boy and his mother strolled by after their trip to the top. He said, "I am tired. I want to go home now and sit on the couch. That is enough adventure for one day!" Shortcake and I had all we could do to contain our laughter.

When we too had endured all we could, we packed up and headed on our way. We still had 3.4 miles to reach our home away from home for the night, with a short climb before then. As if Clingman's Dome wasn't enough, the trail designers had to add Mt. Collins, and I loved every step of the way, even if it was hard.

It was another beautiful day in the Smokies. We had great views, the hike was fun and challenging, and I finally found ramps, a wild, garlic-oniony edible plant I carried all day for Shortcake. And then she forgot to add it to her supper.

We were being extracted by Batman in the morning. We got up early, which was our new norm, but this time we did it so we could have as long a nero day as possible. I loved nero days. We still managed to enjoy a lazy 4.3-mile hike that took us forever to complete because there was so much to photograph in that short distance.

One such item of interest was a blown-down tree whose roots had been ripped out of the earth. The massive, ten-foot-high by fifteen-foot-wide mass of roots gripped a giant boulder in its center. It looked like the tree was laying a ginormous dinosaur egg.

Batman hiked in to meet us. That was his standard MO. He had arrived at the parking lot before we were even up. He wasn't sure which was north and which was south from the parking area, and he accidentally went north for a mile. He still managed to cover more miles than Shortcake and I. We took our time taking photos, de-layering, snacking, and whatever else we felt like doing. We were relaxed, knowing we had a short distance to cover and all day to do it if we wanted.

Since it was Easter Sunday, every now and then I placed jelly beans along the trail, strategically arranging them for hikers to see. It was fun. To this day, I feel a little bit of guilt about doing that. At the time, I thought it was cute, but as I have grown in my outdoor appreciation, I now realize I violated the Leave No Trace principles of pack in and pack out and leave the environment the way I found it. I personally don't like to see artwork out in the wilderness, such as painted rocks, displays of artistically placed natural debris, or anything else along those lines, so why did I think it was okay for me to leave jelly beans?

Batman parked at Newfound Gap. There we were greeted by a friendly chap who was eager to feed us, and it was perfect timing—lunch time. Anytime food is being offered at no cost is perfect to a hiker though.

Newfound Gap is another tourist attraction, where the border of Tennessee and North Carolina runs through a huge parking lot. It is also home to the Rockefeller Memorial and the site where President FDR formally dedicated the park in 1940.

Reaching Newfound Gap meant we were halfway through the Great Smoky Mountain National Park. The second half would have to wait. With our tummies full, we thanked our trail angel and Batman whisked us away. Winding roads took us back to base camp. But not before we stopped at Cracker Barrel for an Easter dinner out.

Zero days are so crucial to a long-distance hiker's success. A day off serves so many purposes, but no matter how a hiker uses their zero day, the result is the same—time off the trail to refocus in order to go back at it. And that's what we did. We cleaned up, we fueled up, we stocked up, and probably most importantly, we had alone time. Even good friends need to get away from each other to decompress. Shortcake's home was spacious enough for all three of us to find our own little place to rejuvenate.

I did a happy dance when Shortcake went through her mail. A package from her sister, Susanne, contained a surprise for me—jelly beans. They became my signature candy for this hike. It was a bag of jelly beans I was holding in 2015 when I fell the first time. I should have been holding both poles to help me stay upright on the snowy trail, but no, I had to have my jelly beans. I ended up on the downhill side of the trail, grateful I didn't tumble farther down.

I am fussy though—not just any flavor or brand will do. My favorite is Brach's Speckled Jelly Bird Eggs. (They come in a blue bag, just in case you want to send me any.) I thought I had stocked up pre-hike, but my supply was dwindling faster than I could replenish. Then the stores ran out. In a rash, selfish haste, I put out a post on Facebook asking friends to send me jelly beans. I wasn't serious.

I have the best friends though; packages of sweet pebbles were coming in from all directions. By the time the deliveries made it to my restock supply, I had enough to last the rest of the hike. Even Short-cake surprised me with a stash of jelly beans she bought while she was out doing her resupply.

Our first three days through the Smokies had been hot and mostly sunny. When we arrived back at Newfound Gap, it became apparent why this mountain range also qualifies as a rainforest—and not the one at Disney's Animal Kingdom, where fake thunderstorms and rain are just part of the dinner and show at the famous Rainforest Café.

I did not want to get out of the car. Shortcake was all too excited to start our second half. I boast about being an avid outdoor adventure seeker, but truth be known, I'm kind of a fair-weather gal. I don't mind if inclement weather sneaks up on me while I'm out there, but I truly despise starting out in it. Shortcake didn't really like unfavorable elements either, but this day she was ready to try out her new piece of gear, a rain skirt by Zpacks. I also had one, but I wasn't so eager to test its quality. We had a 1,000-foot climb I didn't want to tackle when it was wet.

We were already at 5,045 feet of elevation and had to get up and over 6,036 feet. From there, we would spend the rest of the hike hovering between 5,300-5,500 feet, with one bump up to 5,800 feet and then back down to 5,500. The final effort would take us to 6,200 feet then we would finish at almost 5,900 feet at TriCorner Knob Shelter. The elevation profile in the guidebook again resembled a serrated knife.

It was our longest day with 15.1 miles, most of it in the rain. We had a late start since we were coming from base camp, and I prolonged it by whining and complaining about the weather. Thankfully, the sun came out at 3:50pm. We arrived at the shelter by 7:30, and this was probably the first day we were actually looking forward to spending the night in a shelter. The thought of cramming two soggy bodies and gear into my tent was not a happy thought.

But there was no room in the inn. The shelter was tarped closed. Before I could squeeze through the narrow opening, voices from within announced that the shelter was full. I retreated, shook my head in disbelief, and tried a second time. I made it a little farther inside and noticed that there was plenty of ground room we could set up, but everyone was adamant that we could not come in. Never had I encountered such rude and thoughtless hikers. All my other experiences were if a hiker wanted in, hikers made room.

So tenting it was. We could handle that. It wasn't what we wanted, but oh well, we would survive. To make matters worse, all the "good" spots in the vicinity were already occupied. I managed to find a small piece of earth that was sloped the least. I strategically erected the tent so the person on the downhill side had a tree to brace against to keep from rolling out.

I chose the downhill side. I didn't want to squish Shortcake since she was much smaller than me. I am not exaggerating when I say we slept on a slope. Our chosen spot had no business having a tent placed on it. It was the best we could find with the diminishing daylight, and we were exhausted after our longest haul to date.

It was a long, uncomfortable night. We were out of camp by 8:04am. No rain, just cloudy. We arrived at the first shelter by noon-thirty and our intention was only to rest, have lunch, and dry things out. We were the first ones there, so we claimed two spots, just in case our plans changed. And they did. We had only hiked 7.7 miles but decided that was enough. We called it a day, and as the afternoon hours ticked by, more and more hikers took refuge there with us. By 4:00pm it began raining. But no worries, we had a spot in the shelter.

That was our last night in the national park. On April 20, we said good-bye to the Smoky Mountains. I was so happy to be rid of them. Not because they are not pretty. On the contrary, the woods offer a variety of flora and fauna. It's the shelter rules that make thru-hiking the Great Smoky Mountains frustrating for me.

Hikers cannot stealth camp. You must sleep in the shelters unless they are full, then you can tent near them. But tenting wherever you want is not allowed, so hikers are forced to do either fewer miles or extra-long miles to hit the shelters. If we could have camped wherever, I would have been able to find us a flatter place to set up the tent.

I get it, though. Rules are set in place to keep the wilderness intact. I do understand the need for such rules. In my home state, Baxter State Park, the northern terminus for the Appalachian Trail, has some of the strictest rules. I get that too. It doesn't mean I have to like it, but I really do understand the importance of keeping "wild" in wilderness.

But combine the rules with the overcrowding on the trail, and it can make for a not-so-fun traverse through the majestic mountains that would otherwise be enjoyed. Another reason why it is so important to find joy in the little things.

Our exit was enjoyable, with a show of pretty flowers and an easy trail topped off with trail magic just yards from the park boundary.

We pushed on and hiked another personal best of 15.8 miles, ended our day with a 2,000-foot climb, and camped at the top of a peak. We were out of the Smokies and could tent wherever we felt like it. It was so liberating. We were alone, the evening was warm, and we were loving it.

BLACK BEAR TIP

Embrace the YUCK!

Trail Log

Day 29 Friday April 21
Time: 7:34am – 7:55pm
Mile: 245.4 – 260.3
Miles hiked: 14.9
Tented at Walnut Mountain Shelter
Weather: Hot, humid, some rain

Day 30 Saturday April 22
Time: 7:12am – 3:00pm
Mile: 260.3 – 273.4
Miles hiked: 13.1
Base Camp
Weather: Wet & rainy

Day 31 Sunday April 23
Time: 11:44am – 2:37pm
Mile: 273.4 – 279.3
Miles hiked: 5.9
Base Camp
Weather: Wet, rainy, windy

Day 32 Monday April 24
Time: 7:20am – 12:43am
Mile: 279.3 – 288.3
Miles hiked: 9.0
Base Camp
Weather: Cloudy, cool, wet trail

Day 33 Tuesday April 25
Time: 7:29am – 4:15pm
Mile: 288.2 – 300.3
Miles hiked: 12.1
Tented at Jerry Cabin Shelter
Weather: Foggy, cool, humid

Day 34 Wednesday April 26
Time: 7:56am – 7:57pm
Mile: 300.3 – 318.2
Miles hiked: 17.9
Base Camp
Weather: Hot & sunny

8

Mud

What a relief to have the Smokies behind us. I do wish I would change my attitude about this fabulous treasure on the eastern part of the USA. I don't know why I am so hard on this beautiful mountain range. I think it's just my own insecurities that cast a shadow over this wonderful place. One day I need to visit them when I am not trying to just get through them so I can reach Katahdin. But they were done, and we were on to our next milestones.

Max Patch was in our sights for the day. It is a beautiful treeless bald at an elevation of 4,629 feet with windswept grass and rolling hills in all directions. It's a popular destination for locals and tourists, and a picnic there is a real treat for hikers. Most of the time we hike in the forest, and in April, most of the forest is still brown and dull with the occasional flowers starting to bloom. Even with the lack of canopy, one still feels confined. It was nice to be on the open bald in the new spring grass. We each claimed a spot and lay on the soft earth as the sun warmed our skin.

There were other thru-hikers partaking in the summit's glory, as well as day visitors. One hiker passed and joyfully proclaimed he had just checked the weather and the rain was done for the day.

The words parted from his lips and 30 seconds later we all yelled, "Here it comes!" All of us except Shortcake saw it coming. She just stayed there mesmerized by the awesomeness of the bald. I had to encourage her to pack up and get going. We could see the rain cloud closing in. We threw on our rain gear and headed off the grassy plateau.

We hiked down to the safety of the forest. It was there I remembered my wrong turn in 2015, again trying to beat the rain. This was just a drizzle that cooled our hot skin. We hiked to the next shelter and took refuge. It was too early to call it a day, so we decided to cook our lunch and watch the weather. As we did, we enjoyed the company of a fellow hiker, Space Jam. He was the one who had given us the faulty weather forecast at the top of Max Patch.

After three hours the skies cleared and we hiked on. We stayed dry until just before we reached the next shelter. Then it rained again, soaking us before ending for the day. We decided to tent. We just needed to wait a bit for the rain to soften. With precision teamwork, we set up our tent as gracefully as synchronized swimmers.

This was nice. I usually set up the tent and packed it away by myself. My negativity just assumed Shortcake was being lazy. It wasn't until 2022 that I found out she let me erect the tent alone because she knows how particular I can be and didn't want to get in my way. Hmm, communication would have been good on both our parts.

Why is it that we put so much emphasis on things in life that don't really matter? We spend hours—at least I do—rearranging the furniture. We spend hours on social media. We make sure our outfits are coordinated for the seasons. We decorate our houses for the seasons. The list of things we focus on is endless. But we tend to neglect what is most important, and that is our relationships with family and friends. The best way to foster those relationships is by having good communication.

Have you ever watched those cheesy Christmas movies or romantic comedies? The main actors meet and become attracted to one another, but usually there is a hidden agenda. Then that hidden agenda is partly discovered by one of the lovers. That person gets in a tizzy and calls off the relationship because they assume the worst in the other. Communication from the get-go would have prevented all the drama. It's best not to assume anything about the other person, no matter how trivial you think it might be, even if it's just setting up a tent.

Time is relevant, mentally speaking. You have the same 24 hours a day that I do, but isn't it weird how when we are doing something tortuous—like working—the time seems to drag on, but when we are doing something awesome, that awesomeness is over in a flash. Or when we were younger, a week seemed like eternity; but as we get older, the months and even years tick away faster and faster with each passing of the sun.

So it was beginning to happen with this hike. The milestones seemed to be adding up quickly. Our first milestone was making it to Neel Gap, then completing our first state, then the first 100 miles. Now the Smokies were done, and we'd soon be to Hot Springs.

Aw, Hot Springs, North Carolina. A quaint hiker town where the trail follows the main street for about half a mile. All we needed to do was hike 13.1 miles and we'd be able to grab a soak in one of their famous hot springs hot tubs and call it a day. Seemed easy enough.

Apparently, the night before I had slept through a raging thunderstorm. Good for me. I don't usually sleep well. But poor Shortcake informed me in the morning that the storm had been so ominous that she almost had a panic attack. Just her admitting that fact meant the storm must have been bad. She was the calm one of our hiking duo. I was the one who usually freaked out and was the fun-sucker—as my nephew James once told me.

The wet night turned into a wet day, making it a long, messy hike. Batman joined us, hiking southbound from Hot Springs. He had tallied almost a hundred miles so far just hiking in to meet us then hiking back out. Some days he hiked more miles than we did.

The trail was a mess, we were a mess, and our attitudes were not so perky either. Under all that dampness, though, we managed to still enjoy ourselves. The trail teaches you to embrace the yuck. It was easy to forget the recent trail grime, knowing a soak in a hot tub was in our near future—the perfect way to wash away all the crud from our bodies and from our souls as well.

To start the day, we had a 2.5-mile uphill. Once we summited Bluff Mountain at 4,686 elevation, it was mostly downhill to Hot Springs, just shy of eleven miles down to 1,326-feet elevation. Remember, it's never just up and it's never just down. On paper, it looked all downhill. Sounds easy, right? Downhill is actually harder. It's harder on the knees and all joints. It's harder to balance the weight of your pack and navigate the ground to keep from tumbling forward. And when things are wet and muddy, the threat of injury is compounded.

We all arrived unscathed, and when we reached the pavement, we sent Batman ahead to rent a tub. That way, all Shortcake and I would have to do was to be pointed to the correct private tub, strip down, and let the healing waters of Hot Springs do their magic.

But you don't always get what you want. Batman met us on the north side of town and informed us the next opening wasn't until 11:00pm. That was eight hours away. Sure, we had the usual hiker town chores to do, but even with that, 11:00pm was way past our bedtime. We skipped the tubs and headed back to base camp for a home-cooked meal and a Dr. Teal's® minty Epsom salt bath.

Long-distance hiking is a tug of war with one's sanity. On one hand, you crave being out in the wilderness with all her unpredictable situations. Then, on the other hand, you crave the luxuries of modern convenience when you have been without such amenities. Then once you have been pampered, you can't wait to get back out and be miserable again.

So there we were, dry in Shortcake's home after several days of sweat, rain, and mud, sometimes all three at the same time. We woke up to rain and wind, and with base camp being so close to many trailheads, we decided to slackpack.

Slackpacking is when a thru-hiker ditches most of their gear and only keeps what they need for the day; then they retrieve their gear at the end of the day. It's a great way to rest your body and still make forward progress. A purist will carry all their gear all the time. I thought about being a purist in 2015. But that didn't last long. As long as I hiked every white blaze and only hiked north, I was good. Shortcake felt the same way. If we had a chance to lighten our load, we did.

Since our gear was still drenched and it was raining, we decided to hike a nero day—5.9 miles—and sleep at base camp again. Ah, the luxuries of platinum-blazing the Appalachian Trail. It was easy to go out into the rain, knowing we would be under a roof at the end of the day.

We enjoyed that so much we did it again the next day. This time, we slackpacked 9 miles. It was easy in hiker terms. But it was not a walk in the park. The profile in the guidebook again looked like an EKG printout with all the possible bad rhythms except flatlining.

Another rhythm that was taking shape was us. We had now been on the trail for a month, and we noticed we didn't ache as much at the end of the day. We didn't complain quite as much. We were laughing more. We felt strong. We were finally beginning to get our trail legs, which made everything else that much more enjoyable.

When I was reviewing my notes, my blog post for April 24 compared hiking to childbirth. I had remembered a thought I had when hiking a difficult section. Some babies are planned, and some come by chance. It is the same with a thru-hike. There are those who plan for months, even years, before they set foot on the trail, and others just fall into it. Then before the baby comes into the world, there is labor. Sometimes it is hard and grueling and sometimes it is quick and easy. One just never knows. The trail is just like that. Some days we huff and puff and drag ourselves up and over peaks one step at a time, breathing and swearing why did we ever do this. Then we finish that one peak (contraction) and slumber down to the gap, gearing up for the next when we begin huffing and puffing all over again. This goes on for hours. But once we make that final push and we are at the last summit of the day with a breathtaking view (or baby), we forget all about the pain we just endured. And some of us forget real fast about all the pain and agony and do it a second time. It's no wonder at all that some of my friends question my sanity.

Three nights in a row in a bed in your own home—Shortcake's home feels like home to me—will do wonders for one's attitude after being in the wilderness for so long. Not that my disposition is bad. On the contrary, being outside restores my soul. The chance to wash off the blood, sweat, and mud is always uplifting. But we were thru-hikers, and if we wanted to live up to that title, we needed to get back to the trail and earn our blazes.

After our third night at base camp, Batman delivered us back to the trail. Jerry Cabin Shelter, 12.1 miles ahead, was our goal. Mother Nature decided we deserved a day without precipitation, but she still kept us in the fog most of the day. Every spot denoted in the guidebook with a camera icon marking a view was nothing but a blank canvas that day.

So what do artists do with a blank canvas? They create. And since we were artists of the A.T., that's what we did. We began ooohing and ahhhing as we looked into the vast nothingness of the fog. We said things like, "Wow! Look at that view! See the way the sun highlights the ridge." Or "Wow! We are so far up." Our views were spectacular and jaw-dropping, if only in our minds.

At one point, a trail sign warned us of an exposed ridgeline and advised us to take the *bad weather trail* if there was inclement weather. I remembered that sign from 2015 and was excited to see this spot again.

In 2015 I was hiking solo at the time, and when I confronted this warning sign, I sat pondering what to do. I am not a risk taker, and to be in a situation that could be dangerous solo is not what I call fun. The weather was fine; I didn't need to blue-blaze. But the thought of traversing an open ridge alone had a panic attack resting in my throat.

Thankfully, the thought of missing white blazes was more worrisome to me then sliding off a cliff. I gave myself an out. I would go on until I no longer felt safe, and then I could always backtrack to the bad weather trail if necessary.

Little tests in life that push our comfort zone are what increase our confidence and show us that fear is nothing but *False Evidence Appearing Real.* Maybe that is why I endure the rigors of long-distance hiking and why the trail keeps calling me back. It is there I am tested and gain confidence to grow and learn as a person.

While we didn't have to hike in the rain, the bad weather from the previous days and nights had chewed up the trail. It was a muddy, soggy mess. There was so much mud. So let's talk about mud. Not all mud is created equal.

There is greasy mud. This kind is only about a quarter inch thick with a firm surface beneath, but when you step on it, it acts like a lubricant, and you go slip-sliding and away.

Then there is pie crust mud. This is greasy mud that has dried out and will cling to your boots or bottom of your tent in sheets like pie crust.

There is the pleasant mud that I call brownie mix. It is black and with the same consistency as your favorite brownie mix. It doesn't cling to anything, is dry-ish so it doesn't soak your footwear, and it is soft to walk on. But it can be tricky to traverse depending on its depth. Unlike brownie batter, you won't want to lick your boots clean.

Then there is the baby-poop kind of mud. This disgusting kind is black like brownie mix mud but is more like a newborn's first poop. It is black, tar-ish and sticks to everything.

There is soupy mud. This has a layer of water on top and is thicker beneath. This kind you must poke and prod with your hiking pole to find a spot that is safe to cross. Its depth can be very deceiving, as Shortcake has found out many times.

The last kind of mud is the never-ending mud. It can be a combination of any or all the varieties already mentioned and even some not yet discovered. But this type stretches for yards, miles, and even days. There's no going around it, so most hikers just surrender to it and tread right through. I find it one of those simple joys of being in the wilderness—playing in the mud.

We added another milestone to our resume. We hit 300 miles. I could see the pride in Shortcake's face. She is a gal of few words. One seldom knows what she is feeling or thinking. Not knowing can be challenging sometimes since communication is so vital, but when you are friends with someone, just being with them is enough. But that day as we artfully placed small stones forming the number "300" with little yellow flowers dotting the center of the zeros, it was crystal clear how happy Shortcake was.

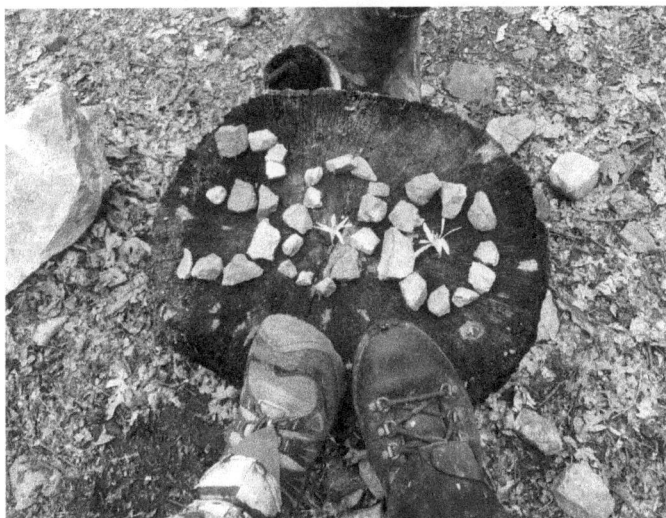

Celebrating another centennial was a great way to end our day's hike. We stopped at Jerry Cabin Shelter and gave it a five-star review for the best tenting area around a shelter to date. The flat, semi-open landscape provided non-shelter-dwelling hikers with comfort. It was true wilderness luxury provided by Mother Nature herself. We arrived early enough to enjoy the rainless evening. Blue hues played peekaboo with the cloud cover. We hoped for promising weather the next day.

Ask and you shall receive. Hot, sunny, low-humidity weather graced us all day. Good thing it did; we cranked out the miles—seventeen—our most yet. Another big accomplishment for Shortcake. You could see her confidence grow almost daily now.

Lots of interesting sights filled our adventure in those seventeen miles. We saw a rock formation that resembled the mouth of a blue whale breeching out of the ground. We passed an old, manicured graveyard. We saw strange metal objects cast out from an era gone by and oxidized from years of exposure to the elements. A simple yet beautiful cascading stream. Several different varieties of flowers. And a view we didn't have to create in our mind's eye.

Big Butt Mountain was the tallest summit of the day at 4,812 feet elevation. The trail doesn't traverse the top, so we didn't go there. We chuckled at the name. There are some doozy monikers on the Appalachian Trail. Another not-so-nice one is Chunky Gal Trail. They make me laugh though, probably because the boot fits.

At mile 15.5 for the day, we had a decision to make. Since it was getting late, should we call it a day and camp at Hogback Shelter (another doozy name) or add one more accomplishment to our resume, that of night hiking? If we pushed on another 2.4 miles, we could sleep at base camp again and begin our double zero days early. It was a no-brainer.

BLACK BEAR TIP

Be patient with your own growth—it will happen.

Day 35 Thursday April 27
Zero

Day 36 Friday April 28
Zero

Day 37 Saturday April 29
Time: 7:04am – 4:00pm
Mile: 318.2 – 331.6
Miles hiked: 13.4
Base Camp
Hot & sunny

Day 38 Sunday April 30
Time: 7:33am – 3:15pm
Mile: 331.6 – 343.0
Miles hiked: 11.4
Tented near tracks in Erwin, TN
Weather: Hot, sunny, occasionally
breezy

Day 39 Monday May 1
Time: 7:41am – 12:45pm
Mile: 343.0 – 351.1
Miles hiked: 8.1
Base Camp
Weather: Humid, rainy, windy

Day 40 Tuesday May 2
Time: 7:01am – 6.20pm
Mile: 351.1 – 368.9
Miles hiked: 17.8
Tented at Clyde Smith Shelter
Weather: Cool start, windy, no rain

Day 41 Wednesday May 3
Time: 7:41am – 6.50pm
Mile: 368.9 – 384.5
Miles hiked: 15.6
Tented at Overmountain Shelter
Weather: Warm, sunny, windy

Day 42 Thursday May 4
Time: 7:35am – 12:57pm
Mile: 384.5 – 393.7
Miles hiked: 9.2
Roan Mountain B&B
Weather: Hurricane-force winds

9

What a Difference Two Years Can Make

*W*e liked to get off the trail at least once a week. Some people think that is wimping out. But I figured if pro athletes get a down day, then we should get one also considering that our workouts last six to twelve hours a day.

So what does a hiker do on a rest day? (We call them a "zero" for "no miles covered.") We do as little as possible. But our rest days are always filled with something. First, we went to a sporting goods store. Shortcake needed new hiking shoes. Her current "new" ones did not pan out to her liking. The treads were more like racing slicks. She wanted something that would help her stay upright. I am not saying that she spent time on the ground, but there had been a few close calls that had her dancing not so gracefully down the trail. Funny for my entertainment, but not hers.

Chores such as laundry, drying equipment, and repacking occupied our time. Then there was the never-ending eating that took more time than the usual rehydrating pouches of food or layering pepperoni slices between crackers and cheese. No zero day would be complete without a nice shower and, why not, a soak or two in the tub with Dr. Teal's® to rinse away the trail grime we had collected since our last shower.

I love the song and dance of trail life. Living on trail and living in civilization are polar opposites, and the shuffle between the two is invigorating. It's a dose of medicine that surpasses anything any pharmaceutical company could ever cook up. Sure, it's hard, it's dirty, it's exhausting, and sometimes it's just plain awful. But after a bout in the fresh air, with mud between the toes, under the fingernails, and in every other spot on the human body, I have never felt so *clean* and alive.

We needed our weekly renewals so we could refocus, only to get back out there to commune with nature all over again. But sometimes, one down day was just not enough. That's when two in a row were on the agenda.

Of course, our second free day was hot and sunny. It would have been nice to have had that weather the previous week of hiking. The forecast for when we were to head back to the trail was supposed to be wet again. We were hoping the weatherman was wrong, as they often are. But what I have noticed is that with 20 percent chance of rain, it is more likely to rain. So why, then, *why*, when it's 20 percent chance of sun, doesn't the sun shine?

Most of our chores were done, allowing us to rest on our consecutive zero day, but we still had to resupply our food bags. It took stops at Publix, Ingles, and Walmart. Most hikers get by with one stop at a Dollar General. But me and my special dietary needs made resupplying challenging. Have you wondered what a thru-hiker eats while on trail? On a normal day, I consumed the following:

> **Breakfast:** 2 bars of some kind and a few pieces of precooked bacon or a couple spoonfuls of Jif.
> **Lunch:** Cheese, crackers, pepperoni or beef stick.
> **Supper:** If I cook, it's pasta or a rice meal. If I am stove-less, it's a peanut butter sandwich.
> **Snacks:** I usually have four to five snacks packed for each day, consisting of any combination of trail mix, pretzels, Stroopwafels™, bars, crackers, and dry cereal.
> **Treats:** Always a handful of jelly beans. Sometimes cookies.
> **Vitamins:** Glucosamine, calcium w/magnesium, a multi, and echinacea and energy supplements as needed.

Food was our heaviest item. The average hiker packs about two pounds of food per day and must carry four to five days at a time. Mine was gluten free, which is harder to find in items that taste good, provide nutritional value, and are low-weight and packable. I made it work. On days we headed out from base camp or were slackpacking, I got creative and carried fresh fruit and foods like a real meat sandwich. Mmmmm.

Hiking requires 4,000-6,000 calories a day, and there is no way we could carry that many calories. Hence, long-distance hiking is a great weight-loss and strength-building program. You can eat whatever you want and still lose weight. No gimmicks. The only drawback is that you can't continue to have the same menu when you get off trail. It is great, though, being worried about not eating enough rather than having to quit after round one at the buffet. And desserts—make those a double, please! Hiking is great.

Slackpacking followed our double zero days. And even better, a night at base camp again. It was an easy 13.4 miles up and over the mountains. With that said, the last two miles of the day, no matter how *easy*, are so slow and painful. The body just wants to quit.

We traversed a beautiful bald even larger than Max Patch.

Just as we descended back to the tree line, Batman popped out. He had hiked in south to meet us.

He continued to the bald as Shortcake and I kept moving forward. We waited for Batman at the shelter where we all had lunch together before hiking out the six miles to the car.

It was another uneventful day. They are common on the trail, and we could have easily become bored. But we didn't. To keep things exciting, Shortcake and I paid attention to the details. We loved the flowers, insects, birds, and trees. It's fun to notice how they grow differently at varying elevations. Big, mighty trees that grow 60-70 feet and more at an elevation of 3,000 feet work hard to stretch their branches a mere 25 feet at 5,000-feet elevation.

One reason it took so long for us to reach our day's destination was that we took so many photographs. We were always apologizing to the other for taking so long to capture that perfect picture of an insect, flower, cloud, or whatever else caught our eye. What we did not say sorry for any longer were the noises our bodies produced. That was another form of entertainment.

The food we eat on the trail wreaks havoc with our systems, whether the results are belching or noises from the back door. After our second day on the trail back in Georgia, we stopped saying "Excuse me." We each said one final apology and said it was for the duration of the hike. There is just no way to be polite about it. So we laughed, and we laughed hard. You'd think we were immature 12-year-old boys. I won't go into details; I am sure you can imagine the sounds we produced. All is fun and games until a silent, deadly one escapes and engulfs the poor soul who walks into its plume. But that's just another part of life on the trail.

Batman slackpacked us again; we took that luxury whenever he offered it to us. The next day our packs would be full for a five-day stint without amenities of any sort. It was feast or famine in all aspects out on the trail, a small price to pay to be so fortunate. Living in the wild was a gift we took for granted, just like most things in life. I think most of us did not realize just how truly blessed we were.

The day's hike included lots of ups and downs on a gentle path. The lighter packs were also a treat. We were headed for Erwin, Tennessee. The drop into the sleepy little town was long. It took seventeen switchbacks to carry us safely to the Nolichucky River bridge. Across the street is Uncle Johnny's hostel, a cute little place with resupply options and shuttle services. The cabins need lots of TLC, but it's a hiker-friendly place with a party atmosphere that is easy to get sucked into. We skipped it, choosing to camp just inside the woods on the trail north of the parking lot where Batman gave us all our gear.

Our packs seemed the heaviest they had been so far on the trip. I'm not sure if that was a fact or just our perception after double zero days followed by two slackpacking days. After meeting Batman and retrieving our gear, our intent was to hike another mile or so, then camp. But burdened with our gear, we made it about 150 yards. We crossed a railroad track and a beautiful campsite lay before us.

"Looks good to me. How about you, Shortcake?"

She agreed and we dropped our cumbersome loads. Batman set foot farther to see if there was anything else. He was gone so long, we decided to pitch the tent. We were not going any farther.

I love trains, and we were so hoping to see one pass as we camped. We built our first fire, an easy task since whoever stayed there previously did not extinguish their fire. Red hot coals lay hidden under the ashes. Shortcake awakened them with a few leaves and sticks. Soon we had a blazing inferno. The fire seemed alive. It was this fire that inspired another devotional which is also in *As Fresh As Daisies.*

Shortcake and I sat around relaxing and waiting to hear the mighty roar of a diesel engine, but none came. Even though it was a relatively short day, I was tired and ready for bed early.

———

The warm night morphed into an even warmer morning. It was the first night we didn't need to be zipped tight in our mummy bags. As we were getting ready to throw on our packs and start the day's hike, we could hear that diesel engine. Excitement raced in our veins. We both love trains. Instead of grabbing our packs and poles we snatched our iPhones and headed to the rail bed. We finally got to see our choo-choo.

As usual, that day was uphill right from the get-go. Straight up terrain on our left flipped to straight down on our right with an intense forward incline as we hiked north. Then when we rounded a corner, the up switched to our right and the down was on the left.

Our hiking pace was slow and steady; Shortcake required few stops. I am the one who yelled forward to her, "I need water" or "I need to rest." So after a couple of hours, I requested a hydration stop at a stream. The rest was quick, and we continued onward.

Our next stop was at a shelter for a snack and another drink. That was quick also. A few other hikers darted in. We discussed the weather, and we all agreed it didn't look too bad. Boy, were we wrong! Soon after we resumed hiking, it started to sprinkle—which felt good, since it was so humid. We decided to forego our raingear. With each step, the rain increased and the wind blew more fiercely. Then, to add insult to injury as we continued to climb on a semi-exposed trail, rumblings occurred overhead.

We marched on, wet and cold. Finally, the rain eased just as we walked into a tenting area that happened to be near a road. We threw up the tent in between raindrops and crawled in to wait it out.

I let Batman know we had stopped shy of our planned destination and requested a weather update. Not liking what he sent back, I asked him if he could find the road we were near and extract us. It was nothing like the rescue of 2015. This was easily doable.

The warmth and humidity of the day had drained our enthusiasm as we had hiked in the rain. I am sure once we put dry clothes on, we could have toughed it out, but who wants to do that when you can be dry and warm inside? This was at 1:20pm, and Batman had us by 3:00pm. Every hiker should be so lucky to have a Batman. Back to base camp we went.

So much for a five-day stint without amenities.

We might have chosen luxury over wilderness sometimes, but after 40 days on the trail, we were seeing our growth. After Batman returned us to the A.T. the next day, we covered 17.8 miles. It made up for our low mileage the day before.

Our daily mileage average was ever so slowly increasing, but it wasn't without the side effects of sore feet. My feet still ached. I preferred 12-14 miles a day, but sometimes we had to push on for one reason or another.

After one thru-hike, you'd think I would have figured out my issues. But I hadn't. I still agonized with excruciating pain in the metatarsals. That was the main reason I needed to rest more often. I preferred a pace a little faster to cover more distance so I could rest every couple of hours. As the day went on, I needed to rest more often. I didn't need to rest long, but I did need to rest. Shortcake was just the opposite, and it was a challenge to find a rhythm for both of us to be comfortable at the same time. I didn't complain. I wanted it to be about her hike and her needs. But gee, my feet were hurting.

The miles were filled with a variety of sights. We saw open balds, dense spruce forests, a bunny, and lots of other interesting things. What amazed me the most was the beautiful, lush green grass that grew deep in the forest and way up in the mountains without any chemicals or tending to by human efforts. Why can't my lawn be that nice? The grass looked like it was planted along the trail on purpose. In other spots, it stretched deep into the woods like a 70s shag rug. I resisted the temptation to dig up a clump to send home.

According to my blog at EmilysEscapades.com, Day 41 on the trail was my favorite day so far. What a difference two years can make. In 2015, this stretch was one of the worst, yet most memorable. It was absolutely miserable in 2015. Yet, this time the day was magnificent. We conquered Roan Mountain. The hike was much nicer without the torrential rains and flooding of 2015. There was even a spectacular view to be had. I apologized to the mountain for cursing her the first time we met.

The crown jewel of the day was Jane Bald at Carver Gap. To me, balds on top of mountains are an anomaly. My paradigm of a mountain has jagged peaks with stomach-churning drops. But the southern Appalachians are dotted with open fields at several thousand feet of elevation. Basking in the sunshine on one such summit makes all the pain and agony forgotten.

We would have preferred camping right there on top of Jane Bald as several other hikers chose to do, but we pushed on. Bad weather was coming the next two days. These peaceful highlands may be serene when Mother Nature is favorable, but we did not want to test fate when she became cantankerous.

Making it to Overmountain Shelter set us up for under 10 miles the next day. The shelter is an old red barn. There is nothing glamorous about the structure. It's ancient, dilapidated, and breezy. But its charm and beauty are in its age. The worn structure tells of an earlier time when life was hard but much simpler than the fast-paced, high-tech world we live in today.

Most of the hikers made camp in the field in front of the barn. It was like tent-city, with over a dozen fabric abodes dotting the grassy approach to the shelter. We set up our tent on the covered deck on one side of the barn. The shelter was built on the edge of the mountain at 4,657 feet elevation and looked down into the valley eastward. We were hoping for a sunrise.

Before crawling into our sleeping bags, we made a reservation at a B&B where we would end the next day. With bad weather forecasted and our 5-day stint ending, we wanted to make sure we had a place to get out of the elements and to resupply.

OH MY GOSH! How can we go from having the best day so far to one of the most terrifying? What we went through in 9.2 miles tested our resolve and showed us what we were made of. In two hours of the most intense hiking I have ever done, we experienced every emotion fathomable—and we only hiked two miles in that time.

We crossed Little Hump and Hump Mountains, which were open bands that topped out over 5,500 feet. The wind whipped and howled and tried to whisk us off the mountain. Gusts at 75 mph were no challenge for Shortcake and me. Well, that's what I said later as I sat in the safety of the B&B, warming by the fire.

I have never in my life experienced winds so horrific.

At first, it was fun. Then it became work. When the wind gusted, our bodies, ladened with our packs, acted like giant sails catching the wind. We used our hiking poles as props the best we could to prevent being toppled over. We did twice as much walking as needed. We'd take two steps forward then literally get blown off the trail sideways and have to take four steps back to the trail.

In many spots the trail formed a trench several inches deep caused by years of hikers treading on the soft earth. When you are vertically challenged, as in Shortcake's situation, that trench was almost knee high and acted as a stumbling block. I lost count of how often the wind knocked her over. I would grab her by her pack and hoist her back up, barely missing a beat.

At times we were fearful. Not only did I have to deal with the physical exertion caused by the climb and wind, I was also running on no sleep. I had slept terribly at Overmountain Shelter. That wasn't all. I was tired and exhausted, and then another hiker kept hiking too close to me. I offered to let him pass, which he did. But when Shortcake stepped aside to let him pass, he wouldn't continue. He stayed between us, acting like our buddy. We didn't want to be social. We had all we could do to stay upright.

I passed him again so I could be in safe range of my buddy, and then he kept crowding me. As all my close family and friends know, I don't handle unfamiliar people behind me well. I was on the verge of a panic attack caused by this yo-yo of a hiker, and the elements were only making things worse. Finally, after the third time I frantically asked him not to be so close, he got the message, and we didn't see him the rest of the day.

Once we reached the safety of the tree line, Shortcake and I stopped to collect ourselves. It was then I said, "I need a hug. That was more than I could handle." I broke down and cried as the release of adrenaline filled my body. I needed to keep it together to traverse the hurricane-gusted bald and to restrain from beating the encroaching hiker. It was an emotionally wild and fun, scary and thrilling hike.

With all that, we crossed another milestone. Two states done, twelve to go. Enough adventure for one day.

BLACK BEAR TIP

Listen to your body. It will tell you when you need to rest, and it will tell you when you can push on. And when it needs to stop and cry—let it.

Day 43 Friday May 5
Time: 7:14am – 1:25pm
Mile: 393.7 – 404.1
Miles hiked: 10.4
Roan Mountain B&B
Weather: Perfect, then cloudy, cool, rainy

Day 44 Saturday May 6
Time: 8:14am – 4:11pm
Mile: 404.1 – 418.4
Miles hiked: 14.3
Black Bear Cabins
Weather: Cloudy, cool, sleet, rainy

Day 45 Sunday May 7
Time: 7:15am – 3:30pm
Mile: 418.4 – 431.4
Miles hiked: 13.0
Black Bear Cabins
Weather: Cold & brisk

Day 46 Monday May 8
Time: 8:40am – 6:30pm
Mile: 431.4 – 447.5
Miles hiked: 16.1
Tented near TN91
Weather: Sunny, breezy, cool

Day 47 Tuesday May 9
Time: 7:42am – 6:30pm
Mile: 447.5 – 470.1
Miles hiked: 22.6
Base Camp
Weather: Humid, rainy, cloudy

10

Hiking the A.T. is an Enormous Treasure Chest

*G*rowth comes through adversity. Lessons are drilled home by the mistakes we make, hardly ever by what we do right. And strength grows from overcoming obstacles. Gold is tested by fire and diamonds are made from billions of years of intense pressure. A baby chick must peck its own way out of its shell. If it is helped, it won't develop enough strength to survive.

Humans are no different. Hopefully we don't have to survive fire or years of pressure. And we aren't born encased in a cage. But we too must be challenged in all aspects of our being if we want to grow, learn, and become stronger. We won't know what we can do until we are put to the test.

That day crossing Hump and Little Hump mountains in hurricane-force winds, Shortcake and I gained unshakable confidence. It wasn't a life-threatening situation, but it was grueling and at times quite scary. Once the drama of the situation was over and we had time to recover in the safety of the trees, we beamed with pride at our accomplishment. Did we want to do it again? No! But we knew if a similar situation came up, we'd be okay.

You know growth is taking place when you endure a struggle, come out the other side, and choose to continue instead of retreat. Batman was there at the end of the day to resupply us. We could have gone home and said enough is enough. But we didn't. We gathered our things for the next several days and continued with our plan to overnight at the B&B.

———

I love how the serendipitous choreography of the trail unfolds. You never know what is in store for the day's hike. You consult guide-books, maps, and weather reports, but none of that is insurance of what things will actually be like. Resources are needed for safe planning, but it's the action that produces the gifts of the trail. Without making the decision to continue, we wouldn't be able to experience the day's offerings.

After the hair-raising day, we were treated to a fantastic rest day for our bodies, minds, and spirits. We didn't zero; instead, we slackpacked ten miles over gentle terrain and a smooth trail. The only obstacles were blown-over trees and debris from the previous day's storm.

Beauty surrounded us as we strolled on the Appalachian Trail. The views were bright even though it was overcast. We saw a huge magnolia tree. I was astounded to learn magnolias weren't just shrubs. Sometimes I wonder where my notions about things originate. We are never as smart as we think we are.

We stopped and had snacks at two different waterfalls. Shortcake found her prince in toad form. But she didn't kiss him, so she'll never know if he was the one. We passed our 400th mile. And we didn't complain when the rain returned.

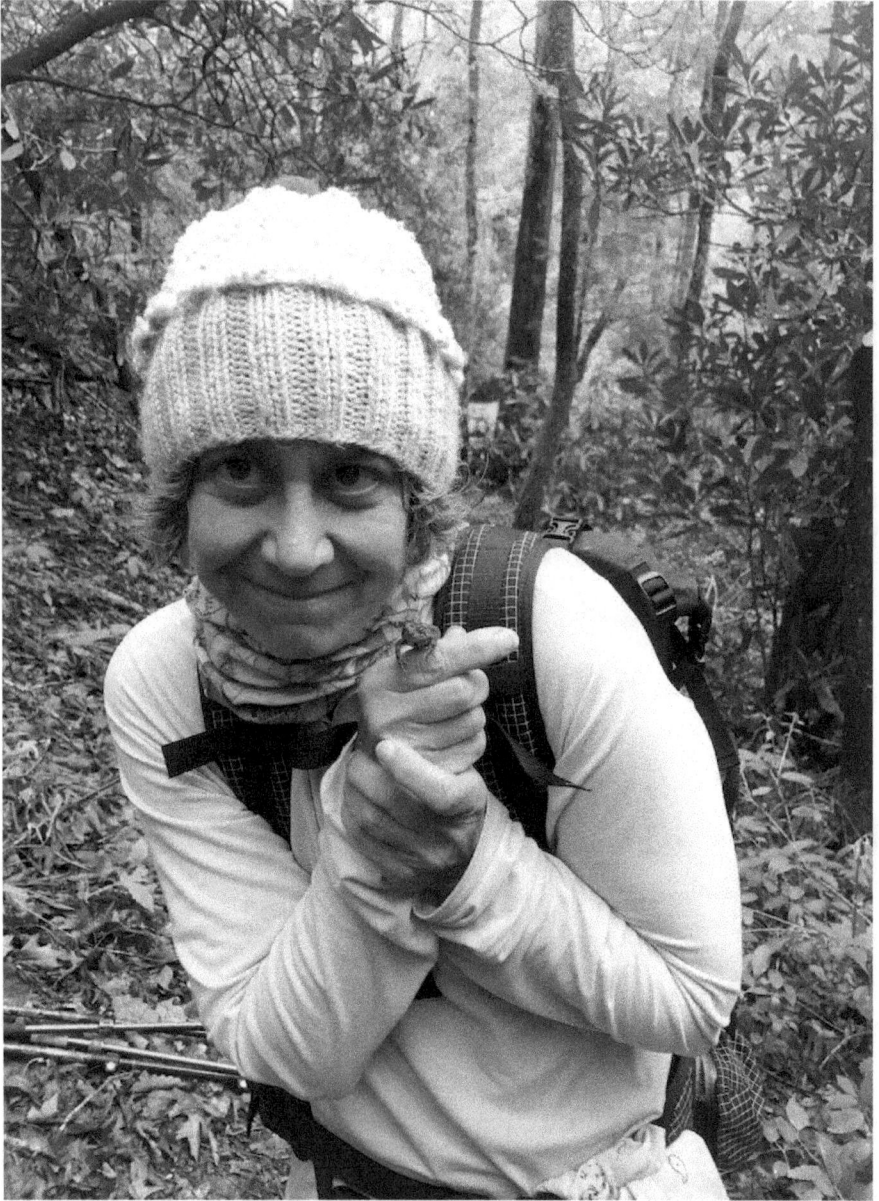

The best treat of all was getting to see some dear friends, Jimmy and I Believe, whom I met in 2014 when I Believe hiked the A.T. They spent most of their spring out on the trail doing trail magic. They made sure to catch up with us to help out for the day. They were the reason we were able to slackpack.

Jimmy does hiker videos and posts them to YouTube. You can check out his channel @jimmy4766. He interviewed us, and I love what Shortcake said: "Hiking the Appalachian Trail is like an enormous treasure chest filled with amazing, spectacular, incredible, and magical things. Each day on the trail, a new gem or treasure is revealed to us." That pretty much sums up why we hike the A.T.

After our treasure-filled day, we returned to Roan Mountain B&B for one more night. Another shower washed away the dirt and mud from the trail. The only thing left to do for the evening was to wait for the other guests so we could all enjoy a Cinco De Mayo meal.

We continued the flip-flopping trail choreography; one day nice weather, the next day not so. Thirty-six degrees and overcast at the start of the day is chilly but manageable and even welcomed while hiking. But the temps dropped slightly as we climbed and the overcast mountains dripped with cold sleet, thawing again to rain.

It was a cold day on the trail with little to report. Our stops were brief. We needed to keep moving to stay warm. Action produces the experience, but we used our knowledge gained before heading out and made reservations when we saw the forecast.

We set our mileage to end at the Black Bear Resort Cabins. The trail may have been cold, but we were greeted with warm hellos and friendly smiles. This is definitely a place to come back and visit. We loved our cute little cabin so much we booked it for a second night.

The next morning, we slackpacked ourselves and the resort shuttled us. Normally, the staff drop hikers off at a trailhead north for hikers to hike south back to the cabin, eliminating a shuttle at the end of the day. But that wasn't our MO. I'm not sure if that was Shortcake's MO, but mine was to only hike northbound. I'll slackpack, but I will not blue-blaze or hike south when on a NOBO hike.

The shuttle dropped us off bright and early. We had thirteen miles to cover. The morning was cool, brisk, and breezy. We meandered around Laurel Falls. Climbed a peak, then descended to Shook Branch Recreation Area at Watauga Lake. Seeing so much water that wasn't falling on us was refreshing.

But the real treasure for the day came when we met B.B. King. Shortcake and I were enjoying a break when this rugged, joyful young girl hiked up to us. She had passed us the other day, but we had only exchanged pleasantries. This time, she approached and said she recognized me. She had seen me in the documentary *Walking Home*.

We chatted and hiked several miles together. What a great gal. She was a recent high school graduate and not sure what she wanted to do. B.B. was fearless and tenacious, yet kind and caring. After our brief encounter, I deduced that whatever she decided to do, she would thrive.

The day ended cold, so we were glad to have our shuttle rescue us and deliver us back to our warm and cozy cabin. I was becoming soft. Nights at base camp, hostels, and B&Bs were turning me into a spoiled hiker. I preferred hiking during the day, tackling whatever Mother Nature had to give, knowing I would be inside for the night. But like all great things, it came to an end. The next night we would be squished together in my two-person tent that was really meant for one.

I didn't want to leave the cabins. I kept thinking of every way possible to justify staying there another night. But we hiked on. We had sixteen miles of ridge walking. We finally left the view of Watauga Lake. After that, the views weren't too interesting, but we did see another snake. Shortcake almost stepped on it. Glad it wasn't poisonous.

I don't mind days lacking in stimulation. Hiking the Appalachian Trail isn't just hard physically. If I was good at math, which I'm not, I would summarize that the trail is over fifty percent mental and the rest physical. Even if my math is wrong, the mental game plays a huge part in a hiker's journey on the A.T. When we have days with little stimuli, it is a chance for the brain to rest also.

As we strolled by the waters, our noggins recovered from the abundance of excitement of the last several days. But I was still trying like heck to go back to the cabins. It would have been fifty-eight dollars just for the shuttle. Ouch. So we tented, with a forecast of 40 degrees and rain. My favorite, NOT!

The rain pitter-pattered on our tent all night. I may have wanted to go back to the Black Bear Resort, but honestly, the rain was a soothing and comforting sound that helped lull me back to sleep each time I woke in discomfort.

The rain stopped just before we got up. Thank goodness, because I despise packing up in the rain. It's one thing to have a wet tent to stuff away. It's a totally different task to have to do it in the rain.

Our luck was short lived. We had everything packed except the tent. We were just about to enjoy our trail breakfast of smushed and crumbled snack bars when the pitter-patter started again. We grabbed our stuff and dove into the tent to finish our meal.

Once the shower passed, we once again emerged from our quarters and were able to pack up in between droplets.

Soon after we started our day, the rain began falling from the sky in a cloudy mist. We had almost 22 miles to hike, and I was so excited to start off like wet dogs. At least it was warm out. But we would not only look like wet dogs—we'd also smell like them.

––––––

All night, we had heard mooing cows. We knew we were near a pasture, but as we entered it, we could not see the bovines. In the morning, we walked up and around the field, following the trail. We could smell them and had to navigate strategically to keep from stepping in cow patties, but we could not see them.

We marched forward for about a mile through the pasture and still wondered where the cows were. Then just as we crested a hill, there they all were, herded together at the north end of the fence, looking pathetic. They seemed even more unhappy to be in the morning's wetness than we were.

The trail proceeded over the fence right next to them. As we approached, they all stared at us. They didn't move. Big ones and babies, as in a trance with eyes focused on us. It was a little creepy. Shortcake wore brightly colored leggings, a bright orange raincoat, and a knit hat that looked like a cupcake. We joked that the cows were saying, "Hey, Ethel, this grass we are eating is way too strong. Did you see that flower walk by? Flowers can't do that, can they? I think we should stop the weed and become carnivores."

We safely exited the field before the herd awoke from their daze. We continued north. The rain stopped after only three miles. I was very grateful. In 2015 when I hiked into Damascus, 23 of 26 miles were in the rain. That was my longest day then, and it was our longest day this time.

––––––

With over 20 miles for the day on our schedule, we had a quicker-than-normal pace. Thank goodness there was not too much to see. It took us forever when the weather and scenery were good. On this day, we had our breaks down to a minimum, and since I had been there before, I knew certain spots where we could stop for longer rests.

But twice when we arrived, another hiker had already claimed the prime spot for their beauty break, foregoing any chance for us having a nice time for ours. The first was at a shelter marking the halfway point of the day. We planned to have lunch there to fuel up. Mr. Happy Hiker was smoking weed, and we didn't want to be around it. So we walked on a bit and sat alongside the trail to have lunch. Maybe that's why the cows were so weird. He must have shared with them.

The second time was at the Tennessee–Virginia state line. Another huge milestone. But when we got there. Mr. Happy Hiker was there again. He had passed us. He was again partaking of his drug of choice, but this time with two others. So Shortcake and I had our photo shoot, then again proceeded up the trail before having a rest someplace else. Later, when he passed us again, the hiker said how tired he was. My thoughts were, *Gee, I wonder why?*

We eventually made it to Damascus, two days earlier than our original schedule, drug-free and rain-free. But it was a close call on both those accounts. First, we needed to distance ourselves from Mr. Happy Hiker; and second, with each step we took toward Damascus, the clouds grew darker. Rumbling started overhead. There is nothing like a little noise from the heavens to change Shortcake's two-miles-per-hour pace to three miles per hour. We were off that mountain, out of the woods, and across town to the safety of a store's awning before the first raindrop and the lightning show.

There we waited for Larry, our shuttle driver. Our plans had been to take a double zero when we reached Damascus. We were just going to hang out in the quaint little trail town. But since we arrived two days early, that would have meant four nights in a hostel. We also were waiting for Batman to return from a business trip. We weighed the costs: Stay in town? Or take a shuttle back to base camp several hours away? Base camp won. Larry entertained us with trail talk as he drove and we relaxed in his van.

The treasures of the Appalachian Trail differ from hiker to hiker. What each one of us finds to be a gem varies, just as each hiker is unique. One may enjoy the solitude; another may thrive on the friendships made. Others delight in both. Some like the climbs while others prefer the descents. Insects, creepy-crawlies, and strange noises pique interest in the curious but give shivers to others.

No matter what tickles your fancy, you are sure to find it when you spend any time following those white blazes. Our last few days had it all. We had thrills, we had quiet. We had the good and the bad. Shortcake summed it up best when she said the A.T. is like an enormous treasure chest, and "each day on the trail, a new gem or treasure is revealed to us."

Arriving two days early meant that we would collect on a rare gem of thru-hiking the A.T.—a triple zero. Larry dropped us off at base camp where we dried out, rested, and waited for Batman to return.

BLACK BEAR TIP

Find treasures in everything you do.

Day 48 Wednesday May 10
Zero

Day 49 Thursday May 11
Zero

Day 50 Friday May 12
Zero

Day 51 Saturday May 13
Time: 9:40am – 7:50pm
Mile: 470.1 – 486.1
Miles hiked: 16.0
Tented near VA US-58
Weather: Cloudy then sunny

Day 52 Sunday May 14
Time: 8:40am – 5:45pm
Mile: 486.1 – 497.6
Miles hiked: 11.5
Camped near Thomas Knob Shelter
Weather: Partly cloudy & breezy

Day 53 Monday May 15
Time: 7:27am – 5:29pm
Mile: 497.6 – 510.9
Miles hiked: 13.3
Tented near VA-603
Weather: Sunny, breezy

Day 54 Tuesday May 16
Time: 7:20am – 6:10pm
Mile: 510.9 – 526.2
Miles hiked: 15.3
Tented at mile 526.2
Weather: Sunny & hot

Day 55 Wednesday May 17
Time: 7:04am – 10:45am
Mile: 526.2 – 532.4
Miles hiked: 6.2
Slept in Partnership Shelter
Weather: Hot & sunny

11

Good-Bye Base Camp

*T*riple zero days—unheard of. Were we thru-hiking the A.T. or were we just glamping our way north?

Why can't it be both? Shortcake's proximity to the trail was too good to pass up. While we were in the area, we took full advantage of the comforts of her home . Soon we would be too far away to come back to base camp. In 2015, I had the opposite mindset. When we reached Maine, I did not want to go home at all. I was afraid that if I did, I wouldn't return to the trail. I didn't have that concern in 2017.

Scorching heat kept us confined inside the walls of Shortcake's home. We were happy it wasn't raining, but the drastic change in weather was too much to adjust to. But it was just as hot inside. I spent time in the kitchen, cooking. It was worth every degree of heat and drop of sweat. We made sure we ate as much as we could. Calorie loading is just awesome.

We each had already lost ten pounds and were counting calories. But not in the normal way. Instead of making sure we were under a certain number, we focused on how many calories we could ingest on our days off to help make up for the deficiency while on the trail. Hiking lots of miles has its advantages.

We did the normal chores of repacking and preparing resupply bags for future drops by Batman. Since we had three days, we were able to relax and not rush around to make every second count. I took another wonderful soak in the tub with Dr. Teal. I also polished my boots.

I wonder if I am the only hiker who actually cleaned and polished their footwear every chance they got. I wasn't in the military, but I do come from a long history of family members who served and still are serving. My dad used to scrub, clean, and polish my soccer cleats after every game for four years of high school and soccer camps. Footwear is the foundation of most sports. I continued this task for myself on the trail. In a way, it brought me closer to my dad, even though we were apart.

Besides eating, the highlight of the triple-Z was FaceTiming with a fabulous group of students from Glenburn Elementary School in Glenburn, Maine. My coworker Darnel's daughter Elyse had been following us. She invited us to speak to her class next chance we had. Shortcake's and my early arrival into Damascus gave us three days at base camp, so we scheduled a call.

———

The class had wonderful and inquisitive questions. It was so much fun sharing our adventure with them remotely. It also reminded us why we were out there. Sometimes when you set out on a journey, it's exciting in the beginning. Then, after a while, you forget what made you do it in the first place. Challenges and struggles start to cloud your vision. But answering all their questions and retelling stories brought back all the joy we had been having before the wet, cold weather got in the way.

It is so important to keep the dream alive if you want to succeed. There will always be bad weather no matter what you do in life. It's how you handle yourself in the storm that will determine where you go. Don't let it control your direction. If you must, turn your sails around and find another route or mode of transportation. That's okay. Just don't lose sight of your goal.

Not only did the FaceTiming revive our attitude, but it was also a chance to give back. We had been so focused on ourselves—which is important to do at times, but joy is compounded when it is shared and misery is divided when it is shared. Thank you, Elyse, for inviting us to your class.

Another bonus of multiple zero days is that one has a chance to re-member forgotten gems of the journey. On trail, the tasks of packing, unpacking, drying, resupplying, laundry, and eating get in the way of the memories that are made.

The trail always provides. It is a saying often used by hikers because it's true. I haven't mentioned how often this has happened. In my spir-itual growth, I don't believe in coincidences; I do believe that things happen for a reason and that all good things come from our Creator, no matter how insignificant.

On May 9, we were hiking along when Shortcake stopped abrupt-ly and retraced a few steps. I just watched curiously to see what she was up to. Then I saw it. A deflated mylar birthday balloon caught in a tree next to the trail. The next day was her sister's birthday.

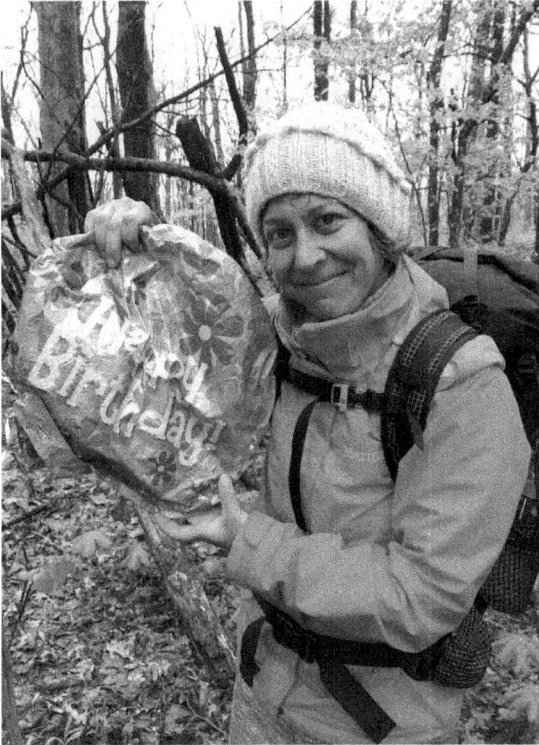

Shortcake was missing several of her family members' special days while she was out on our adventure. Cell service wasn't always possible, and neither were gift shops and post offices when you needed them. Nor did she pre-plan. So we captured a photo of Shortcake holding the birthday greeting, and she was able to send birthday wishes from the trail to her awesome sister, Susanne, the next time we had service. It may seem insignificant to most, but the trail gives these serendipity experiences often. You just have to be open to receive them. Just like in life. The world can be full of harsh realities, but if we try to not dwell on the negative and search for little treasures, we can find them. They are everywhere.

We left base camp for what would probably be the last time. We had hiked too far north to have the luxury of returning to zero again. The only reason to drive that far off trail would not be a good reason. North we went, back on the trail.

Batman dropped us off at the Dollar General in Damascus, where Larry, our shuttle driver, had rescued us from the storm three days earlier. This little hiker town was bustling by the time we arrived at 9:30am. It was their annual community yard sale day and people were out in droves. Batman drove to the north end while we followed the white blazes through town. It was a short mile walk, especially without our heavy loads; we were slackpacking again. But with all the shops and yard sale vendors, it took us much longer than expected.

The hike out of Damascus was nice and easy as it followed close to the Creeper Trail, an old railway bed. There were lots of hikers and bikers out enjoying the weather and town festivities. We had roughly 13 miles planned for the day. A long day, considering we didn't get started until almost 10:00am.

After Batman left us again on the north end of town, he jumped ahead to the rendezvous point where we would stop for the night and camp. I planned this spot. I remembered seeing it on my 2015 hike. The area was close to a stream, there was parking for Batman, and a toilet, all the amenities to make our first day back after a triple zero even easier. But what I didn't know was that the area was closed to overnight guests. So when we arrived, we had to make alternate plans. Plan B usually involves hiking on. And that's what we did. We ate our suppers, emptied even more gear from our already empty packs, and hiked on 3 more miles to the next spot. Our day ended close to 8:00pm. It was long but wonderful.

————

I love cold nights. They make for good sleeping. But they make mornings tough when it comes time to get out of the tent. Not only were we cold, but the car remote failed to work also.

All long-distance hikers know that in cool and cold weather you need to sleep with your electronics. And when you get up at night for whatever, zip up the tent to conserve heat. And on really cold nights, sleep with your puffy jacket on as an extra layer. The key words are "long-distance hikers."

Batman, my beloved hubby, did none of those things, and consequently he was cold, he let the heat out of the tent, and the remote died. We couldn't get into the car at first. The key fob had a valet key attached, so I removed it from the housing; but when I used it to unlock the door, it set off the alarm. Which I could not shut off because the remote was dead. After a while, it turned off, but I set it off five more times. Oops! Eventually, the key warmed up and we were able to start the car. I didn't need it to start. I was hiking. But Batman needed it. I teased him about being a day-hiker and not seasoned like Shortcake and myself.

————

Once we headed north on the trail, it was a mere 100 yards when we spotted a bouquet of lady slippers lining the trail. A beautiful sight for two moms on the trail that Mother's Day. Other gifts of the day were wild ponies at a distance. We were close to the Grayson Highlands State Park, home to herds of wild ponies.

We explored Grayson Highlands State Park in Grayson County, Virginia, on a bluebird sunny day. The park lies next to Mount Rogers National Recreation Area within the Jefferson National Forest. The Appalachian Trail traverses through eight national forests and six sections of the national park system. Grayson Highlands area is a must-see for all. But aren't all the state and national parks worth our time and money?

Mount Rogers National Recreation Area is a busy place along the Appalachian Trail. The main attraction is not the endless hiking trails or the spectacular views. The stars of the show are the feral ponies that reside in the park. They are wild in the sense that no one owns them, but they are far from skittish like most other creatures. Just rustle the wrapping of a snack bar, and you'll be mauled by these adorable equines. They will approach you, hoping to score a tasty treat. Oblivious visitors to the park ignore the signs of "Keep the Wild in Wilderness. Do Not Feed the Ponies." I will admit, in 2015, I didn't see the sign until after I had shared my oats with them. They are also quite photogenic and will pose with you for that perfect selfie.

We saw over 30 of these guys on our trek through their habitat. My favorite was a baby who could only have been a few days old. He walked on unsteady limbs. I wasn't a baby, but I walked similar to him by the end of most days on the trail.

Part way through the park, we reached a significant milestone. We crossed the 500-mile mark, and I did a little trail art to mark our milestone—with horse poop. We thought it was a fitting medium.

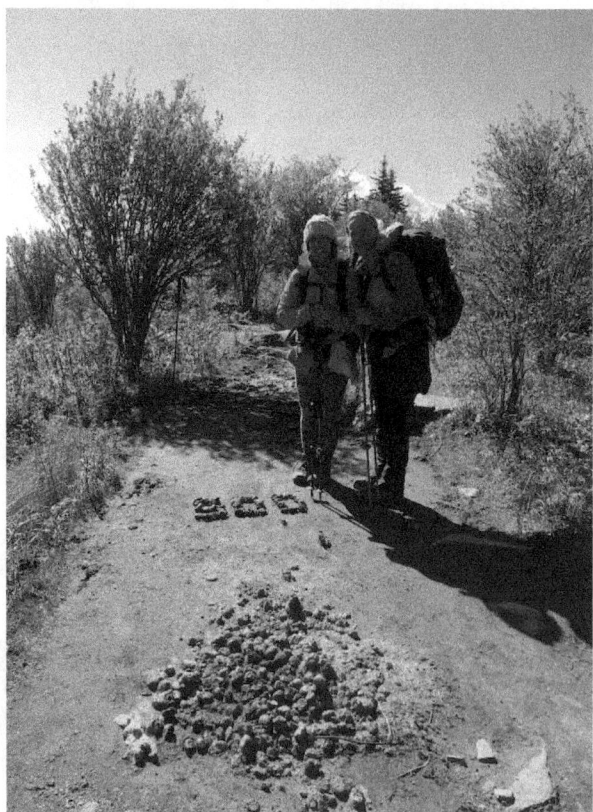

Our exit out of the park was uneventful. It was a rocky day, but another one with sunshine. I didn't care what the trail bed was like as long as the day wasn't cold and wet.

Lately it seemed we were having to hike more miles than we'd planned for the day. That day, it was because there were so many hikers on the trail. There were three options in the guidebook for tenting. When we arrived at each one, they were full. So we kept trucking until finally we found a spot.

I need to control my environment. You know the type—high A personality. I had no idea why I kept hiking. Because if there is one thing you can't do out there, it is control your environment. Weather, people, conditions, and even the guidebooks are so unpredictable. But with all those variables, the trail did teach me that I can control my attitude. And that makes all the difference. I can choose to make a bad situation worse or better, just by how I think and react.

All those longer-than-expected days allowed us to have an easy and short stroll into Partnership Shelter, which just happens to be one of the nicest shelters on the trail. It is a hundred yards from the Mt. Rogers Visitor Center. The two-story log structure comes complete with a cold shower and even a sink out back. The cold shower was awesome to wash away the accumulated sweat, grime, and dirt from the past several days.

The visitor center was a pleasant detour, with its small gift shop, outlets to charge devices, and real bathrooms—items we take for granted in our everyday life. The best part was their binder full of service providers. We grabbed the delivery sheet. Shortcake ordered pizza and I did my usual, a burger, fries, and a salad instead of a milkshake. Delivered in under an hour. We spent the afternoon just hanging around the center and shelter, relaxing and talking with other hikers who were doing the same thing.

The miles were flying by. Soon our journey would be half over. It had seemed like it took us forever to hike a hundred miles. Now after 53 days on trail, on May 15 we had completed 500 miles—almost one-quarter of the trail done. We were becoming seasoned hikers. Things we struggled with in the beginning were becoming habit, like cooking our meals, setting up and breaking down camp, finding water and filtering it. And even hanging a bear line was becoming easy. There seemed to be more smiles than frowns, even on "bad" days. Life was good.

BLACK BEAR TIP

When challenges discourage you on your journey, step back
and share what you are doing with others. It will remind
you why you are chasing your dreams.

Day 56 Thursday May 18
Time: 7:00am – 6:00pm
Mile: 532.4 – 546.1
Miles hiked: 13.7
Tented at mile 546.1
Weather: Hot & sunny

Day 57 Friday May 19
Time: 8:04am – 3:30pm
Mile: 546.1 – 556.6
Miles hiked: 10.5
Tented near VA-42
Weather: Hot & sunny

Day 58 Saturday May 20
Time: 8:04am – 6:30pm
Mile: 556.1 – 574.3
Miles hiked: 18.2
Stayed in a hotel
Weather: Hot & sunny,
then storm threat

Day 59 Sunday May 21
Time: 9:47am – 6:15pm
Mile: 574.3 – 590.1
Miles hiked: 15.8
Hotel in Wytheville
Weather: Cloudy, rainy, humid

Day 60 Monday May 22
Time: 9:47am – 4:10pm
Mile: 590.1 – 602.0
Miles hiked: 11.9
Camped at Jenny Knob Shelter
Weather: Rainy, misty, overcast

Day 61 Tuesday May 23
Time: 7:57am – 5:15pm
Mile: 602.0 – 616.5
Miles hiked: 14.5
Tented at Wapiti Shelter
Weather: Rain

Day 62 Wednesday May 24
Time: 7:30am – 11:40am
Mile: 616.5 – 623.7
Miles hiked: 7.2
Woods Hole Hostel
Weather: Drippy, wet, rainy,
breezy, cold

12

An Attitude Adjustment is in Order

*H*ot and sunny days had kept our spirits up since we returned to the trail after our triple zero. The beautiful weather was a real treat. What I did not enjoy was waking up to several bites that itched like crazy. Partnership Shelter had given me more than I bargained for. I don't know what it was. I was the only hiker affected, and it was maddening.

The rhododendrons bloomed in mass along the trail, creating beautiful gardens curated by Mother Nature. The most talented landscape artist could not design something so splendid.

The Appalachian Trail does not just weave through secluded wilderness with mountaintop vistas, rolling hills, balds, and quiet forests; it also leads hikers to sleepy little towns not on any top-ten vacation destination list. But these places are gems, with their appreciation for the simple life and respect for the past.

The Settlers Museum of Southwest Virginia is a 67-acre open-air museum about the people who settled in the Virginian mountains. Scotch-Irish and Germans settled in the area and developed farming as a way of life. The museum consists of a restored farmhouse, nine preserved outbuildings, and the building that catches most hikers' attention—an 1894 schoolhouse.

We didn't enter the historic building for a lesson; rather, we partook of the many goodies and supplies in totes donated by the generous West End United Methodist Church of Wytheville, Virginia. In 2015 when I came upon this place, I needed cold gear. I had sent mine home too soon. I was able to grab some necessities to get me through until I could retrieve my own. This year, I limited my takings to leave more for the next person. I did enjoy a cold drink and fruit. That was too good to pass up.

The schoolhouse was a step back in time, which was fitting for throw-back Thursday. We didn't visit any of the other structures on the property, but we did take time to read everything in the schoolhouse. We chuckled at the teachers' and students' rules. Some made us cringe, some made us laugh, and others we thought would be good if still implemented today.

1872
Rules for Teachers

Teachers each day will fill lamps, clean chimneys. Each teacher will bring a bucket of water and a scuttle of coal for the day's lesson.

Make your pens carefully. You may whittle nibs to the individual taste of the pupils. Men teachers may take one evening each week for courting purposes, or two evenings a week if they go to church regularly.

After ten hours in school, the teachers may spend the remaining time reading the Bible or other good books.

Women teachers who marry or engage in unseemly conduct will be dismissed.

Every teacher should lay aside from each pay a goodly part of his earnings for his benefit during his declining years so that he will not become a burden on society.

Any teacher who smokes, uses liquor in any form, frequents pool or public halls, or gets shaved in a barber shop will give good reason to suspect his worth, intentions, integrity, and honesty.

The teacher who performs his labor faithfully and without fault for five years will be given an increase of twenty-five cents per week in his pay, providing the Board of Education approves.

The next day I woke up to more bites. They were driving me insane. My friends would say it's not a long drive for me to arrive at insanity, but the itching was unbearable. I scratched my skin off in places. I was thinking Partnership Shelter had given me bedbugs or fleas, or I was the chosen delicacy for the nighttime gnats. I couldn't wait to meet up with Batman, who got the urgent message to bring Benadryl.

The heat and humidity were only making my derma condition worse. My skin felt like it was on fire. Thankfully, we only had 10.5 miles to go before possible relief. So much can happen in such a short time, though.

Cow sightings were abundant as we trudged through their pastures. Lady slippers stood gracefully along the trail, and we even saw a rattlesnake. Another trail artist had decorated the trail with a progress marker. This time, it consisted of sticks and bark, with the 25 percent symbol letting hikers know we had passed the official ¼-way mark at mile 547.45.

The trail crossed a dirt farm road with an interesting water-level sign. The top measurement reached five feet. We stopped to wonder if the area was prone to flooding. If so, we also wondered how devastated the surrounding areas would be if flood levels did reach that depth. Shortcake stood next to the sign, proving her vertically challenged stature.

All the heat and humidity produced another storm. Hot and humid days had been the norm lately, and in our short ten miles, we weren't able to avoid being drenched yet again. With only two miles left, the cloudy sky opened with one bolt of lightning, a dose of hail, and buckets of rain.

We chose to stay in the cover of the trees rather than proceed across the open pasture. Once the thunderous music and light show stopped, we continued. It stopped as quickly as it began, but not before our rain gear was soaked through. The only good thing was that the cool rain put out the fire on my skin, at least for a while.

It was always a great day when we got to slackpack. Since Batman had joined us on the previous night and would see us at the end of the day, we gladly handed over to him everything we didn't need. In fact, while we were hiking, instead of meeting us from the north like he enjoyed doing, he spent his day slaving away, washing, treating, and repacking my gear. I thought for sure I had contracted bedbugs or fleas from Partnership. I couldn't explain where all the bites were coming from, so Batman treated all my stuff.

The sights for the day included numerous bridges of all types. Old ones, new ones, high ones, and low ones. Green mossy structures and dry rotted ones that make you wonder if your passing will be its last.

We evaded another storm most of the afternoon. We hurried over a bald again instead of being able to bask in the openness. It seemed like we were always hurrying through some of the best-view spots, avoiding potential danger.

The weather had been so stormy. Sure, we had a stretch of hot and humid weather, but at least once a week, we were threatened by and/or exposed to thunder and lightning. Good thing was, it hadn't been too close, yet.

The forest always had a surprise of some sort. I saw strange mushrooms growing. I know the very nature of mushrooms is strange, but I had never seen these before. Shortcake mentioned that they looked just like candy corn. I didn't know that's where the sweet treat came from. Not only does the trail provide, it also teaches in so many ways.

On May 21, orange seemed to be the designated color of the day. It actually began the day before with the tree candy corn.

Everything of interest seemed to be some hue of orange. Short-cake started the day in her orange raincoat. Then we saw flaming azaleas, as they set the forest ablaze with their vibrant colors.

Throughout the day we saw orange newts. These little lizards littered the trail. We stopped counting at 30. We needed to be careful not to squish them.

Then there was an orange toad. Shortcake didn't kiss him either. The hunt for Prince Charming was still on.

We found a penny at one trail magic and nacho cheese Doritos at another. We couldn't get orange off the brain that day. When I went to bed, I dreamed in shades of sunset.

My itchiness slowly lessened, and only two new spots erupted. Hopefully, Batman's slaving to tend to my gear took care of the mystery. We would be spending the night at a motel, so I was able to clean up and hopefully ease my discomfort.

The place closest to the trail was booked, which meant we had to drive to the next town, Wytheville, Virginia, to get a place out of the rain. Batman dropped us off and scheduled Bubba to shuttle us back to the trail in the morning. So far, we'd had a Bubba and a Larry as drivers. All we needed was a Darryl.

It was Shortcake's turn with insects. Just as she crawled into her bed, she felt something on her leg. Yikes! It was a tiny tick. Not attached, thank goodness. We both did another tick check before climbing into the rack.

We reached another milestone, 600 miles. Even though I have hiked that many miles before, it still seemed surreal that we had done that many miles—and that we had just completed 500 playing in pony poop. A different artist marked out the 600.

The motel may have been lacking in newness and even cleanliness, but it was dry. Unfortunately, we started the next day in rain, which turned to a mist, then just an overcast sky, but it was always extremely humid. At times the sweat was pouring off my face and arms. If that wasn't bad enough, the gnats in the air were sticking to my bug-repellent, sweaty skin. They had no chance. I was a walking bug strip. Then there was the seasonal caterpillar invasion. They suspended from trees and dropped on us; always seeming to land on the backs of our necks. Another addition to my derma dilemma.

There was a comical sign at a trailhead. We finished a road walk then re-entered the woods. Trash cans were scarce out there. What we packed in, we packed out. At this location, a trail angel maintains a receptacle for hikers' convenience. Above the can was a note: *No deer carcasses.* Really? If there is a rule for it, then at some point it must have happened.

Other than earning another milestone, the day was uneventful. One could easily get bored walking the trail. It's the same thing day after day, week after week. But I believe boredom is a personal problem. It's a choice, and it's my fault if I am bored. Only I can do something to change that.

It makes me think of our kids today. Parents feel they must provide stimulating activities constantly to their kids so they won't be bored. But that just makes matters worse. Kids aren't allowed to entertain themselves and learn how to explore on their own. Even worse, they never learn to just sit and be in the moment. There needs to be a healthy balance between activities and stillness. It's no wonder our youngsters grow up and have stress-related health problems so early in life.

But the day was a little stagnant in trail entertainment, even for us. So Shortcake and I played a word game, the game when one person says a word and the other has to say a different word beginning with the last letter of the previous word. The theme was anything related to the trail. We played that game for over two hours while hiking. It was so much more fun than a video game.

Milestones were racking up but so were the rainy, stormy days. Bad weather was out-weighing the nice weather. The only good thing about hiking in the rain was that I didn't have to work. But after days of being soaked and filthy, I regretted refusing the invite by an elderly man named Kermit to stack wood as a work-for-stay at his house.

The drizzly day concerned us only slightly. When one has a goal, the facts don't matter. The forecast may have been for scattered showers again, but we had our eyes set on Trent's Grocer, a small convenience store half a mile off trail at a road crossing. I had stopped there in 2015, and they had the best little lunch counter and milkshakes. So off into the misty fog we hiked.

We had tried several times to get a good shake at various establishments along our trek. Hikers crave lots of things, and one of the most common is a milkshake. I don't drink milk at home, but out on the trail, I can't get enough of it. When we entered Trent's, I asked for a strawberry milkshake, and the lady taking my order apologized and said they don't make them anymore. I held back the disappointment and tears.

Our attitudes plummeted. We were damp from the drizzle and now were told there was no treat. Instead, we filled up on a burger for

Shortcake and BBQ with slaw for me. I will say, the South does know how to do BBQ.

Back to the trail we headed. We had eight miles to our destination. Thankfully, the drizzle had lifted shortly before we reached Trent's, giving us a chance to dry out. But that didn't last long. With a mile and half left for the day, at 3:30pm the scattered showers turned to a downpour. At 7:21pm, there was still no sign of it stopping.

We managed to set up the tent without allowing too much water inside. Shortcake wiped it dry while I went to the creek to fill our water bags to filter later. I don't get discouraged too easily, but I really was getting tired of all the rain.

It stopped pouring about 1:30am, then picked right back up at 2am. By 4:30am, the only drizzle was the drops from leaves shaken by the breeze. We had stayed dry in our tent, but it was difficult to pack things up. We needed to do so inside our little home, but with two bodies trying to maneuver bags and gear without dragging in muddy, wet leaf-litter, it was quite challenging.

Then came packing up the tent. There was no sense in even wasting any effort in trying to shammy it dry. I just broke it down and rolled up the soaking shelter and stuffed it into its sack. I swear the rain-soaked tent weighed twice as much as it normally did. Into my pack it went.

I wanted a new tent. My dream tent is the Pyramid 4 by Hyperlite. It is spacious and, since it's Dyneema®, it won't retain water. Plus, it is lighter than the one we were using. More space but less weight and bulk—can't go wrong. But since I didn't work outside the home and Batman did all the heavy lifting for our family, I did like my dad always told me when I requested new stuff: I wanted in one hand and pooped in the other and waited to see which filled first.

Four days of showers plus the night's downpour had left the trail in terrible condition. The streams were overflowing, making crossings tricky. Rocks and roots were slippery, and the trail bed was muddy. My attitude was not where it should have been. In fact, I was not a happy hiker at all.

I hated everything. I was tired. The continuous days of being wet and gross were wearing on my nerves. My skin still itched. My feet hurt. I hated being crammed into a tent. I hated having to carry a soggy, dirty tent. I was even feeling lonely when Batman wasn't with us because Shortcake didn't talk that much. We were hiking together but didn't really converse. I just wanted to quit and go home.

But I couldn't. That would leave Shortcake solo, and I wasn't going to do that to her.

Since I couldn't change the weather, my surroundings, or even the lack of communication between Shortcake and myself (even though I constantly tried to), the only thing I could adjust was the six inches between my ears. Just as boredom is a personal problem, so is a bad attitude.

I despised the rain, but the flowers loved all the moisture. New blooms adorned the trail. Lilies of the valley, pink azaleas, and many more varieties I couldn't name, reminded me of why I was out there.

I prayed to God, asking for help with my attitude. In my heart, I loved the trail, but the current circumstances were robbing my joy and I needed a fix. He heard me, and His gift was all the beautiful flowers.

In 2015, I had a similar attitude meltdown—several, actually. Hiking 2,189.2 miles taught me so many wonderful things. The lesson I am most grateful for is the skill I developed at noticing all the treasures around me, no matter how small. I learned to enjoy the little things, a lesson that is now my tagline.

Shortcake was correct in saying the trail is a treasure chest. I like to add that God is the one who fills that chest over and over. All we need to do is be aware of our surroundings and be open to those gems and realize they are not just coincidences.

Woods Hole Hostel, a self-sustainable farm located not far from the trail, would be home for the night. It wasn't in our original plan, but we needed to get out of the elements, not just to dry out but, more importantly, for our mental status. Flowers were a great start, but a larger intervention was needed. The charming old chestnut log cabin from the 1880s was just what I needed.

BLACK BEAR TIP

Relish the stillness of boredom and enjoy the little things.

Day 63 Thursday May 25
Time: 7:00am – 2:30pm
Mile: 623.7 – 634.3
Miles hiked: 10.6
Holiday Lodge Inn Motel
Weather: NO RAIN

Day 64 Friday May 26
Time: 9:37am – 2:50pm
Mile: 634.3 – 643.7
Miles hiked: 9.4
Tented at mile 643.7
Weather: NO RAIN

Day 65 Saturday May 27
Time: 6:57am – 2:30pm
Mile: 643.7 – 657.1
Miles hiked: 13.4
Tented in a parking lot
Weather: NO RAIN

Day 66 Sunday May 28
Time: 5:57am – 7:30pm
Mile: 657.1 – 676.5
Miles hiked: 19.4
Weather: Cloudy, rainy, humid

Day 67 Monday May 29
Time: 7:57am – 3:30pm
Mile: 676.5 – 687.0
Miles hiked: 10.5
Tented by a nice stream
Weather: Warm, humid, cloudy

Day 68 Tuesday May 30
Time: 7:27am – 7:10pm
Mile: 687.0 – 702.4
Miles hiked: 15.4
Hostel Hens and Rooster
Weather: Hot & wonderful

Day 69 Wednesday May 31
Time: 8:03am – 8:10pm
Mile: 702.4 – 718.7
Miles hiked: 16.3
Tented at Lamberts Meadow Shelter
Weather: Hot, partly sunny, sprinkles

Day 70 Thursday June 1
Time: 7:35am – 1:35pm
Mile: 718.7 – 729.6
Miles hiked: 10.9
Hotel
Weather: Partly cloudy & hot

13

The Lists

I had a great night's sleep in the loft of the hostel. I was pleasantly surprised. My first impression upon entering the bunkhouse was *Oh no! This is nothing more than a barn with mattresses crowded on the floor in a hayloft! Without heat even!* It was just a converted barn, and I was just happy to be out of the rain. The hostel turned out to be quite charming, especially since a few of our hiking friends were there. It wasn't as bad as I had thought it would be. But then again, I think my standards were lowering.

Shortcake and I skipped the family-style breakfast. We wanted to get to Pearisburg as soon as our tired feet could get us there. We were the first hikers out. We were only gone an hour before our hiking friends caught up to us. Oh, the powers of youth. Our standard practice was to step aside and let faster hikers pass. But that morning I stopped, turned, stretched out my poles and blocked the path. I gruffly said, "Not today! You are not passing us already this morning. It's a troll road!" And I growled like a bear.

Bananas was in the lead, followed by The Machine and then Atticus. The trio had been leapfrogging with us the past several days. Bananas acted tough and rough, clanging his poles together as though to scare away Black Bear—the behavior you should do if encountering a real black bear on the trail. When he did so, his pole snapped in half.

The Machine and I burst into hysterical laughter at poor Banana's humiliation. We couldn't stop laughing. I told him, "That's what you get when you mess with Black Bear." That was a fun start to an already nice day.

———

It had poured buckets while we snoozed in the barn, but the downpour ceased by morning. The skies may have been dry, but the trail was not. The last four days of drizzle and storms had left the path a soggy mess. Most of the day we hiked in a river. At one point, Yoda quipped, "I feel like a salmon swimming upstream, getting ready to spawn."

I couldn't help myself. As much as I have tried to clean up my mind, the words left my mouth before I could slam the gates closed, and I replied to his comment with, "Not right here! Not right now, I hope!" We all laughed.

This was one of those days I was happy to be wearing my heavy, full-grain leather hiking boots. My feet stayed dry thanks to my trusty Cresta boots from L.L.Bean. Shortcake wasn't so lucky. All that runoff produced some gorgeous waterfalls, though, which we enjoyed listening to and seeing.

My favorite product of all the rain was the rhododendron explosion in the forest. Everywhere we looked, the trail was lined with pink shrubs tall enough to form a tunnel around the trail. It was easy to forget the misery of the conditions while strolling through such beauty.

We ended the day in Pearisburg, Virginia. A reroute confused me a tad. In 2015, I remembered weaving through a residential area before the trail dumped me off onto the road to town that was a short half-mile walk. This time, we ended at a trailhead parking area with little indication of which way to go. Thankfully, someone was leaving in a vehicle as we arrived. I asked the occupants of the truck for a lift into town. With an affirmative yes, we threw our gear in the back and climbed in the bed of the truck for an open-air ride. We were headed for a hotel. Another night of not having to sleep in wet conditions was a-okay for us. At this point, I didn't care if I glamped my way to Katahdin. As long as I walked every white blaze, I was good.

———

Unfortunately, glitz and glamour were not available. We were up way too early the next morning for our planned "sleep in." But since our luxurious accommodations were a step below a "dive," in Shortcake's words, I couldn't get out of there fast enough. The place had an odd smell upon check-in, but at the time, it seemed better than the rain. However, after sleeping in the room for several hours, my lungs had all they could take and woke me up at 1:30am with a burning sensation, a headache, and chest congestion. I suffered through, in and out of sleep, until I saw Shortcake awake about 6:30-ish.

We packed up and were out of there. On our way back to the trailhead, our road walk took us past a Dairy Queen. Finally, we could quench our milkshake desire. At least, Shortcake did. I was too ill for that kind of treat. The only thing I needed was lots of fresh air.

We were a mile off trail. The day before, we'd had the good fortune to snag a ride from a nice elderly couple leaving the trailhead just as we showed up. They let us climb in the back of their pickup. That was fun. But in the morning, no fortuitous shuttle appeared to deliver us back to the trail. We didn't mind. We had a short 9.4 miles planned for the day, so one extra mile of road walking would make a nice warm-up.

So much for the fresh air. An hour into the hike, the trail took us along a landfill. I had forgotten about this feature. It was bad in 2015 and just as rank in 2017. For half an hour our nostrils filled with the stench of decomposing trash. Breathing through our mouth didn't help. The odor was so strong you could taste it. Our need for fresh air compounded with every minute.

We hiked on, and as we did, the sights and smells of Pearisburg vanished. Soon we were back in the healing atmosphere of the forest. Our lungs and senses returned to normal as we enjoyed a second day in a row without rain.

We saw a doe bound gently a few leaps away from the trail then stop. She turned and watched us. When there is one deer, there is often another. So we looked around, and on the other side of the trail we saw a yearling. We stood still, letting him cross the trail to join his mom. It was such a pretty sight. That's why we put up with all the misery—just so we can get to see stuff like that.

A long-distance hike is a microcosm of the real world. Or is the hike the real world? I heard Dixie, in an interview on The Hiking Radio Network Podcast hosted by Steve "Mighty Blue" Adams, say it best when she said hiking is the real world and everything else is synthetic. On the trail, life is raw. There is no room for pretending. There is no need to impress. There is no desire to one-up the next hiker. You do what needs to be done as efficiently as possible to save energy for the next task at hand. There is a freedom to just be. You are accepted as is and you accept others for who they are. You may not like everything about everyone, but there is an acceptance on the trail that breaks down barriers and allows friendships to develop that might not do so in everyday life.

In the synthetic world (as coined by Dixie), we tend to avoid people we don't like or who differ from us. We shy away from people with dissimilar thought processes. I'm guilty of it. It's easier and more comfortable not to deal with others who strain our emotional, mental, spiritual, and physical well-being.

On the trail where life seems more real than any other place, I find it oddly refreshing to be surrounded by a mix of characters who are so far from my way of thinking. It doesn't mean I want to be like them, but I value the insight a different perspective has to offer.

No matter which world one finds themselves in, one thing is common in both. It happens in the synthetic society and in the microcosm of the trail. It happens in family life and in work life. It happens in organizations big and small. That is having to do things you don't want to do in order to have the things or do the things you want to do.

We all want or need money, but we don't necessarily want to work. I love to eat but I despise doing the dirty dishes. I loved teaching but didn't care for all the non-teaching stuff that went along with the job. In order to accomplish what I really wanted, I had to do the not-so-pleasant. Life on the trail is no different. Shortcake and I had many dislikes. Here is the short list.

Shortcake's List

- Uphills
- Feet hurting
- Being wet and wet gear
- Camp chores after a full day of hiking
- Packing and unpacking
- Getting dressed in the tent
- Getting up early

Black Bear's List

- Being wet and cold
- Sleeping after a hot sweaty day and no shower
- The humidity
- Pot and cigarette smoking
- Dogs not on a leash that try to steal your food
- Downhills
- Smelly hikers
- Graffiti on trail signs
- Gross privies

It seemed so easy to ramble off our dislikes. But as much as we may not like a lot of the stuff we go through on the trail, those dislikes don't outweigh our likes. It's no different out on the trail than when we're pursuing any other dream or goal. We must do the things we do not really want to do in order to have or accomplish the thing we desire.

In order to experience what the trail has to offer—like a deer crossing the trail or a spectacular view at the golden hour—we must endure the parts of the trail that we don't necessarily prefer.

What would a dislikes list be without a likes list? After all, it's going through the negativity that gives value to the positive. If everything was hunky-dory, how would we distinguish between the good and the great?

After dwelling on the not-so-nice things that were irritating us, we decided to make a list of the things that kept us going.

Shortcake's List

- Each day's sights
- Being outside
- The critters
- The views and vistas
- Being self-sufficient
- The cows (love them!)

Black Bear's List

- The challenge
- The actual hiking
- The spectacular views
- The sun on my shoulders
- Morning hiking
- Ridge hiking

Both Of Us

- Meeting people
- The wonderful smells in the forest
- Seeing wildlife
- Tenting near a babbling brook or waterfall
- Trail magic
- Big or small waterfalls
- Flowers

You are probably surprised how simple our lists were. Nothing on either of our lists was out of this world. But that's what worked for us, and it's the perfect illustration of how important it is to enjoy the little things life has to offer.

Since we had started the day early, we covered our distance earlier than normal, but it was too late in the afternoon to push on another five miles to the next tent site. We called it a day and enjoyed a lazy afternoon. After the dreadful accommodations the previous night and the foul air at the beginning of the day, it was nice to hang around and recuperate in the fresh air on our second day in a row of good weather.

No rain again for the next day. It was cloudy and humid, which meant we were still wet, just from sweat instead of rain. A precipitation-free day wasn't the only treat for the day's hike. The trail was comfortable, hovering around 3,300 feet as we ridge walked until just before the end of the day, when we dipped to 2,500 feet at Stony Creek VA-635. There we found trail magic and met up with Batman, neither of which ever got old.

Another day ending in the early afternoon allowed for another afternoon of rest. We would need all the R&R we could get. The next day we had 19.4 miles planned. To accomplish those miles would require one of Shortcake's most dreaded tasks—getting up early.

Mornings were tough for my hiking buddy. That's another area in which we differed. I absolutely loved mornings and was excited to see what the day would bring. Shortcake thought morning should start around 8:00am, which is not late, but is much too late to start a 19-plus-mile hiking day. She was not a happy camper with the 5:00am wake-up call.

We were making tracks by 5:57am. It's easy to get out of camp when Batman is around to help and is slackpacking us.

The first half of the trail was easy. It was the warm-up we needed to tackle the rough second half. Midway through, a steep decline followed by a steep and rocky incline slowed our progress before we finished with another long, steep descent.

Sights were limited, which was probably a good thing. Too much to see on a long day makes for an even longer day. Blooming orange azaleas and mountain laurel colored the forest. We encountered the most precious creature of the whole trip—a fawn curled up, half on the trail and half in the tall grass. We captured a few photos and were careful not to touch the baby deer.

Later we learned a hiker had picked up the deer and moved it. Then it was reported a dead baby deer had been found in that vicinity. According to deerassociation.com, it is best to leave a baby deer where it is unless it is in a dangerous place. Right on the trail may not be the best place for a newborn, but its mother knew where it was. As hikers, we are guests in the forest and should respect all aspects of wildlife. We are in their home. Of course, I sing a different tune when giant spiders or snakes invade the spot where I want to sleep.

I was happy the 19-mile day was over, and I was looking forward to a hot meal. Batman was taking us to town to eat. But we went without Shortcake; she chose to stay at the trailhead. It was a small, grassy parking area, and we set up our tents there, along with a few other hikers. When Batman is with us, he and I share the double tent and Shortcake takes the single. It gives her time to be alone.

It was late when we returned. We pulled into the parking/tenting area, shut the car off as quickly as possible to kill the lights, and went right to our tent as quietly as we could. Nineteen miles hiked and a tummy full of Mexican food made it easy to fall asleep, content and happy.

I slept like a lead brick, a rare occurrence for me. I usually sleep like a rotisserie chicken. It doesn't matter if I am in a five-star hotel with a dump truck load of pillows or on the hard floor of a shelter, nighttime is not my friend. But the next morning, I woke refreshed and had apparently missed the late-night show. Not the one hosted by Johnny Carson, Jay Leno, or whoever is the star of that program now. According to Batman and Shortcake, the stars were the couple in the adjacent tent.

It was a good thing I slept through the neighbors' romp in the sleeping bags. I have just enough crudeness in me to have made a snide joke that surely would have made everyone uncomfortable while I would have laughed myself back to sleep. But I missed it all while I was deep in slumber. It didn't stop me from mentioning something cute to one of the guilty parties when I saw him days later. Sometimes I just can't leave well enough alone.

My mood soared with a great night's sleep and the continued good weather. It would have been nice if Shortcake's attitude paralleled mine. But it didn't. She had been in another funk for the past several days, and she wasn't sharing the cause. I've known her long enough to know when she feels like opening up and when she clams up. She tends to do the latter more often than not.

Her food bag being left out was enough to break her silence. When Batman and I got back to camp after dinner, we had been focused on turning off the car and getting into our tents without disturbing anyone. We did not see her food bag waiting to be put into the car. It was an honest mistake, but it set the stage for a very upsetting morning for all of us.

On that beautiful Memorial Day morning, Batman did his normal routine of hiking and moving the car ahead. With happy faces on, some real and some forced, we hiked out for a mere 10.5 miles.

Batman wanted to see the old tree mentioned in the guidebook. It is the largest oak tree on the Appalachian Trail in the south, second only to a Dover Oak in New York. With an eighteen-foot circumference, the Keefer Oak has stood watch for over 300 years. She is amazing. As I stood under her wide, expansive canopy, I let my thoughts drift, thinking about all the history she has seen. Her massive branches, disfigured and failing from the battle scars of life, keep the secrets of past generations, the larger and more numerous injuries indicating the larger tales.

Even though we were carrying almost-empty packs and did only 10.5 miles, it took us thirty minutes shy of eight hours to complete the day's miles. Sometimes the short days are the longest. I don't know why it was such a difficult day. The terrain wasn't particularly difficult. As a matter of fact, it was quite enjoyable, scenic, and easy. Maybe the morning's turmoil soured the day. I do remember the conversation with Shortcake was limited. I regret letting one incident overshadow the whole day. That's time wasted that can never be retrieved.

While on a ridge, I had full cell service and spent my time calling Stephen and Patch and texting while I hiked. I don't usually do that. I like to focus on hiking and on the person I'm with, but I was feeling alone at the time even though I wasn't alone.

Batman had hiked back out to the car earlier and drove around to our rendezvous point. His services included scoping out the perfect tent site for us next to a stream, right off the trail, and only 100 yards from the road. But because it was down over a very small hump, it was undetectable to passersby. It was perfect!

I love to camp by water. There is something soothing about the sound of it. The air always seems fresher, and gazing upon the shiny surface washes away any strife that clings to the heart. It also cooled the fire on my skin caused by… unknown causes. Yup! My itching had returned and it was driving me insane once again.

Batman's long weekend escape from work ended. He made sure we had what we needed from our resupply then headed back to base camp. Shortcake and I tended to our own needs as we geared up for another night on the Appalachian Trail. I was engrossed in calming the bites or rash that was acting up again. We had a big day ahead of us, and I didn't want the night's rest to be interrupted by derma issues again. I tried rinsing off with stream water. I tried lotion. I tried stream water again. Nothing helped. Finally, a couple Benadryl pills knocked me out until morning.

The smooth, steep trail switchbacked as we climbed 1,500 feet to start the morning. As I rounded one switchback, I had a flashback to my first hike. There I saw Walking Man sitting on the side of the trail, resting. Just prior to that, I thought I was going to die if I took one more step. My raggedness must have shown on my face, because he said "Here, have a seat" as he scooted over to make room for me on a rock. As Shortcake and I passed my 2015 resting stone, I glided my hand over its surface, remembering the wonderful time I had hiking with Walking Man and his son, GQ.

Shortcake and I continued the climb. As we huffed and puffed our way to the top, the trail eased as we joined an old roadbed. At the junction was a very nice park bench to rest on. I knew it was there but kept it a surprise for Shortcake. Unfortunately, when we reached the bench it was already occupied by two other weary hikers. We stopped briefly and continued another half mile to our first highlight for the day, the Audie Murphy monument.

Audie was the most decorated American soldier of WWII. He died in a plane crash close to this site. There were two more park benches at the monument. We dropped our packs, and each claimed a bench as our reward for completing the ascent. After my snack and hydration break, I placed the *Gratitude* stone I had been carrying since Day 1 on the monument for a photo. Then I carefully repacked the stone to continue on the journey with me.

One major climb done for the day. After we left the monument, we headed for Dragon's Tooth, ten miles away. The trail turned ugly—or fun, depending on how you perceive it. I thought it was fun. Of course I did. I also like uphill, early mornings, and hiking in the rain.

"Where did all the darn rocks come from?" That isn't quite what Shortcake said. I had to edit one word to keep this family-rated.

It took us awhile to hike to the popular monolith rock outcroppings known as Dragon's Tooth. Just before we arrived, we hit the 700-mile mark. I created a little more trail art, written this time with mountain laurel petals from the abundant, wild flowering bushes that had exploded in bloom.

We explored the adult jungle gym created by the gigantic stones and boulders of Dragon's Tooth. I wanted to climb the behemoth landmark, but my fear of heights prevented me from doing so.

We finished playing around and continued our descent. We had 2.5 miles to our destination. The ridge up to Dragon's Tooth was quite rocky but the incline was easy. The descent would be a lot more rapid and tricky. I couldn't wait for it. I had thought it was fun in 2015, and it was just as exciting this time around, except I was a little more concerned for Shortcake. It wasn't hair-raising or death-defying, but we did need to take our time and concentrate on our footing to prevent a twisted ankle or face-plant. But no worries needed. We both came through unscathed although worn out.

Our 15.4-mile day produced another Shortcake quote: "It felt like 30!" A great day, nonetheless, completed on the Appalachian Trail with my good buddy Shortcake as we limped our tired bodies to the hostel.

McAfee Knob is the most photographed spot on the Appalachian Trail. The iconic spot draws visitors from all around, and Wednesday, May 31, was no different. It was like a hiker super-highway up to the summit. At one point, I just wanted to stop and go hide behind one of the house-sized rocks along the trail until rush hour was over. If I've said it once, I have said it a thousand times: If you want peace and solitude, don't hike the A.T. Or at least, don't hike near tourist traps.

The day marked a full week without rain, and we were loving it. We were so excited to have clear skies for our McAfee photo shoot. That all changed by the time we reached the overhang where only the strongest-willed souls dare sit. Angry clouds gathered overhead as a dozen or so hikers patiently waited their turn for selfies and pictures.

Since I had my turn in 2015, I let Shortcake go first. I skipped sitting with my feet and legs dangling over the edge. I wanted to do something different. I chose a "Strong Girl" pose on the edge instead.

The forever view was shadowed by gloomy, ominous-looking clouds with rain over the valley below, but the storm hadn't reached us yet. We took in the panorama for a few more minutes, then decided to have a quick snack since the rain was far off. Just as we retrieved our packs and gobbled a few bites, the pitter-patter started, and we were once again chased off another summit.

We gathered our packs and headed down. It was so hot we didn't bother with rain gear. Silently, I welcomed a little shower to cool me off. It was over before we realized it, so not much cooling took place. We out-sweated the raindrops that fell as we descended and then ascended Tinker Cliffs.

It was late in the afternoon; we were far from the hustle and bustle of the tourist attraction of McAfee, but the sight that stretched out before us was more magnificent than the highly acclaimed McAfee Knob. As the sun lowered, its golden rays filled the horizon. Looking out from Tinker Cliffs, we had the spectacle all to ourselves, except for two deer we saw on the walk up. From our viewpoint, we could see McAfee and the ridgeline we had just hiked across. No wonder we were tired, and we weren't done yet. But we were in no hurry as we sat silently and alone, warming our skin with those golden rays.

We hiked on to our scheduled destination, but at 4:15pm we decided to push on six more miles to the next shelter to make the next day's hike shorter. This was a bold move for us. We aren't the fastest cars in the garage, and we already had a full day. We claimed our decision and set out. We arrived at 8:10pm and set up the tent just in time for the return of the pitter-patter. This time, it continued all night, ending our weeklong dry spell.

––––––

We had been eagerly waiting to get to Daleville, Virginia. The trail exits the woods on US-220, and within a very short walk there are eateries, motel choices, an outfitter, a grocery store, and several other businesses of interest to hikers. This was our destination for our next scheduled rest. We had not had a break in 20 days. We needed real food and lots of it. We also needed clean clothes and clean bodies. Most importantly, we needed rest.

Our initial plan was to hike to Daleville, eat, go to the outfitter, then hang out and wait for Batman to meet us. He'd take our gear, and we would easily stroll empty-handed 1.5 miles through the woods to Troutville, where we would all camp in the town park. But that all changed.

I had a bright idea. Instead of hanging around in the hot sun, sweaty and gross, while we waited for Batman to arrive, we checked into a cheap motel close to the trail. It was a dive. You get what you pay for. At least we were clean.

After we washed away the trail, we went to the outfitter, then to Three Little Pigs, a wonderful restaurant specializing in southern BBQ. I ate until I couldn't move. The real treat was a hiker-only free dessert. Since it wasn't gluten-free and Shortcake was also stuffed, we took dessert to go. I saved mine for Batman.

An hour before Batman's arrival, he called. That was our signal to put on our hiking shoes. We did just that. Leaving our packs in the room, we headed across Route 220. With nothing but our phones and my *Gratitude* stone I carried every mile, we continued the 1.5 miles to Troutville. It was a lovely stroll. It's easy by anyone's standards, a wide, mowed path connecting the sister towns of Daleville and Troutville. Within that short distance, we saw two deer and a bunny. Batman joined us from the north end, and the three of us completed the mini-hike. Once at the car, we all hopped in and he drove us to Cracker Barrel for our second supper. It's good to eat. What's even better is to end a long hard stretch with food, a zero day, and better yet, a night with a roof over our head.

BLACK BEAR TIP

Step out of your comfort zone; doing so will build confidence, teach you about yourself, and help you learn to think on your feet.

Day 71 Friday June 2
Zero

Day 72 Saturday June 3
Time: 8:54am – 5:10pm
Mile: 729.6 – 743.6
Miles hiked: 14.0
Tented at mile 743.6
Weather: Sunny, warm, no humidity –
Perfect

Day 73 Sunday June 4
Time: 7:32am – 2:30pm
Mile: 743.6am – 756.3pm
Miles hiked: 12.7
Tented near Jennings Creek
Weather: Sunny

Day 74 Monday June 5
Time: 7:37am – 12:30pm
Mile: 756.3 – 765.0
Miles hiked: 8.7
Tented at Cornelius Creek Shelter
Weather: Rainy & chilly

Day 75 Tuesday June 6
Time: 7:57am – 3:30pm
Mile: 765.0 – 779.5
Miles hiked: 14.5
Tented by Gunter Ridge Trail Jct.
Weather: Partly cloudy, warm, breezy
– Perfect

Day 76 Wednesday June 7
Time: 7:25am – 10:30am
Mile: 779.5 – 784.9
Miles hiked: 5.4
Stanimal's Hostel
Weather: Cool start, then cloudy

Day 77 Thursday June 8
Time: 7:52am – 5:15pm
Mile: 784.9 – 800.0
Miles hiked: 15.1
Tented at mile 800.0
Weather: Cool start, then cloudy

Day 78 Friday June 9
Time: 7:24am – 4:15pm
Mile: 800.0 – 813.0
Miles hiked: 13
Tented at Hog Camp Gap
Weather: Partly cloudy, humid, &
breezy

14

Bridges

I got up early while my two sleepyhead companions slept in. What can I say, I just love mornings, even on a zero day. I did our laundry so it would be one less thing to do.

Once we all were up, fed, and packed, we checked out. While Daleville had just about everything a hiker could want, choice of hotels was limited.

A Sheraton hotel in Roanoke, fifteen minutes from the trail would be our real place of rest. Finally, a place to relax where we didn't fear catching something. That is how we did zero days.

We started with an early check-in of 9:30am that included free breakfast vouchers for their buffet. It made Shortcake's third breakfast that morning, all before 9:45am. She had consumed a buffet at the Howard Johnsons before we left Daleville. On the short drive to Roanoke, she ate her free dessert from The Three Little Pigs, then topped that off with the free buffet at the Sheraton. For such a little gal, she sure could eat. Hiker hunger does not discriminate; it affects every long-distance hiker.

After our zero day, we slackpacked out of Troutville and arrived at our destination with energy and time left over, allowing us to hike two miles farther than we'd planned. We tented off a parking area on the Blue Ridge Parkway near Bobletts Gap Shelter. The parking area came with high-value amenities such as a picnic table and a bear-proof trash can.

We decided we loved slackpacking and car camping. We carried on our backs only what was essential for the day's hike. Batman met us at the end of the day and we'd gather our gear. We would set up camp close to the car and then store our things in the car for the night. No hanging food bags in a tree. No filtering water. Batman brought us water. It was a great way to hike the trail. I wished he didn't have to work so he could join us all the time.

We had the luxury of slackpacking and at the end of the day had the comforts of a picnic table, and we felt guilty calling ourselves thru-hikers. With such amenities, I felt energized enough to cook for everyone. I whipped up gourmet trail rice with cheese, bacon, and turkey sausage bites. If that were all I served at home, my family would turn me in to the authorities for neglect. But out on the trail, it was a five-star meal.

The sun burned a hole in the horizon with an orange fireball that etched its color onto our retinas. A perfect sunset ended a perfect day on the trail. We retired to our cocoons while the warmth of the day still lingered.

Soon after we had fallen asleep, Batman and I awoke with a sense of déjà vu. We heard the steady walk of a large animal in the trees next to our tent.

"You've got to be kidding me!" I said to Batman. I grabbed the headlamp, unzipped the screen, and scanned the trees to make sure it wasn't a bear. Shortcake was next to us in her tent. I wanted to confirm our safety from any hungry beast. It wasn't a bear. Instead, it was a very large deer about ten feet away.

In 2015 Batman and I were tenting in the exact same spot, and at roughly the same time of night, we heard an animal. That year it circled our tent all night, but we could never see it.

Exhaustion kept hitting me midday. I'd wake up strong, then struggle to finish the day. As much as I loved the heat, I thought it was affecting me. If not the heat, it was a combination of a few things such as not getting a good night's sleep, to having to take Benadryl to stop the itching, to lack of good food. Who knew? What I did know was that I was tired all the time. On the days when the fatigue was the worst, I plodded one foot in front of the other, praying for the day to be over and wondering how I was ever going to make it to Katahdin.

I kept going and drew strength from the little things, like the sight of a beautiful doe right in the middle of the trail. We watched from close by and let her do her thing, only continuing when she disappeared over the ridge.

Despite my tiredness, sometimes things worked out. I had wanted to take two zero days when we were at the Roanoke Sheraton, but it didn't happen. I was beyond tired, but we hiked on.

Surprisingly, the third day back on trail after our last zero day, I woke up refreshed. I had gone to bed at 6:30pm, though, and slept until 6:30am. I guess I was getting caught up on some much-needed rest.

We started the day in the rain. It was only a drizzle, but as we hiked on and up in elevation, it rained harder and the temperature dropped. By the time we came to the second shelter, we decided to stop for a second break, and we never left. We dried out—mostly—and I rested more.

We had stopped 5.3 miles short of our goal. We didn't want to end the day wet, exhausted, and at over 4,000-feet elevation. I may not have gotten my extra zero day back in Roanoke, but three days of easy hiking had allowed me to rest on the move, and I didn't want to undo what I had gained by pushing at the end of the day. So we called it quits early and stayed at Cornelius Creek Shelter.

———

We started the next morning with golden sunrays beaming through the forest. It's hard to have a bad day when those streams of light from heaven beckon you forward with each step. The trail is a never-ending roller coaster of good and bad with a whole lot of not much in between. Some days Shortcake was grouchy. Some days I was grouchy. Other days we both were miserable. Sometimes the weather stunk.

Other days it was glorious. No matter what, we just kept walking and the scene changed.

That morning all was well. We were rested, we were happy, and we were communicating. The trail was pleasant, and God was lighting our way for another fantastic day.

We passed an alien telecommunications site (a.k.a. an FAA tower) at the tallest peak for the day. Every time we passed a federal aviation tower, we said it was the government communicating with outer space. I have an overactive imagination, and my story detailed alien invasions supported by our very own leaders and if we stayed on the mountain too long our brains would be snatched for research.

The trail had just the right amount of up and down and never a time when we wished a particular section was over. We did stumble upon two young hikers who were so tired they took a nap right on the trail. As exhausted as I got, we never did that.

The day ended with a dream path. After fifteen minutes of smooth hiking and peekaboo views of the lush green valley below, I asked Shortcake to strike me with her pole. I must have been dreaming. This couldn't have been the A.T.

We set ourselves up for only a 5.4-mile hike to the road in the morning and then a 6-mile shuttle to town. We scheduled a driver for that task before we went to bed.

Rumblings in the distance invited us to call it a night. We dashed into our castle, my new term for our tent. We were still sharing sleeping quarters. That might be one of the reasons for sleepless nights. But that night, I crawled into my spot and dreamt about lunch and supper the next day.

Well, I had done it again. In 2015, I sent home my sleeping bag and all my cold gear way too early. I'd had a long spell of hot weather, so I wanted to lighten my pack. This year, I vowed to hold on to it much longer, which I did. But we had been having hot nights, so the previous Sunday I had sent my sleeping bag packing with Batman and replaced it with a small fleece throw. And just like that, the temperatures changed. And not just a little bit. They dropped to the low 50s.

Thankfully, I had kept my down puffy, wool pj's, and a sleeping bag liner. But for two nights I was chilled, even with two bodies generating heat in the tent.

Our initial plan for our stay in Glasgow, Virginia, was to camp in the town park. But our shuttle driver, Bob, asked if we were going to the town's hiker shelter or to the hostel.

"Hostel? There's a hostel?" I asked. "How much? And is it close to food?" All his answers were within budget, so we decided to stay at St-animal's Hostel. Bob and his wife just happened to be the caretakers.

Shortcake and I were not particularly fond of hostels. We knew that's all part of a thru-hiking experience, and it wasn't that we were snobs. We just did not like the filthy, grungy hostels. We weren't ger-mophobes either, but we also understood that it only takes one bout of giardia or norovirus to ruin one's thru-hike. So we were a little re-served at first, not having any prior knowledge of Stanimal's.

One quick look around, and we were hooked. The older two-bed-room home with four cute bunks in each bedroom was clean and invit-ing. Free laundry and local shuttles were added perks. Bob and Donna were the sweetest hosts. She even folded our laundry.

Before catching our shuttle to Glasgow, our short morning hike carried us across the James River footbridge, made just for the Appa-lachian Trail. It's one thousand feet long, making it the longest foot-bridge on the trail.

There are many types, shapes, and sizes of bridges constructed along the A.T. Bridges are fascinating in their designs, from a simple debarked tree laid across a creek to a well-engineered structure that cost thousands of dollars. But whatever shape or size, they serve the purpose of helping people to cross from one side to the other. They connect two separate sections.

Bridges can also be metaphorical. One of my favorite sayings—*Never burn bridges; you never know when you will need them*—doesn't necessarily mean the physical bridges we use to cross a body of water or divide. Instead, it refers to a chasm that can happen between individuals emotionally.

Relationships are like the lakes and rivers of our lives, and just like those bodies of water can be used for navigation, we use our relationships to navigate through life. That's not a bad thing. It's just the way our species works. We are dependent on others. Sometimes our relationships are tested; and if we are not careful, we can damage the emotional bridges we have with those we are close to, must work with, or need to interact with. And the more we damage the structures, the greater the chance that eventually they will not be able to hold up and will crumble. Then we are left with a great divide separating us from the other person and no longer any way to connect.

We all have traveled over a bridge that may have put our sense of danger on high alert, wondering if it should be closed. It's an eerie feeling. It's even worse to have that gut-wrenching sensation when you feel the emotional wear and tear of a friendship's bridge. You have two choices when that happens: give up and set the bridge afire because you *know* you are right and hope you never will need that relationship again, or you can close the bridge temporarily for repairs and work on rebuilding the damages.

When I cross bridges hiking, I am in awe no matter how simple the structure is. Someone took the time and money to build that for me. I also ponder how I tend to the bridges in my emotional world. Am I just using them for my own gain? Am I repairing the ones that are worn? Do I appreciate the ones I have?

Stanimal's Hostel was worth our change in plans. The little gem spoke to our needs and checked off all the boxes to satisfy weary hikers. Our caretakers, Donna and Bob, made us feel at home. When we were done resting, Bob delivered us back to the trail so we could continue our journey north.

Good thing we were rested up. Two-thirds of the next day's hike was uphill. I liked it! I loved it! I wanted some more of it! I was feeling strong. My exhaustion was hiding for the time being. Even though the roller coaster of emotions, strength, and health continued, I took it as it came.

What a journey it had been so far. We passed the 800-mile mark the day we left Glasgow. It was only because we had seasoned legs, bodies, souls, and minds that we easily climbed the peaks of that day. The previous 799 miles, uphills, descents, obstacles, and challenges prepared us for that eight hundredth mile. And each additional step we took got us ready for what was to come.

As I said in Chapter 13, we may not like some of the things we have to do, like work, getting along with difficult people, cancer, sickness, loss of employment, etc., but each challenge we face prepares us for bigger hurdles. All that's needed to succeed is to put one foot in front of the other, get back up when knocked down, do not quit, and build bridges.

Eventually, you will make it through the rocky sections of life—just to do it all over again. Remember that without struggle there is no growth. But unlike other species who usually struggle alone, we can have help. We can use our bridges connecting us to each other to carry us over life's challenges together.

800 miles under our boots, but who's counting? You betcha we were counting! The next day we took our first steps toward another mile of preparation for whatever peak, valley, or challenge awaited us.

———

Shortcake and I hiked at a speed barely recordable. We were strong hikers in the fact that we put in the miles; we just took longer to do it. We had great stamina. One reason for our slower-than-most pace was that we took so many pictures. Seldom were the days I did not feel like capturing the day in Kodachrome. But Friday, June 9, started out as one of those days. I just wanted to enjoy the hike and take it all in without the added burden of trying to frame that perfect shot.

The trail was easy to navigate, making it even easier to get lost in thought. But I will admit that with one mile to go on the longest climb of the day—almost 3,000 feet of elevation gain over 6 miles— my quads were asking for a break. Once we stopped, rested, and had lunch, I was ready to finish the day strong.

Exhaustion no longer had its hold on me. Sure, I still got tired— how could you not get tired doing what we were doing?—but I reached a point where my fully loaded pack no longer seemed cumbersome and awkward. I still enjoyed slackpacking. Just because my back may not have noticed the weight, my knees and feet noticed, especially at the end of the day.

The almost-bare bald at the top of the climb was a great surprise. I hadn't read about it in the guide. Our resources were full of information. They contained so much information it was sometimes overwhelming. On many days, I only focused on the destination and water sources, letting the day unfold. Often, this lack of attention to detail caused me to miss a point of interest. At other times, I was rewarded by a surprise. Sometimes, not knowing is a gift.

When we reached the open air of the bald at 4,059 feet, my desire to take pictures returned. The view was spectacular. The blue sky, dotted with happy white fluffy clouds made the perfect backdrop for the tall meadow grasses and wildflowers. We could see for miles, in almost a 360-degree panorama. I couldn't stop taking pictures.

Perfect days on the trail are the bridges connecting the challenging times and the humdrum days. While it's important to find the joy in the little things to help keep our spirits up, those jaw-dropping experiences keep us wanting more. Hiking on a bald at over 4,000 feet, attainable only by blood, sweat, and exertion, is a feeling like no other. Your legs burn with the power in your muscles. Your lungs expand and deflate with each step you take. Your ears are filled with the songs of the earth. Your heart beats with pride as you watch your friend in front of you experiencing what you are feeling. Hiking the Appalachian Trail is so much more than a walk in the woods.

BLACK BEAR TIP

Build bridges instead of burning them. You never know
when you will need them again.

Day 79 Saturday June 10
Time: 7:42am – 5:55pm
Mile: 813.0 – 828.0
Miles hiked: 15
Tented at mile 828.0
Weather: Sunny, warm, breezy

Day 80 Sunday June 11
Time: 7:18am – 6:00pm
Mile: 828.0 – 842.8
Miles hiked: 14.8
Tented in a field on BRP
Weather: Very hot – 90 degrees

Day 81 Monday June 12
Time: 7:21am – 5:55pm
Mile: 842.8 – 856.9
Miles hiked: 14.1
Tented at Paul C. Wolfe Shelter
Weather: Mostly sunny, hot, & humid

Day 82 Tuesday June 13
Time: 7:04am – 9:35am
Mile: 856.9 – 861.9
Miles hiked: 5
Stayed at the Lutheran Church hall
Weather: Extremely hot & humid

Day 83 Wednesday June 14
Time: 9:15am – 6:40pm
Mile: 861.9 – 874.0
Miles hiked: 12.1
Tented at mile 874
Weather: Extremely hot & humid,
T-storm

Day 84 Thursday June 15
Time: 7:33am – 3:45pm
Mile: 874.0 – 888.7
Miles hiked: 14.7
Camped at Loft Mt. Campground
Weather: Hot, humid, T-storms

Day 85 Friday June 16
Time: 7:42am – 4:00pm
Mile: 888.7 – 906.1
Miles hiked: 17.4
Tented in parking lot / Then went to
hotel
Weather: Cloudy, misty, T-Storm

15

Shortcake Gets the Boot

My mind and body had decided to work together lately. I didn't know why. I still wasn't sleeping well at night, and we certainly didn't eat properly. Even though I was hiking with my bestie, I was sometimes lonely. But despite all that, I was strong. I like to analyze things. I figure if I can make sense of a situation, it is easier to accept. But most of the time situations rarely make sense, and it's better just to let things be and ignore the facts. So I did. I was feeling great and didn't want to question why.

Spy Rock was a nice blue-blaze adventure. I skipped it in 2015 because that day I was not feeling strong and did not want to climb anything that was not a white-blazed trail. But that day in 2017, we dropped our packs and blue-blazed out to the behemoth outcropping. With 360-degree views of the Blue Ridge Mountains, we enjoyed our detour as we snacked and rested on the warm rock.

Batman met us on the trail. His doing so was the highlight of my weekends. Living on the trail, one day is the same as any other and it was hard to keep track of the days of the week. But weekends were extra special because I got to see my hubby, and it made it easier for me not to lose all track of time.

Shortcake and I had completed our spying at the rock and were hiking north. We still had almost five miles to complete for the day.

Batman met us just shy of Spy Rock. We told him he had to go see it, since he was so close. We continued north while he hiked out to the attraction.

The day was hot, and when Batman reunited with us, we were all in need of a break. We sat along the trail and sipped our warm waters in the cool shade of the trees.

As we rested, a hiker came along and stopped. He took one look at me and said, "I know you..." I thought it was the usual recognition from seeing me in the *Walking Home* documentary on YouTube. But he said, "No, we met in 2015. I was low on food, and you gave me most of your food." I was astounded. It was a serendipitous meeting. What were the chances we would meet again two years later? It was like trail magic.

Things like this happen often on the trail. It's one reason so many people are drawn to endure all the yuck of the trail. No matter how bad and miserable the trail can be at times, the challenges are forgotten and replaced with all the good memories.

We camped just north of The Priest Shelter at mile 828.0, making the next morning's hike out to the car only four miles long.

It was nice camping with Batman. I missed him, even though he joined us almost every weekend. He was so much fun to be around. His excitement gushed from him as he left his work at base camp to rejuvenate in the wilds of the woods. Shortcake and I were usually tired from living several days in those wilds and liked to get off the trail. It was an amusing matchup.

At the car, we emptied our packs of anything not necessary for the remainder of the day. Yay! Batman was slackpacking us again. He would drive the Batmobile around to the day's ending point and again hike south to meet us. Chores filled the rest of his day. Every thru-hiker needs a Batman.

Shortcake and I hiked out. The easy downhill out to the car had warmed us up for the huge climb out. It went up for six miles. We rested every hour; we could have done so every 30 minutes. Like most things in life, when there is great effort there tend to be great rewards. The views we had each hour were incredible. I know I use that adjective often, but it's true. We just couldn't get over how awesome and amazing the scenery was. I so wanted to throw away our mileage agenda, set up camp at one of those overlooks, and call it a day.

We finally managed to hobble our way to the car, arriving at 6:00pm. We weren't done, though. It was resupply time. Batman had all our stuff in the car, and we sat on the curb, adding food, wipes, tissues, and swapping out clothing. Poor Shortcake had to add one more piece to her gear.

Up until then, apart from a handful of nights, we had been sharing a tent. It had been hot lately, so I gave her the boot, kicking her out of my tent. Not for any wrongdoing on her part. Squeezing in the tent when it was cold was one thing. Doing it when we were stinking and sweaty was more than I could handle.

We had started with sharing a tent so Shortcake wouldn't have to sleep alone. We made it over 800 miles. During those miles, she grew and developed into a seasoned backpacker. It was time for her to leave the nest. And just like little eaglets are thrown out of the nest in order to learn to fly, it was time for Shortcake to take that last step to being truly independent on her Appalachian Trail thru-hike. Besides, I was just too hot at night and couldn't stand the hot mess of two bodies in the tent with hot smelly clothes and gear. I had to deal with it when Batman joined me. But he was also going to get the boot if he didn't quit farting at night while we were crammed in our little abode.

Waynesboro, Virginia, was a mere nineteen miles away when we woke up. Our goal for that day was 14.5 miles, but I was secretly hoping to push on to the town. The elevation profile in the book looked gentle. I had hiked over 3,000 miles using the same book and digital app, and I continued to believe all their lies.

The day was another uphill marathon. At one point, the GPS said we were at the peak, yet we continued to climb for another 30 minutes. My hopes of reaching town for a shower and real food were foiled by early afternoon. Our bodies went on strike for the rest of day. All the younger hikers were passing us and pushing on. At one point, we said we could do it, but why bother? Sleeping one more night in the woods was okay with us.

We arrived at the Paul C. Wolfe Shelter. The water source, a shallow stream cascading gently around rocks as it made its way to lower elevations, stopped the strike our bodies had picketed earlier. The cool pools refreshed our feet and hydrated our thirst. We hoped the stream would lull us to sleep later that evening.

We ate dinner in the shelter with other hikers. I was just going to sit on the ground by the tents and listen to the stream, but while I was setting up camp a tick joined me, and I wasn't impressed. Ticks—my biggest fear out on the trail.

I filled my tummy from my boring food bag and said good night to all. I was so hot, I just wanted to zip up in the tent in my birthday suit, dust the humidity off with layers of Gold Bond®, and journal.

After a few minutes, Shortcake came a-knocking. I warned her of the view she'd have upon entry, but she stuck her head in anyway. She had news. While she was still hanging out at the shelter, another hiker who arrived after I had left informed her that we were tenting next to a crazy person. Oh, great. There goes our restful night.

Several hikers had earlier had some not-so-good, even dangerous, encounters with the so-called crazy person. We digested the information given to us. We even thought about night hiking the last 5 miles. But that thought caused each of our bodies to hold up picket signs again in protest at such a thought. We decided just to be on guard and we'd go to bed and sleep with one eye open.

Armed with my SOS device and cell phone, I fell asleep fast, with little concern about the crazy hiker just a few yards away.

About 11:45pm, bright lights startled me awake as they flashed through my tent. I sat up, ready to attack and defend myself and Shortcake. Thankfully, at some point I had put on my pj's and I was no longer naked. Why is it when the sun goes down our paranoia goes up? All those scary movies we watched as kids come back to haunt us.

I slowly unzipped my tent and peeked out. I could see a headlamp from the crazy hiker's tent shining haphazardly with no clear intention on direction. The beam of light cut through the darkness as if signaling a distant aircraft. Then the beam would swing drastically downward. Then left and right in a zigzag pattern. After the hiker scanned every compass point, he flashed it in our direction—and seemed to be coming closer. *Oh great!* I thought. *He's on the move!*

I went back to the false safety of my tent but left the vestibule open so I could keep an eye on the situation. After an hour of watching the weird light show and wondering if the "psycho" was going to slice through my tent, I managed to drift off to sleep—only to be startled a second time at 1:30am.

This time, lights were on the other side of my tent, but closer. The fear factor was overloaded; I was ready to wake up Shortcake if needed. I jumped out of my tent on the far side, tucking between our two tents. I peered over the top and saw a headlamp uncomfortably close. I quickly ducked back down so I wouldn't be caught witnessing a possible crime. Then slowly peeked above again. I bobbed up and down several more times, holding my hiking pole and feeling like a Samurai warrior ready to defend to the death. I probably looked more like Shaggy and Scooby-Doo hiding from a ghost.

My eyes finally adjusted to the nighttime light, and I realized it was only a new hiker who had just arrived and was setting up his tent. Once my heart stopped racing, I relaxed and crawled back into my tent. Just as I was zipping up, crazy-hiker lights returned, and my guard went back up. Morning didn't come fast enough.

Morning did come, and I reported the night's fiasco to Shortcake. She had heard and seen nothing. Embellishing the best I could so as not to make myself out to be a scaredy-cat, I went on to tell her how I kept her safe so she could sleep peacefully.

When story time was over, we packed up fast and headed to town. We had three goals to accomplish by noon: the post office, a shower, and Ming's Chinese buffet. We completed them all.

Once those were done, we needed to decide on a place to stay. The town offered free camping at their park. That was our first choice, but bad news of an incident that took place the previous night caused us to reconsider. Having had enough crazy, we chose to stay at the Lutheran Church hostel. It was the safer option and turned out to be much more fun, reminding me of the teen retreats I attended as a youth. Only this time we were all adults who had no desire to sneak out after lights-out. We went from a night of hell to a peaceful night under God's roof.

I am sure by now you have probably wondered what it must be like to hike the Appalachian Trail. To help you understand what it's like, let's play a game. Close your eyes. Oh wait, you can't, you must read. Okay, instead, picture in your mind…

First, you wake up early, ready to greet the day with wild anticipation (like me). Or you wake up and hope your hiking buddy doesn't hear you and you can sleep a few more minutes (like Shortcake).

Once your eyelids are open, you immediately start packing up. Hiking clothes are put on, no matter how wet, cold, or smelly they are. You only have one set of hiking attire. Everything else gets neatly placed back into your backpack, hopefully before it starts raining.

Did I mention that the clothes you put on are still wet, stinky, and/ or cold from a week of hiking? Yes, I did. But it's important to say again to drive home this fact. They don't dry out. Nice! That means 5 to 7 days of sweat and mildew buildup. Oh, it feels so good on the skin!

Once the morning chores are done and the pack is stuffed, it's hoisted onto your back. Your pack too is wet and smelly. Well, the straps and hip belt, anyway. The pack is dry because you have a nice waterproof pack, but the harness system is a different fabric, and it stinks worse than your clothes. You check the time and clank your poles together in your pre-hike ritual as you set off.

Twenty minutes into the hike, you are dripping with sweat. As the brush, branches, and cobwebs touch your skin, you cringe. It's awful! With a layer of insect repellent, you are one slick chick. As the morning progresses, so does the southern heat. Add that to the never-ending inclines, and the sweating only worsens.

Picture walking on a treadmill at a 35-degree incline, carrying a small dog on your back, with the heat turned up high in your house. The lights are dim, since you are in the canopy, but every so often a heat lamp is turned on right over your head, instantly raising the temperature 10 to 15 degrees. You walk like this for two hours nonstop until you have sweat out more than you have put in, and it's time to hydrate. But you can't have your fill because you are only allowed two liters of water every 10 to 12 miles.

With all that agony and discomfort, believe it or not, that's not what you focus on. Sure, it's hot and hard work, but the sight of a bunny in the brush, a deer in the middle of the trail, a strange insect half-bee and half-housefly, or a view that takes your breath away, makes the former insignificant. It's easy to be miserable when you focus on the wrong thing, but just a little change in thinking can make a world of difference between discouragement or enjoyment. It's important to find joy in the little things. The choice is yours.

We slept well in the basement of the church. It really was a pleasant experience, and a first for us on the trail. Our stays up until then had been hotels, motels, regular hostels, and bed and breakfasts. The Lutheran Church ran a tight ship, and keeping to their time schedule was a must. To make sure sleepy hikers rose and shined in a timely manner, they had a wake-up call, and I was able to assist.

Everyone thinks I am nice and kind; I do well fooling them. I gladly volunteered to be the light-switch guard to turn the lights on by 8:00am. I am a morning person and do my best to see to it that everyone enjoys their morning as much as I do. One can't enjoy those earlier hours, though, unless one is up, so I found joy in helping any hiker who was still tucked in snugly and asleep on their cot to wake up. Plus, I was helping the hostel by seeing that we were all out by the scheduled time of 9:00am.

Shortcake and I were ready to get back to the trail. We would be entering the Shenandoah National Park (SNP), another one of America's gems. I loved the SNP in 2015 for its "gentle" trails and "easy" terrain. Everything is relative on the trail, but I did remember the SNP to be kind and enjoyable. And with the current weather being so hot and miserable, I was hoping to have some reprieve by having an easier hike.

Batman had returned to base camp instead of staying at the church with us, so when we were ready, we grabbed a shuttle from Leonard. Leonard was a kind old man who loved to talk, tell stories, and help hikers. You could tell he thrived on being around hikers. Hikers were accommodated by him, and being needed filled a purpose in his life. What he gained by offering services to hikers was just another example of how the trail provides for those in need.

June 15, Day 84, was another dreadfully hot day. The week's heat and humidity brewed up thunderstorms. The air felt and smelled of bad weather. The morning's white, fluffy, happy clouds clustered together as the day progressed. Storms were so frequent they were inoculating us to their true danger. We barely took notice of them anymore. It was just something else we learned to deal with.

Shortcake was in a silent mood again. Something else I had to deal with. On the flip side, maybe she had to deal with me never shutting up. I got that she was quiet in the morning; she didn't really like mornings. We were opposites. She needed her space in the morning; I needed mine in the evening. It would have been a little more fun, though, if we conversed more during the day's hike or at break time. Trying to get Shortcake to hold a conversation was sometimes like drawing blood from a turnip.

I would get lonely. I was out there with my hiking buddy but felt so distant from her and everyone. I don't mind being alone. I enjoy hiking alone. But since I wasn't physically alone, I felt the pressure of trying to fill the uncomfortable silence between us, and I didn't know how. Since we were hiking together, we didn't really make any connections with other hikers to develop a "trail family" as is so prevalent on an Appalachian Trail thru-hike.

Silence can be healing, and maybe that's what Shortcake was needing. It was just difficult for me because I couldn't figure out her needs and she wasn't giving any clues even when asked. So when I found it too uncomfortable, I would add a tiny bit of distance by lagging back. This space would give me the physical distance I needed for my own mental health to be alone without feeling I needed to figure out my buddy's issues. God knows I have enough issues of my own.

———

We were almost to our destination, Loft Mountain Campground on Skyline Drive. We were hiking together yet alone again, each one of us deep in our own thoughts. Shortcake was submerged dangerously low. So low that she strolled right passed a large rattlesnake just inches from the trail.

When I noticed the creature curled up bathing in the sun next to the open path, I let out a holler to Shortcake. I truly feared for her lack of awareness. It startled her also to realize what she had just done. She came back to peek at what she had missed, in hopes of being able to recognize it in the future.

With hearts pounding and our fight or flight awareness on high, we breezed the half mile to our destination. Grabbing one of the open tent sites close to the trail, we set about doing our day's-end chores. Shortcake took advantage of the coin-op laundry and shower. I skipped it. I didn't want to walk or spend the money on something that wouldn't last. A bird bath and clothes rinsing in the bathroom sink were good enough for me.

That night we were lulled to sleep by those clustering clouds partying. One terrifying crack of thunder had me wondering if this would be the storm that would end our hike, but the thought didn't last long, and I was back to sleep as a light show lit up my tent in random shadows and rumbles played a symphony of percussion.

The next day started out great. For once, we had dry clothes. Well, mine were almost dry. I used the hand dryer in the ladies' room to get most of the moisture out of my shirt. Shortcake was dry and clean. That feeling lasted about thirty minutes into the hike. That's about when the morning's incline heated us up to full-on drippy sweat. And that's why I didn't spend the extra effort and funds for laundry or bathing.

In the first hour, we had lots to photograph. Not too far from our campsite, a tree turned into toothpicks by the night's storm lay in splinters across the trail.

It had me reconsidering my unsafe comfort with thunderstorms. Next, we saw a cute bunny. What is it about these sweet creatures? You can't help but smile when one crosses your path. To end the first hour, we had a beautiful view.

By 1:00pm, our sweat-drenched clothing was rinsed clean by a rain shower.

It poured for over an hour. Just as we began to dry, the heavens opened up again, making the first soaking seem like the desert. I have never been outside in such a torrential downpour, with thunder thrown in just to make things interesting.

For the two-hour rinse cycle, I repeated *Hail Mary*s and *Thank you, Jesus, for keeping us safe*! It was hair-raising.

We arrived at the Hightop Hut, our destination for the day, only to find it full. How surprising. Did we actually think there'd be room for us? Batman was going to park at the road two miles ahead and hike in, but he wouldn't arrive until late. I sent him a message to sleep in the car. One wet hiker in my tent was enough, and we'd see Batman in the morning.

But once the rain lightened up, Shortcake and I decided to hike the two miles and stealth camp. Stealth camping is allowed as long as you are hidden. Once we arrived at the road, I walked on to find a suitable spot close to the parking area for our tents. None were found. I suggested we set up on the grass next to the parking lot. We weren't even close to being hidden.

We managed to erect our tents in between raindrops and stashed our wet gear under our vestibules. We peeled off our wet clothing and put on our dry ones. Just as the sun began to vanish, lights pulled in and we heard a friendly hello. I knew it was the park ranger. Shucks! We'd been discovered.

I explained our situation that our ride was late and we were trying to keep dry. He said no problem as long as we didn't stay there all night. Which meant when Batman finally did show up, we needed to pack up and disappear somewhere.

Batman showed up close to midnight. We had one choice, and that was to seek shelter at a hotel. We repacked all our gear, then he whisked us away. The little motels in the rural area were closed tight with no late-hour service, and we had to drive to the larger city of Harrisonburg, Virginia, home of James Madison University.

It was 2:30am by the time my head hit the pillow. We didn't care. We were away from the storms, we were dry, and it was the end to another day on the Appalachian Trail.

BLACK BEAR TIP

Take the side trails. It may slow you down,
but the rewards will outweigh the delay.

Day 86 Saturday June 17
Time: 3:30pm – 8:00pm
Mile: 906.1 – 915.7
Miles hiked: 9.6
Harrisonburg Courtyard Hotel
Weather: Cloudy & hot

Day 87 Sunday June 18
Time: 10:35am – 4:00pm
Mile: 915.7 – 925.0
Miles hiked: 9.3
Tented at Big Meadows Campground
Weather: Cloudy & hot

Day 88 Monday June 19
Time: 6:53am – 6:00pm
Mile: 925.0 – 938.8
Miles hiked: 13.8
Tented at Byrds Nest #3 Hut
Weather: Cloudy, T-storms, & rain

Day 89 Tuesday June 20
Time: 6:42am – 5:45pm
Mile: 938.8 – 956.3
Miles hiked: 17.5
Tented at Gravel Springs Hut
Weather: Sunny, warm, & breezy

* Day 90 Wednesday June 21 *
Time: 7:13am – 6:45pm
Mile: 956.3 – 974.9
Miles hiked: 18.6
Tented at Jim and Molly Shelter
Weather: Sunny & hot

Day 91 Thursday June 22
Time: 7:04am – 6:45pm
Mile: 974.9 – 993.3
Miles hiked: 18.4
Tented at Rod Hollow Shelter
Weather: Cloudy, hot, & humid

Day 92 Friday June 23
Time: 6:58am – 2:30pm
Mile: 993.3 – 1003.2
Miles Hiked: 9.9
Sheraton Hotel
Weather: Miserably hot, cloudy,
& humid

16

Naked Hiking and The Crazies

*W*e slept in, but when you go to bed after 2:00am, is crawling out of the sack a few minutes before 9:00am really considered sleeping in? The hands on the clock ticked away as we used our time wisely, completing the normal hiker chores such as laundry, drying wet gear, resupplying, and a trip to the clinic to get checked out.

Oh yeah, can't forget a visit to Krispy Kreme donut shop. Batman and Shortcake loved that. I can't eat that stuff. My treat was lunch at Chili's. No menu needed for this girl. Fajitas are a no-brainer for me when I visit that eatery. And their chips and salsa with fresh guacamole are always a plus.

Did you notice in two paragraphs up I added a trip to the clinic, or did that fact slip by you? Yes, one of us had to go to the clinic. It wasn't me. Unfortunately, Shortcake noticed a bite on her leg. When she showed us, my heart sank. I tried not to let my face show how worried I was, but I never have been good at lying. The classic red bullseye tattooed her skin so perfectly it looked drawn by an artist.

Shortcake, the ever-so-calm personality of our hiking duo, refused the initial offer to be driven to a clinic. But after further debating with myself and Batman, she caved. Batman to the rescue. I stayed back and did chores, and that's when the two of them indulged in the sticky, glazed pastries of Krispy Kreme.

"Positive for Lyme disease" was the diagnosis. Thankfully, she had decided to have that bite checked out. Lyme is nothing to fool around with, and having it out on the trail, far from health care, is dangerous. Armed with her prescription, she never missed a white blaze.

Even though our plans to stay close to the trail the night before had not happened, it was for the best. We had things we didn't realize needed to be done—and they wouldn't have gotten done if we had not been kicked out.

Since our day started significantly later than planned, we decided a short nine-mile hike would be perfect, ending at a campground. When we started this hike over 900 miles before, a 9-mile day was a struggle. Now, when planning our weekly distance, a 9-mile daily goal rolled off our tongues as easily as we could erect our tents.

Growth. It's a wonderful thing. When tackling any major adventure—whether it is hiking a long trail, starting a new job or position, beginning new relationships, having a family, or going through an illness—struggles arise. We do what we need to do to successfully traverse the challenges of life. It's those struggles that make us smarter and stronger and nurture growth in whatever it is we are doing. What started out as difficult becomes routine and easy. We grow. Our new norm is at a higher level than when we began. We aren't aware of these changes on a daily basis, but at some point, we realize what used to be hard is now a piece of cake. In our case, we could hike 9 miles starting late in the afternoon, and it was no big deal.

Nature dazzled us in those 9 miles. First, a baby fawn dashed through the woods and across the trail, almost running us over, then disappeared on the other side of the trail. It made me think back when I was a kid and Mom would ring the bell signaling it was time to come in. My brother and I developed acute hearing. The better our auditory senses, the farther we could roam from our yard. But that also meant the faster we had to run. We dashed across the neighbor's yard, across the road, or up a trail by our house, just like that baby deer. I pictured the fawn being beckoned by its mother to come home.

We saw a ring-necked snake, a tiny salamander, and two other deer who couldn't have cared less that we were there. It was a doe and a young buck whose new antlers were fuzzy with velvet.

We arrived at the campground close to sunset. To our disappointment, not one campsite was available. Clouds draped the sky in early darkness, making it risky for us to hike on and stealth. Our strong bodies propelled us along the trail as planned, but our minds still needed an increase in fortitude. If we had to go to a Plan B, night hiking to find a place to camp was not our first choice. Since it was the weekend and Batman was with us, there was a Plan B. Back to Harrisonburg we went.

I don't like being so far from the trail unless I get to take a zero day. It's way too much driving and checking in and out. But at least it's dry and warm. And when it was dark, we could flip a switch for light to do our evening chores.

I also don't like it when my plans don't come to fruition. It's very frustrating. One lesson the Appalachian Trail taught me was that when plans fail, do not get upset. What would losing my cool accomplish anyway? Nothing, and it would probably only make the situation worse. Plans fail all the time; that's life. I have learned to chill out and not sweat the small stuff. So the drive from and to the trail was longer than I preferred. Big deal! I could have had to set up my tent in the rain instead. I am still learning that most of the time when there is a change in agenda on trail or in my synthetic world, the alternate plan usually works out way better than I could ever have imagined.

Happy Father's Day! Poor Batman had to spend it without our kids—who were young adults—and help Shortcake and me. At least we took him to Cracker Barrel for breakfast, even though he drove. The next best thing to spending his day with our awesome boys, though, was being able to spend it in the woods, hiking with me.

Before he could do that, he had to secure a tent site. After the last two nights of leaving things to chance and our planning gone wrong, we decided to be more prepared. After Batman dropped us off at the trailhead so we could continue north, he drove to Big Meadows

Campground to reserve a tent site before they filled up. Then he hiked south to meet us.

Our late start determined fewer miles hiked for the day. After Batman did our chores, he had limited time for boots on the trail. But it was just the right amount of time needed to see the best sighting so far on this journey.

The three of us hiked together. The clouds kept the sun away, but the day was still hot. Shortcake was in the lead. Suddenly she stopped. She was so excited. Her quietness ceased, and her emotions were obvious. I saw it too! Not one, but two bear cubs and their mom about twenty yards ahead just off the trail.

Woo-hoo! All three of us were excited. Mama Bear gave a grunt, and the two little ones scrambled up the tree like toddlers being scolded and running to their room to avoid a spanking. Then a third rascal cub ran into view from our left, climbed the tree, and joined his siblings.

Mama Bear kept watch from the ground at the base of the tree. We couldn't pass—they were less than ten yards from the trail. We watched them and she watched us with even more intensity. I tried bushwhacking a wide berth off the trail to the right. But as I proceeded to go forward, Mama Bear took two leaps up the tree, let out two ferocious roars I could feel in my chest, dropped from the tree, and bluff-charged me.

We backpedaled to safety, then backtracked a quarter mile, where we hung out and had a snack. After our unplanned rest, we continued. The cubs were still in the tree, but the mama was nowhere to be seen. I did not even stop the second time for a picture. The first encounter reminded us you don't mess around with Mama Bear. And since we did not see her but still saw the cubs, we knew she couldn't be far away.

The wind blew ferociously as we slept in our tents at the campground. It was hard to sleep. I thought I was going to end up somewhere in Kansas. When morning came, I packed up what I could while still inside my tent. When I was ready to emerge, I unzipped the screen, and I was a little confused. My water bottle was missing and so were my poles.

Every night I placed my hiking sticks parallel with the tent on the ground and placed my water bottle on top of them, so it would not roll away. I found it hard to believe an animal or a person could have taken them without me hearing. But I assumed that's what had happened. I then reached farther out to unzip my vestibule. I flipped the nylon fly back and was completely confused by what I saw.

It wasn't the same view I had seen when I went to bed. My brain put two and two together—missing poles, missing bottle, strange view. *I must still be sleeping.* I shook my head to wake up.

Nope. I was awake. I looked back outside, and this time paranoia set in. I had no idea where I was! All I knew was that it wasn't the same place where I had gone to bed. Maybe I had been blown to Kansas with Dorothy instead of Shortcake.

It seemed like eternity as I sat there frozen, staring at the unfamiliar view outside my tent. I was afraid. I didn't know where I was, and I had confirmed I indeed was awake. Then my smart brain kicked in and reminded the panicky brain that she had two openings on her tent, a left side and a right side.

I had gotten turned around in the tent without realizing it. I swear, some days I should be on medication. A brain should be used for good things, not paranoia. It's amazing how our thinking can lead us astray. It happens so often to me. Usually, it isn't as bad as that morning. Usually it's jumping to conclusions or thinking the worst. It's a character flaw I am always working on. My kids say I need more work.

After my episode from the Twilight Zone, the rest of the day went well—for a while. We were having a great hike, then we heard the thunder and saw the rain coming across the valley toward us on the ridge. I suggested we set up our tents at the next possible spot. That was a pipe dream. There hadn't been too many random tenting spots in the Shenandoahs.

But twenty paces after I suggested we take cover, we crested a plateau, and there were two beautiful sites. We threw up our castles just as the rain began. It was only 1:30pm. We were dry and happily settled in to wait out the rain. The storm grew more intense as it closed in on our plateau. I was hoping to capture an afternoon nap, but with the ruckus of booms and clashing overhead, that wasn't going to happen. Instead, I assumed the safety pose, crouching down while balancing on the balls of my feet and making myself as small as possible. When I tired of that position, I sat on my boots with the rubber soles down, making sure my butt did not touch the ground. I hugged my knees. My feet were in front of me, shoved into my Crocs. I hoped the layer of rubber under my bottom and around my feet would serve as protection. I didn't know if either of these positions made any sense, but I figured it was much safer than full-body contact with a possible electrified earth.

The rain had stopped. I checked the weather forecast, and rain was anticipated for a few more hours. I asked Shortcake if she wanted to call it a day and just get up early and hike extra miles the next day. I think the words *get up early* scared her, and she voted to pack up and hike on.

That's what we did, and twenty yards later, the heavens opened for round two. So much for staying dry.

I didn't sleep well. Thus, awakened even earlier than normal, I packed up quickly and headed out. I rarely left without Shortcake. Since my clothes were still wet and the air was cold, I too was cold. Hiking was the only way to warm up. I went slowly, and she caught up to me quickly. Hiking warmed me up and my clothes almost dried in the morning breeze, but it wasn't long before they were saturated with sweat.

The trail was very busy, but not with people. Hikers are just some of the traffic on the trail. There were several piles of different kinds of scat. There were also snakes, butterflies, insects, and deer, as well as several different kinds of animal tracks in the soft mud.

At one point after Shortcake regained the front position, a southbound hiker informed me a deer was following me. I turned around and there she was, acting like she was part of our trail family. I didn't even know the animal was there.

June 21 was our ninetieth day on trail and Naked Hiking Day. I bet you were wondering when I would make the connection to the chapter title. Yes, naked hiking is a thing, and it happens on the summer solstice. One must be totally nuts to participate in this ritual.

In an article written by Mary Beth "Mouse" Skylis for *Backpacker Magazine* dated June 23, 2021, Mary states what one should consider before participating in this ritual. Possible sunburn, bug bites, abrasions, and embarrassment are just a few negatives of baring it all on the trail. Then there are the legal ramifications if one is caught in their birthday suit. The type of fine given depends on if the land is privately owned or regulated by the state or federal government. Despite the risks, every year crazy or brave hikers free themselves of their attire to experience nature close up and personal.

In 2015, I purposely took a zero day on the summer solstice. I did not trust myself. I was out there, doing something wild and crazy and wanted to test all my abilities, but I am a rule follower and was afraid to step out of my comfort zone and try something new. Besides, how could I go naked, write about it in my blog, and then have to answer to the teachers and parents as well as my church family who all were following along on my journey? So I played it safe and stayed in a hotel with Batman.

In 2017, I was hiking with Shortcake. She is very modest, more so than me. Weeks prior, when discussing this activity with other hikers, Shortcake strongly expressed her choice of *not* participating in Naked Hiking Day. So when that day came around, I didn't think it would even be an option.

I couldn't have been more wrong. Good friends keep you out of trouble. But when certain things are too tempting, they will dive right in with you. When we woke up that morning, we packed up as usual and Shortcake said to me, "You know what today is?"

I had forgotten and was so glad she reminded me. Because while I think one must be nuts and crazy to hike naked, I didn't want to skip it this time around.

Guess what? Yup! Black Bear went bare! We hiked out after a few of the men had left. Good thing. After a mile or so, we came to a beautiful overlook. I said to Shortcake, "Okay, here goes." I stripped down to nothing but my boots, socks, and kneepads.

Monkey see, monkey do. Shortcake soon ate her words and joined in the fun. She wasn't quite as committed. She could only manage to let the girls out. I must admit it felt so good! I stood on the cliff and gave a big hoot as the breeze caressed my skin and Shortcake snapped a few tasteful pictures. Then I did the same for her.

We threw on our packs and headed out. I strategically placed my bandanas to hide the downtown district and the moon shot as well as the girls. But after a few hundred yards, the girls were liberated. We had intended to go only a few yards, just enough to say we had participated in Naked Hiking Day. But we soon realized naked felt really good. Oh, no! What had we unleashed?

We changed our "few yards" to "hiking until the first person saw us." We weren't done having fun yet. So we kept going in the buff.

When a couple of young dudes in their mid-20s approached from southbound, we saw them before they saw us. We started laughing so hard we could barely walk.

The first guy politely tried to keep his eyes down. But the smile on his face showed he had great peripheral vision. The second hiker didn't hide the fact he was looking and said "Oh, Naked Hiking Day!" Shortcake and I stumbled our way passed them. For a moment, I thought I was going to fall into them. Good thing I didn't, because they probably wouldn't have known where to grab—or maybe they would have known.

We continued in the nude for almost two hours. Honestly, I didn't want to get dressed, but we did. We decided to spare humanity from any more indecency. We'd had our fun.

Less than two miles after we put our clothes back on, we met a park ranger hiking south. She had a grumpy look on her face. We didn't think she would have appreciated our carefree exhibition. Timing is everything.

There was no happy medium. We were either drowning in rain and thunderstorms or drowning in our own sweat. The past week had been miserably hot (one of the reasons hiking naked felt so good). I always thought I could handle the heat better than the cold. I discovered I can't do either one.

Same with the bears. First, we saw no wildlife, then we saw an abundance of it. After being roared at and bluff-charged by Mama

Bear several days before, I didn't care if I ever saw another bear in the wild. But we had three different sightings on June 22. One bear ran through a field and climbed a tree. The third one ran through the shelter area just before bedtime. That made falling asleep hard to do. Thankfully, in each of these sightings the creature ignored us and hurried away as fast as it could.

I lost my cool on that day—not just physically due to the heat, but mentally, also due to the heat. As we climbed the inclines, the humidity had us gasping for air and sweat stung our eyes. Branches and brambles brushed and scraped our sticky, sweat-covered skin as the trail narrowed.

Then hiking behind Shortcake had me feeling closed in even more. It took every fiber of my being to keep from screaming. I just needed to get out of the woods. But that wasn't going to happen for over 20 miles.

We came to a trail junction at a state park boundary in the middle of nowhere. There was even a seat to relax on. A clearing about the size of a small foyer opened up. I could breathe. We sat on the bench and consumed calories and drank water. As we did, a honeybee kept buzzing me like Maverick of *Top Gun* buzzing the tower. It would not go away.

I lost it!

I roared as loud as I could at the bee. The mama bear we'd seen the other day would have been frightened. Shortcake's eyes met mine briefly as she froze, not knowing what was going to happen next. Then we both blurted out laughing. It was a great release.

That told me I needed to get off the trail for a day or two. It's one thing to chat with birds and squirrels throughout the day. It's a whole different diagnosis when you go diabolical on a honeybee.

We cranked out 18.4 miles, arriving at Rod Hollow Shelter just in time to snag the last two tent pads, eat, and go to bed. While we were doing so, we were thrilled to reconnect with B.B. King, the young gal we had met earlier. She was a tough nut, fun, and easygoing like us, just much, *much* younger.

That's another great thing about thru-hiking. The trail breaks down barriers between classes, races, religions, genders, and whatever group you can think of. It also closes generational gaps. The trail does not discriminate, and neither do most hikers. All that stuff is irrelevant in the real world of the Appalachian Trail.

Just when we thought it couldn't get any more humid, the weather app said it was 73 degrees, but it felt like 83 degrees. They didn't ask me what it felt like. Who decides that anyway—someone sitting in an air-conditioned dark room hammering out algorithms on a keyboard? They'd be more accurate if they stuck their head out the window or hiked a mountain in that so-called 73-degree weather.

To this Mainer who loves to escape our cold winters, 83 degrees sounds nice. But that day, I think they were wrong. Beads of sweat rolled down my forehead, down my nose, dripping constantly. My eyes stung from salt. We could not drink enough water to satisfy our thirst.

Luckily, signs of heat exhaustion never appeared for either one of us. We were just miserably uncomfortable as we labored our way to complete our second 18-plus-mile day in a row, also crossing the 1,000-mile mark.

As if the humidity didn't make the day difficult enough, we entered a section of the trail that proudly boasted being called the roller coaster. The guidebook says it's a section with sharp ascents and descents compressed together over 14 miles. We were only doing about nine miles of it.

The sign and the guidebook made the roller coaster sound scarier and hairier than it was. It would have been fun on a more favorable day, but as we melted with every step, the carnival ride broke us. Nine miles of the coaster after nine miles of "regular" hiking was enough on that *mild* 73-degree day.

———

Looking back through my notes and photos, most of my pictures show us smiling and having a great time. Those moments captured in time are proof that even when it's bad, it can be fun. But even I struggled to stay positive on the trail. I did manage to snap one selfie that isolated the agony and stress of hiking in grueling temperatures and long miles.

We prevailed through a week of the crazies—crazy bears, crazy naked hikers, a crazy momentary diabolic possession, crazy weather, and crazy trail. Rest was our reward. We were going to take the next two days off in a hotel, Batman-style.

BLACK BEAR TIP

Don't be afraid of challenges and obstacles.
They may produce the crazies, but they will definitely
initiate growth, build confidence, and spark wisdom.

Day 93 Saturday June 24
Zero

Day 94 Sunday June 25
Zero

Day 95 Monday June 26
Time: 7:14am – 5pm
Mile: 1003.2 – 1017.4
Miles hiked: 14.2
Aloft Hotel in Winchester, VA
Weather: Perfectly sunny & breezy

Day 96 Tuesday June 27
Time: 8:11am – 7:05pm
Mile: 1017.4 – 1030.0
Miles hiked: 12.6
Tented at Ed Garvey Shelter
Weather: Beautiful, sunny & breezy

Day 97 Wednesday June 28
Time: 7:50am – 4:15pm
Mile: 1030.0 – 1043.1
Miles hiked: 13.1
Tented at Dahlgren Campground
Weather: Perfect bluebird sky

Day 98 Thursday June 29
Time: 6:45am – 3:30pm
Mile: 1043.1 - 1057.9
Miles hiked: 14.8
Tented at Dahlgren Campground
Weather: Sunny & hot

Day 99 Friday June 30
Time: 6:52am – 4:05pm
Mile: 1057.9 – 1072.9
Miles hiked: 15
Tented at Caledonia State Park
Weather: Partly cloudy, extremely hot

Day 100 Saturday July 1
Time: 6:30pm – 12:15pm
Mile: 1072.9 – 1082.9
Miles hiked: 10
Tented at Caledonia State Park
Weather: Cloudy, hot, & humid

Day 101 Sunday July 2
Time: 7:02am – 12:45pm
Mile: 1082.9 – 1094.9
Miles hiked: 12.0
Tented at Caledonia State Park
Weather: Hot & sunny

Day 102 Monday July 3
Time: 6:52am – 3:15pm
Mile: 1094.9 – 1110.8
Miles hiked: 15.9
Tented at Caledonia State Park
Weather: Hot & sunny

17

Thru-Hiking or Glamping?

What a wonderful day. We slept in until 8:00am. I headed right down to do laundry. Zero days were always full of chores. I know I sound like a broken record, but that's what it was. On town days, we were busy doing everything we needed to do so we could get back out into the *misery*. If, and only if, there was time, we got to rest. That's why we loved double zero days.

Shortcake was also up and joined me. Then we woke Batman so we could head down to breakfast. We filled our tummies with fluffy eggs, greasy sausage, crusty potatoes, oatmeal, and fruits. Yummy.

Then Batman shuttled us to Walmart for resupply. It was crazy busy. I thought Saturday shopping at home in Bangor, Maine, was hectic. I now have a new perspective of "busy" and it ain't pretty. The woods may have lacked in luxury and finer things, but it was peaceful and void of drama—most of the time and when I wasn't cursing a honeybee.

Back at the room, we began the opening, sorting, and packing of our food for the next few days. That always takes time. After we completed our chores, Shortcake chilled in the lounge and I treated myself to an in-room self-pedicure and a soak in the tub complete with bubbles and soothing essential oils. I felt human again.

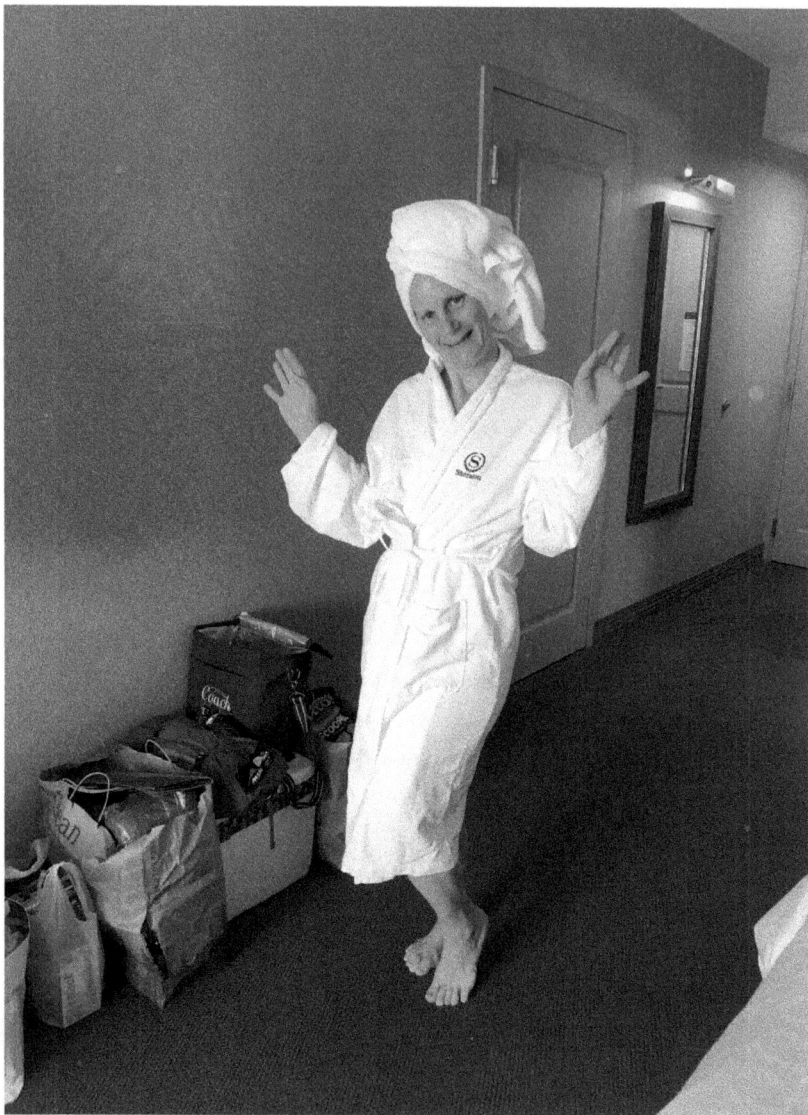

I don't know what Batman did. He probably recovered from being our butler.

With bodies and minds refreshed, we headed to the club lounge for appetizers—or in hiker terms, first supper. Second supper took place at Chili's restaurant.

I never tired of that place. My go-to meal was chicken fajitas, but I switched it up that night. I had their ribs. They were incredible, fall-off-the-bone, finger-lickin' good. I enjoyed them until later, when I realized they come from baby cows. For a few hours I became a vegetarian. Then I got hungry again.

The best part of the meal included meeting up with Wye Knot, one of my hiking buddies, and his girlfriend, Lori. He and I hiked together a significant amount in 2015. Out of the hundreds of hikers I met that year, only a handful stand out. He is one of them.

There's nothing like being a thru-hiker, cranking out the miles week after week, then escaping the trail for two days of no hiking. Our focus was sleeping in and eating. My "sleeping in" would be considered early for most people though. We were up by 8:00 or 8:30am each of our double zero days.

We blue-ribboned the calorie intake also. We had a full breakfast buffet both days. Well, I did. Shortcake skipped it. Chili's still occupied her system, and she wanted room for our next meal since we had lunch plans with friends. I could always eat. My name wasn't Black Bear for nothin'. And the good thing was, I could eat whatever I wanted, and it still wasn't enough. I've said it so many times: long-distance hiking is a great weight-loss program. If you don't believe me, check out my pre-hike photos and compare them to my naked hiking day pics. Or don't.

Our lunch date brought the gang together. Maps, Moxie, and Wye Knot drove over to meet us. Maps and Moxie were a dynamic duo I hiked with in 2015 from the White Mountains in New Hampshire all the way through Maine. It was a blast to hike with them.

They were an answer to my prayers on that hike. Before we met up at Mizpah Hut, I had been hiking mostly alone, especially after leaving GQ and Walking Man. Wye Knot and Kilroy filled a void, but Maps and Moxie were girls my age and we just rocked the trail. It was so much fun having lunch and retelling stories to Shortcake. We all were quite animated.

We still can't believe how much a part of our lives our Appalachian Trail thru-hike is. It's not just something we did and then it was done. The friends we have made will last a lifetime because we all share an accomplishment that relatively few have done. It's a bond that can never be broken.

What a difference a little R&R can make. We hit the trail running the day after our double zero. Okay, not quite running, but we did have a much quicker pace than Friday. We were rested, fed, and ready to take on the day. It's not about the miles but rather the smiles, and the smiles couldn't get any bigger than the ones on our faces that day.

The sun shined brightly, keeping the humidity at bay. I barely broke a sweat, and that's saying something for this menopausal gal who has her own tropical storms every hour it seems. A slight breeze that kept the annoying bugs away added to the day's enjoyment. And to top it all off, Batman joined us on a Monday, whisking us away to a hotel again. We had lots to be happy about and enjoyed every minute of the fabulous weather and amenities while they lasted.

Our night under a roof was just that. No thrills or extras. Our double zero was enough for a while, but it sure was nice to take another shower and not have to set up our tents. The next day we only hiked 12.6 miles.

Harpers Ferry, West Virginia, the unofficial halfway mark and home to the Appalachian Trail Conservancy Headquarters, provided the day's highlights. Here we had our photo taken and received our numbers. When we registered at Springer Mountain, we were hikers number 1065 and 1066. Signing in at Harpers Ferry, we were hikers

1173 and 1174, meaning that over 100 hikers who registered after we did at the beginning were now ahead of us.

But that was okay; hiking the A.T. is not a race. Everyone who even attempts such adventurous journeys is a winner in my book.

We had another hiker reunion. I reconnected with James Sisu, a ridge runner I met on my first day on the trail in 2015. We met again later that year when I arrived at the A.T. Conservancy in Harpers Ferry and James was working behind the desk.

In 2017 on Day 97, June 28, I gave a shout-out on my blog to all the trail maintainers, ridge runners, and rangers. It's a thankless job, but without them we would have no trails to hike. At lunch in Harpers Ferry in 2017, James explained all the duties of ridge runners. They don't just walk up and down the trail, teaching us about best practices. One of their jobs is to knock down the poop cones in the privies and fish out anything that doesn't belong. I bet they don't tell you that in the recruiting flyer. They wouldn't have to do such a disgusting job if hikers weren't lazy. Please think about that next time you use a privy while out in the backcountry. If you pack it in, pack it out. Wow, hats off to the privy fishers!

When I first met James at Springer Mountain Shelter in 2015, he was full of great and useful advice. A lot of people have free tips and tricks to share and most of it isn't worth the breath used to tell it. (But not my Black Bear Tips; those are valuable too.)

What James had to share was also worth paying attention to. He advised when choosing gear for a thru-hike, ask yourself if you are out there to make it to Katahdin or out there to camp. Then choose the gear that will help you the most in reaching your goal. I used his advice then and am still using it today, as well as sharing it with others. I've also carried his advice over into life off trail.

In other words, it was advice on being a minimalist. We can get so bogged down with stuff we think we need, when in reality it is just stuff we want. There is a difference between wants and needs. God gives us what we need, but we usually pray for what we want. Big difference.

Sure, it's comforting to have a beautiful home filled with all the fine touches or a vehicle with all the bells and whistles. Who doesn't love a closet packed with items for each season in all your favorite fabrics? What about your favorite collectibles? We all have those things we love to own. I am no different. But after hike number one, I discovered that having too much stuff gets in the way of what I really want to accomplish. Too much stuff was time consuming and added way too much clutter to my already cluttered brain. Less was actually more.

Decluttering my home from needless items freed up space. And not just physical space, but mental space as well. It also freed up time. No longer did I spend hours cleaning and organizing stuff I thought I *might* use one day. Now I don't have to deal with the useless items since they are no longer in the way of what I might be looking for in a closet.

Becoming a minimalist is like peeling an onion—one layer at a time, or in my case, one yard sale at time. After each decluttering, I would say "There, that's it!" but after living in the *new* clean for a few months, I would find more stuff I could do without, and I would have another yard sale. That cycle continued for several years, but I think it's safe to say I have had my last yard sale. Now I keep a bag in the closet and add unused things to it as I find them. When it fills, I donate it to a thrift store. Batman and I are light-years away from being hardcore minimalists, but we have much less clutter, and it's freeing in so many ways.

—

On the walk into the historic town, we had found wild raspberries growing abundantly. I filled my little snack cup and carried the berries for over a mile. After lunch and the traditional photo shoot at the Conservancy, we headed to the outfitter for repair tape to fix my tent. It had acquired its first hole. Then, with raspberries in hand, we headed to the ice cream shop. I ordered a huge vanilla ice cream and mixed in my berries. The trail provides.

We sauntered out of town with full tummies once again, and pride filled our hearts, knowing that we had made it to the unofficial halfway mark. The odds that had been stacked against us at Amicalola were now reversed. Hikers who make it to Harpers Ferry tend to make it to Katahdin, barring any injury or running out of funds. That is a huge generalization, and many factors still are at play. But just having that knowledge lightened our mental load, at least for the night.

The 6x miles out of town brought us to the Ed Garvey Shelter, where we pitched our tents for the first time in a few days. It was just like riding a bike, though. A long-distance backpacker never forgets how to set up their home away from home.

Nine minutes after leaving the Ed Garvey Shelter, we saw a bear. That's always one of those things you want to see—but not really. It was just one of the thrills of the day. The cloudless bluebird sky made for an enjoyable 13 miles of hiking packed with lessons in history at Gathland State Park. Batman was still around, so he whisked us away again at the end of the day. Not to a plush hotel; rather, to Dahlgren Backpacker Campground.

It wasn't a hotel, but the campground had level tenting areas, bathrooms, showers, potable water, and picnic tables. If you ask any thru-hiker, they will tell you that those amenities are luxurious.

We played it smart the next day by strategically mapping out our miles to end at another road, and then we returned to Dahlgren Campground for a second night. We even left our tents set up, so we'd have one less thing to do after our day's hike.

When you live with very little, you learn to be creative and thrifty, a skill I find to be quite fun at times. In hiking the Appalachian Trail,

I have learned that more isn't always better. In fact, it can be the opposite. The more we have, the more work and responsibilities go along with what we have.

———

In the last few days, we had crossed two state lines and the next day we would cross another. We went from Virginia to West Virginia and West Virginia to Maryland. In 6.5 miles, we entered Pennsylvania. Our slow start in Georgia had progressed to flying. Once we reached the official halfway mark, Shortcake and I really cruised. We'd be home before we knew it.

Before that, though, we enjoyed more sights. And Maryland with its few miles and rich history had plenty to show us. We saw Gathland, a historic state park. Then we saw the original Washington Monument. I love history, and it's so much more interesting when you can see it rather than just read about it.

Woo-hoo! This Yankee made it back home. Well, at least she made it north of the Mason-Dixon Line.

I was torn, though. I was born on a military base in Georgia. I love the southern weather, the people are friendly, and the BBQ is the best, hands down, but my heart belongs in the north. There is nothing like the deep woods, crystal clear lakes, mountaintop views, and coastal cliffs of Maine. With each day—not counting our zeroes—Shortcake and I were closer to those vistas in my back yard.

It was extremely hot and humid the day we left the South, a little reminder of why we endure our long cold winters up north. It wasn't quite as bad as the day we hiked the Roller Coaster—but it was close. We tried to beat the heat by getting up early. We were not successful. We did outrun the afternoon rainstorm. We pitched our tents and cooked dinner just as the first dribbles fell from the sky. Luckily, we were glamping and retreated to the car while the rain passed.

Batman had secured reservations at Caledonia State Park for several consecutive nights. He would shuttle us to and from the trail, and the campground would serve as base camp. We never passed up an opportunity to slackpack and to have running water easily available. And we didn't have to set up tents after a long day of hiking or take them down after the midnight rains. Life was good on the trail.

Shortcake and I had nothing to prove to anyone. With over 1,000 backpacking miles under our feet, we knew what we were doing and could fend for ourselves We were far from experts, but our confidence grew as we hiked the miles.

As much as we were becoming trail wise and adapting to situations, we had a long way to go to match the evolutionary results of nature. We watched a black snake—who is normally very timid and non-aggressive—show a trait it must have learned from its cousin, the rattlesnake.

Shortcake and I loved these snakes. They are so sleek and cool to watch as they slither their way peacefully along the ground and up trees. We pulled out our cameras to snap the perfect photo. As we approached the usually docile serpent, he uncharacteristically coiled up to strike as he vibrated his tail wildly in the leaf litter. Both of us stopped our photo shoot and backed up, thinking we had mistaken the identity of the snake. Once we were sure of its species, we were awed by what we had just witnessed.

Just like the black snake imitating the rattler, in life we too must learn how to evolve if we want to survive. Sometimes it might be in how to get along with others or how to start a new career or any of the other challenges life throws at us. Shortcake and I were adapting to trail life. We knew when we had to push, and we knew when we could take it easy. A few days using a campground as base camp, complete with a swimming pool and bathhouses, was just what we needed.

Hiking the Appalachian Trail is one big party. Not necessarily a binge drinking, substance-abusing shindig (for some it is), but rather, a time to enjoy the little things and celebrate them. Milestones are a huge part of what keeps long-distance thru-hikers going. We rejoiced in getting to camp before dark. We were proud when we beat our personal best-mileage day. We gained confidence when we slept alone the first time and not near a shelter. We did the happy dance each time we completed a hundred miles.

It is this learning to enjoy the little things that I have carried over from the trail to my synthetic world. It helps me to keep things in perspective. Life has very few large and grandiose treasures. But it is full of small, everyday happenings that can be savored but are easily overlooked.

After my first thru-hike when I finally admitted I was suffering from depression, I sought help from my priest and a counselor. Both helped me immensely. But it was the analogy my priest used that opened my eyes to see the gravity of my situation.

I was explaining to him that I didn't understand why I was feeling so bad. I had a great life, a great husband, and great kids. My health was awesome. I had support where I needed it. We were financially stable. I had no reason to be upset. I then went on to explain how I had all these little unrelated issues that troubled me, a bunch of negative things that had taken place over time.

He explained how each item by itself was small, but if you took each one and stacked it on top of the previous one, the negativity mounds up. A light bulb lit up in my dark brain, and I kid you not, I said, "Oh, it's like when my dog goes shit on the lawn, one pile is not bad. But if I take all that shit from a year of shitting and put it into one pile, then that's a lot of shit."

Excited about the revelation, I felt relief rushing over me, but it was quickly replaced with embarrassment as I realized the language I had just used with my priest. It was another indication of how depressed I had become. I normally do not use that kind of language in general conversation. I try not to have a potty mouth. Growing up with four brothers, I learned more than I should have, and sometimes habits are hard to break.

So now, take that analogy and reverse it. Instead of a pile of negative crap, let's have a mountain of small, wonderful things. Let's stop waiting for the big event to make us happy. Life can be so great if we focus on the right little things. They are all around us every day.

July 1 was one of those little things to celebrate. We reached our centennial. No, we were not 100 years old, even though after some days of hiking we felt like we were. We celebrated 100 days on the trail. Wow! It was hard to fathom that we had been out there that long. We decided to treat ourselves to a short 10-mile day and enjoy time at the campground.

Thank goodness we had planned a light day. Our neighbors the previous night didn't seem to care that others were next door. They obviously did not have a mom who taught them to be respectful in public. In turn, they were not teaching their children either. Midnight rolled around and they were still carrying on. Our alarms were set for 5:00am so we could rock out our 10 miles before the heat and afternoon thunderstorms rolled in. It may have been a low-mileage day, but it was still grueling.

Back at the campground, we waited for one of our trail friends to arrive. We had invited B.B. to camp with us. With her, we spent the afternoon relaxing, drying off after a thirty-minute thunderstorm drenching, and—best of all—an hour at the pool.

This is the way to hike the A.T.: hike, then get the heck out of the woods and go swimming in a place without snakes. After our dip in the pool, we were walking back to our campsite and Shortcake said how fresh and clean she felt. We all laughed because *fresh* and *clean* are not words to describe a public pool. In fact, they are more of an oxymoron. But out here on the trail, everything is relative.

There are many traditions and challenges on the trail. Some of the more common ones are a four-state challenge, a suitcase challenge, Naked Hiking Day, and my favorite, the half-gallon challenge. There may be others; these are the ones I am familiar with.

In the four-state challenge, hikers try to hike in four states in one day. They start at the Virginia-West Virginia border, pass through Virginia and Maryland, then cross into Pennsylvania. It amounts to 43 miles in 24 hours. I wouldn't even attempt that one. But our son Patch (trail name, "Cold Brew") completed this challenge when he thru-hiked in 2022.

I am not sure what idiot thought up the suitcase challenge. It must have been a bunch of fraternity brothers. To complete that task, a hiker must drink a suitcase of beer, one beer an hour for 24 hours, hiking 24 miles wearing a suit. I have a brain, so I didn't do that challenge either.

I did participate in Naked Hiking Day on the summer solstice. I stepped outside my comfort zone, donned only my birthday suit, boots, socks, and pack. It was so liberating. I would not have done so if I would have known I could have been jailed and listed on the federal sex offenders list. Really, what's this world coming to?

The best challenge of all, in my opinion, is the half-gallon challenge. I am surprised at the number of hikers who do not participate in this one. Hikers brag about how much food they can eat, and this challenge is a chance to prove it. Shortcake and I crushed it!

Just after the halfway point on the A.T., at Pine Grove Furnace, there is a store where hungry hikers can purchase a half gallon of ice cream. If you finish it, you receive a cheap wooden spoon stamped with the words *Member of the half gallon club* and you get to sign the log.

While reaching the halfway mark and indulging in a half-gallon of ice cream is something to celebrate, my true highlight of the day involved a chance meeting. The trail goes right by the country store, and when we arrived, we checked out the ice cream choices. It was too early in the day to stop. We didn't want to eat that much ice cream and then hike eight and a half more miles to our day's destination. So our plan for the day was to hike our miles and then Batman would bring us back to complete the ice cream challenge.

As we were getting ready to hike our last miles, a nice young man by the name of Colin approached me. He asked my name and said we had met last winter at L.L.Bean. I then recognized him as a customer who had been looking for gear. He had been planning a hike starting in June at Harpers Ferry and ending at Katahdin. What were the chances we would now be at the same spot on the same day at the same time? It was incredible. It was one of those little things to enjoy that the trail provides.

Batman collected us at the end of the day. We went back to Caledonia State Park for our last night at the fun establishment. It really is a must-see for anyone who likes to glamp. Glamping we did, thanks to Batman. Nine out of the last ten nights we had either stayed at a hotel or a campground, all with amenities we tend to take for granted. We were getting used to this and beginning to wonder if we were thru-hiking or glamping our way up the Appalachian Trail. I do think the latter is a great way to experience all the trail has to offer.

BLACK BEAR TIP

Work on minimalism, because less is more.

Day 103 Tuesday July 4
Time: 6:45am – 12:45pm
Mile: 1110.8 – 1121.6
Miles hiked: 10.8
Hotel in Harrisburg, PA
Weather: HOT

Day 104 Wednesday July 5
Time: 8:48am – 5:25pm
Mile: 1121.6 – 1138.1
Miles hiked: 16.5
Hotel: Holiday Inn Express
Weather: Hot & cloudy

Day 105 Thursday July 6
Time: 7:24am – 12:45pm
Mile: 1138.1 – 1149.0
Miles hiked: 10.9
Hotel: Holiday Inn Express
Weather: Cloudy & rainy

Day 106 Friday July 7
Time: 7:48am – 5:35pm
Mile: 1149.0 – 1164.9
Miles hiked: 15.9
Hotel: Holiday Inn Express
Weather: Drizzle, cloudy, rain

Day 107 Saturday July 8
Time: 8:03am – 4:18pm
Mile: 1164.9 – 1180.9
Miles hiked: 16.0
Hotel: Holiday Inn Express
Weather: Cloudy start, warm & sunny

Day 108 Sunday July 9
Time: 7:03am – 2:28pm
Mile: 1180.9 – 1193.7
Miles hiked: 12.8
Stayed at Wood Haven Girl Scout Camp
Weather: Sunny & comfy

Day 109 Monday July 10
Zero
Woods Haven Girl Scout Camp
Weather: Hot & sunny

18

More Glamping

I love mornings but I am in the minority. I still convinced my hiking gang—which now consisted of Shortcake, B.B., and myself—to hit the trail bright and early to beat the heat. We woke at 5:00am. The 30-minute drive from the campground to the trailhead had us hiking by 6:45am. By 7:30am, I was soaked in sweat. So much for beating the heat. At 8:45am, we took our first break, and Shortcake begged us not to let her start hiking in the mornings with her long-sleeved layer on. She runs much cooler than I do and always starts off with multiple layers. We were all happy that at least it wasn't raining.

We began our day early not just to beat the heat but also so we could participate in a July 4th celebration. Yes, we were glamping again, this time at a hotel along the river in Harrisburg, Pennsylvania. July 4th was on a Tuesday, and the Saturday before, I had started wearing my red, white, and blue attire. I am very patriotic—sometimes a little over the top. For three days I wore patriotic gaiters, matching bandannas on my poles, and a headband with star antennas. I was quite festive.

On the Fourth, Shortcake strung streamers to the back of her pack. The tails were a great reminder for me not to tailgate. I added music occasionally. We started the day singing "God Bless America" and the national anthem, then finished with iTunes music with Lee Greenwood's "God Bless The USA." Love that song. That track I played over several times. It always brings tears to my eyes.

We hiked a short 10.8 miles into Boiling Springs, Pennsylvania, where Batman whisked us away again. At our hotel in Harrisburg, we spared no time doing our chores, showering, and even managing to get a mini rest. Then we were off to check out the many food trucks the festival had to offer.

Lots of tourists like us were out for the festivities. The Riverwalk was nice; we enjoyed the stroll on level, firm ground. If only the food trucks had more to offer. There were many varieties, but for some reason, nothing appealed to any of us. For me, the portions being doled out were disproportional to the price. They would have barely sufficed as a snack for my hiker hunger. We waited for the restaurant.

The restaurant of choice has since slipped my memory, and its name didn't make it into my journal either. But I do remember it was yummy and met the tastes of all of us, especially Batman and Shortcake. They were quite happy with the brew selections. I had never before seen my dear friend imbibe so liberally. She was respectfully inebriated and a hoot to watch.

We walked back to the hotel, following the main street instead of the river. We wanted to check out the shops and anything else the strip had to offer. Decorated oversized ducks about the size of a child's carnival ride adorned the sidewalks. I am sure there must have been signs that requested no sitting, but we didn't see any and Shortcake made sure she test drove each one of them.

This may come as a shock to anyone who isn't a long-distance hiker, but going commando is quite common on the trail. And when hikers are in town having their laundry done, it is pretty much a norm. We were no different. Under our short town skirts, we were as free as the wind blowing off the river that night—a fact Shortcake forgot each time she mounted and dismounted one of the ducks. I would stand guard to help provide cover as she giggled and posed for pictures.

Making it safely back to the hotel without causing harm to the fowl or anyone else, we gathered our blankets, headed to the river's edge, and waited for sunset. Then the fireworks began. Explosions of artistically crafted pyrotechnics entertained us for the best light show I had seen in a long time. It was the perfect ending to a perfect day of hiking the Appalachian Trail.

The miles flew by. We enjoyed great weather, hot and humid at times, but still great. The terrain was gentle and kind, and since Batman was on vacation, we had been slackpacking. When he went back to work, we would have to act like real backpackers again. For the time being, we welcomed every minute of glamping we could while we were blessed with his presence.

After we put in our miles for the day and checked into our room, we headed to a local restaurant recommended by the hotel clerk. Upon arrival, we weren't even sure if we had the correct place. The building looked like a hodge-podge of structures pieced together without much thought. But Center Street Grille in Enola, Pennsylvania, lived up to its reputation. You know it's a good place when the parking lot is full. As we approached the entrance, a sign advertised the special of the day, *Wednesdays All You Can Eat Crab Legs.*

There's nothing a hiker likes better than an AYCE. Combine that with king crab legs, and you have one very happy Black Bear. They were phenomenal! I had a plate and a half of those crustaceans. If I had eaten any more, I would have exploded.

As good as the meal was, it paled in comparison to the service. Our server, Candy, was the warmest and kindest person. I wish I could have brought her home with us. It's always such a wonderful feeling to be around nice people. Thanks, Candy!

We actually do hike, and this is a memoir about my second thru-hike on the A.T., with Shortcake, my dear friend. We cover our miles; we don't skip sections. We carry our packs, sometimes with only what we need for the day. But we also enjoy everything we can when it is available. One of the fabulous things about hiking the Appalachian Trail is it brings one through areas not on the beaten path. And some of the best places are local diners that Google Maps knows nothing about.

Each state the Appalachian Trail passes through is known for something. Sometimes the titles are warranted and sometimes they are exaggerated. And those exaggerations are relative to one's own perspective.

Georgia claims the title for northbound starts, the arch at Amicalola and the approach trail, as well as Neel Gap, where many hikers' dreams and aspirations of thru-hiking the A.T. die.

North Carolina and Tennessee have The Great Smoky Mountains and a section of the trail where it flip-flops between the two states, making it confusing to know which state you are in.

Then there is Virginia, the state with the most trail miles—over 500 of them—making it seem like forever before hikers can tally another state in their logs. Here, it is said, hikers catch the "Virginia blues." I did not feel this way. Sure, it takes a lot of effort to add another state to one's tally, but the state has so much offer, how can one get bored?

Then West Virginia, with less than 3 miles (probably because Virginia stole them all), is home to the Appalachian Trail headquarters. West Virginia and Maryland together with their bordering states are part of the four-state challenge mentioned earlier. Both states are also a walking history museum.

And that brings us to Pennsylvania, or what hikers like to call Rocks-ylvania. I honestly think Pennsylvania gets a bad rap. The first 73 miles are welcoming and *easy* with the rolling hills and cornfields. Then right around Duncannon, the rocks begin to emerge. And from there, it seems like someone purposefully dumped loads and loads of rocks onto the trail. Not your smooth stones with rounded edges, but the jagged kind that resemble a shark's mouth with pointy, irregular teeth just waiting to take a bite out of the bottom of your feet, ankles, shins, and even sometimes your face. The need to replace your footwear after traversing through this state is common and often planned for.

On July 6, we officially entered the rock zone of Pennsylvania. The first several days were pleasantly smooth and enjoyable. That ended all too soon. Other states have rocky sections, but the key word is *sections*. For the next several days, the trail was a hazard of rocks to no end. It tested our physical and mental well-being. Due to the rain, I was unable to capture any photos of rocks that first day. The misery caused by the heat gave way to the misery caused underfoot. It might seem we were never happy. But surprisingly, we were.

We had been hiking in a green tunnel for weeks with few views and were quite excited the day before when we had finally seen one. It was a sunny day. On our left, the trail opened to the valley below. A retaining wall made of hewn stones held back the earth on our right. Created in the wall was a bench hikers could rest on as they gazed out over the landscape below. It's always a satisfying reward to be up so high and know you have climbed there. For me, it is like looking back in time to when I was a different person. The elevation gain on the trail represents life's struggles, and the view is the strength and reward I gain by overcoming those struggles.

Since views had been limited lately, we were then once again excited to see a sign with the word *View* carved into it, pointing the way. "Less than impressed" described our feelings when we looked in the direction of the arrow. Visibility reached a maximum of 50 yards. We could see the tree line, separated by a narrow corridor as it dipped down. But all we saw was a white screen. Just like so many other views in the earlier days of our hike.

On a sunny day, I bet a spectacular scene lay out over that dipped horizon. This was not a sunny day, though. We couldn't complain; the weather had been great. I couldn't remember the last day we had hiked in the rain.

We did a short day, knowing Mother Nature was going to be a little uncooperative. And yes, we were still glamping.

Back to the hotel in Mechanicsburg, Pennsylvania, we went. With our miles in, laundry done, and a mini rest, we still had lots of time for eating and resupply. I didn't have crab a second time. I knew my limits on splurging. I had to settle for a salad and chicken.

Being lost for words is not usually a challenge I struggle with. Occasionally it does occur. As I hiked, I thought about my daily blog post; generally, I knew within a few hours what I would like my message to be. When inspiration eluded me, I spent the day seeking elements to build upon.

Batman dropped us three gals at the trailhead, and we preceded north while he did his normal routine. We started in a drizzle, then the drizzle stopped and the day was cloudy with manageable temps and no precipitation. At one point early in the day, we had another famous Appalachian Trail vista. Several gray wires mounted on a massive iron skeletal frame stretched along the opening carved for the power lines, then disappeared at sharp angles into the white foggy abyss.

We knew once again we were up high, not just because our GPS and guidebooks told us, but we could tell we were on a mountain by the way the electrical wires dangled in each direction delivering power to the valley far below. We fantasized about what lay beyond the clouds enclosing the landscape. Our imaginations created our view. Even with viewless summits, the fog was beautiful. The blank canvas had a way of highlighting the most mundane things that we might not have otherwise taken notice of—like the beauty in that manmade structure silhouetted against the nothingness.

Views were still limited, and the rocks increased as the smooth sections decreased. Our few views were mostly fogged in, so we continued to play the imagination game. Our vision of the day was seeing Jason Statham on the beach, then later seeing him delivering us ice cream cones up on the ridge. Poor Batman had to listen to B.B., Shortcake, and myself fantasize as we hiked on. A girl must do what a girl must do to keep up her momentum for whatever task is at hand. And our task was getting the miles done before our aching feet quit.

We dried out as the day progressed and were happy to not be wet from muddy rain, just sweat. As we neared the end of our miles, we could feel the weather turning. We tried hard to make it out of the woods without getting soaked, but less than a mile before we got to the car, it started to rain. Not only was Jason not on the beach or at any summit to give us ice cream, but we were also drenched by the time we reached the Batmobile. No worries though, we were headed back to the hotel again.

At the end of the day, it wasn't our fantasy that was there for us, it was Batman, who hiked 20 miles that day and still had energy to tend to three gals and their post-trail needs for another night off trail.

Thanks again to Batman's accumulated hotel points, we enjoyed the luxury of hiking all day, getting wet, dirty, muddy, and hungry but still relishing in modern conveniences at the end of the day. I'm sure A.T. purists would say we weren't real thru-hikers, but I have found that most of those naysayers when given the opportunity like we had, would also take it.

Cleaned, fed, and refreshed, we cranked out sixteen miles the next day in only eight hours. A great pace for us—meaning Shortcake and I. B.B. could do that with one leg in a cast. The previous day's rains had muddied the trail and made the rocks slick, but it didn't seem to slow us down.

Life's little things amaze me all the time. We say, "It's a small world," and it really is. A highlight of the day was meeting a fellow Maine-iac. His name was DC6, and he knew our neighbors and friends Pat and Doug.

We enjoyed our day. It would be the last day of slackpacking for a while.

Sometimes I live by the mantra *Go ahead and do it. You don't know anyone here—have fun.* But that doesn't always hold true. On this adventure alone, in the middle of nowhere on the trail, I ran into four different people who knew me or someone I knew personally from my synthetic life. My two worlds were colliding. I have lost count of the number of followers who also recognized me from Ryan Leighton's documentary *Walking Home.* So I guess I should care about what I do.

That leads me to my other mantra: *If you always act with integrity whether you are being watched or not, then you will never have to worry about skeletons in your closet.* I struggle with this constantly. I have two voices in my head. One encourages me to do things that challenge my morale compass, and the other voice has me walk the straight and narrow.

In 2021, my editor encouraged me to write a devotional. I laughed at the idea. Sure, I contribute to a series she publishes, the *Boundless* devotionals. But no way am I worthy enough to write my own. Look at all the things I have done. The last one, hiking naked in a national forest! I didn't want the book to be a do-as-I-say-and-not-as-I-do-type of thing.

But I took the challenge, and in 2022 I wrote and published the book *As Fresh as Daisies.* As I reread that devotional, I realize it was written for myself and to challenge me to work on all the things I struggle with. And if that can help others, that's just a bonus.

The devilish part of me loves to have fun and still pushes my integrity, but as I grow and mature—yes, at fifty-eight I am still learning and growing wiser every year—the needle on my moral compass heads in the correct direction more times than not.

Batman's vacation came to an end. We had been glamping for two weeks. It had been just the break we needed to regain some strength after weeks of hiking day after day. Our fifty-something bodies didn't bounce back quite like they used to.

When Batman's vacation ended, so did ours. We left the hotel with our fully loaded packs and headed north. This time we were not met partway through the day by Batman hiking in south. No smiling face to greet us and pick up our tired spirits.

I will admit, the first half of the day was difficult as we readjusted to the weight of our packs. We'd had two weeks of slackpacking. B.B. didn't skip a beat. She set off, and we didn't see her again until we caught up at the end of the day. They didn't call her "the King" for nothing.

Shortcake and I took a little longer to finish our miles. The 1,000-foot climb out of Lickdale, Pennsylvania, was a shock to our refreshed and relaxed bodies. It was at that point we cried out, "What the heck are we going to do without Batman? How dare he leave us to actually hike this trail with our full packs, like all the other hikers?"

We managed, and after our lunch break, we were back to cruising as though our loads were empty. We barely noticed them. We made it to our destination, and there we found B.B. She was waiting at the road, enjoying a stash of trail magic by two wonderful gentlemen, Applejacks and Don Gauntlet. Each man had come solo to provide goodies for hikers. It was wonderful. We filled our tummies with cold beverages and snacks while we waited for our ride.

Our vacation of slackpacking and hotels supplied by Batman may have been over, but our glamping wasn't done just yet. Michelle, my friend who ran a Girl Scout camp close to the trail, offered to host us. One hundred forty-five campers and counselors also inhabited the camp. All we had to do in return was give a talk about our adventure to all the young ladies.

We went swimming, we toured the facilities, and they fed us supper, after which we entertained them with tales of our journey and a very lively Q & A session. The best part of the visit was sleeping in the tree house cabins. No tent again. We truly were three spoiled hikers. On top of all that, we also zeroed the next day.

A huge shout-out to Michelle and all her staffers at Wood Haven Girl Scout Camp near Pine Grove, Pennsylvania. They adopted us into their group and made us feel so welcome.

Our cozy accommodations caused us to sleep in, missing breakfast. Our plan had been to get up, eat, then go back to bed. Hikers love a good breakfast, especially when it is free. Our huge tree house bunkroom had shades that blocked out all light. When I did wake up, I was shocked to see it was 8:50am. Shortcake and B.B. were still in their racks also. So much for the most important meal of the day. Glad I had packed out leftover smiley fries and applesauce from supper.

We spent the morning relaxing and planning our miles for the next section. Before we knew it, it was lunch time. This time we heard the chime of the meal bell giving a half-hour warning. We had heard it ring that morning, but none of us knew what it was and we dozed back to la la land.

After lunch, a counselor approached us and asked if any of us would be interested in riding lessons. I guess the smile on my face answered for me. B.B. and Shortcake accepted the invitation also. Neither one of them had ever been on a horse. My last time was 27 years before, on our honeymoon. I love horses. I may be a Maine girl, but I think in another life I was a cowgirl.

Once we were assigned our lesson time, I took a nap, Shortcake wrote in her journal, and B.B. played ball with some of the staff. At 3:00pm, we met at the barn and were fitted with helmets and given our assigned horses. Shortcake got Bond, B.B. was handed Hopeful, and I had Diamond.

We saddled up inside the ring. B.B. had met her match. It was the first time we had seen any trace of fear on her face. But, champ that she is, that fear turned into pure joy. You never know what you can do until you try. As Eleanor Roosevelt said, "You gain strength, courage, and confidence by every experience in which you really stop to look fear in the face. You must do the thing which you think you cannot do."

The supper bell rang later in the day, and we were just like Pavlov's dogs, salivating and waiting to be fed. Another incredible day off trail.

BLACK BEAR TIP

Work hard. Do what needs to be done to reach your goals.
But also take time to play.

Trail Log

Day 110 Tuesday July 11
Time: 8:53am – 6:10pm
Mile: 1193.7 – 1208.8
Miles hiked: 15.1
Tented at Eagle Nest Shelter
Weather: Cloudy & humid

Day 111 Wednesday July 12
Time: 7:28am – 5:45pm
Mile: 1208.8 – 1223.5
Miles hiked: 14.7
Tented at Windsor Furnace Shelter
Weather: Hot & humid

Day 112 Thursday July 13
Time: 7:44am – 2:00pm
Mile: 1223.5 – 1232.6
Miles hiked: 9.1
Tented at Eckville Shelter
Weather: Cloudy & hot as hell

Day 113 Friday July 14
Time: 8:53am – 1:30pm
Mile: 1232.6 – 1240.0
Miles hiked: 7.4
Allentown Hiking Club Shelter
Weather: Pouring

Day 114 Saturday July 15
Time: 6:39am – 3:30pm
Mile: 1240.0 – 1252.4
Miles hiked: 12.4
Hotel: Sheraton in Scranton, PA
Weather: Cloudy, warm, wet rocks

Day 115 Sunday July 16
Time: 8:51am – 3:38pm
Mile: 1252.4 – 1262.7
Miles hiked: 10.3
Hotel: Residence Inn
Weather: Sunny & hot

Day 116 Monday July 17
Time: 7:33am – 4:03pm
Mile: 1262.7 – 1278.1
Miles hiked: 15.4
Hotel
Weather: Cloudy, humid, & thunder-
storms

Day 117 Tuesday July 18
Time: 7:38am – 5:40pm
Mile: 1278.1 – 1295.3
Miles hiked: 17.2
Stayed at Shortcake's sister's in CT
Weather: Hot & sunny

19

Excuses or Dreams

*H*iking the Appalachian Trail is so much more than a just a hike. We'd had a wonderful easement back to full-on thru-hiking. We didn't want to leave. In fact, B.B. didn't leave. She hung around another week. Shortcake and I were shuttled back to the trail by Swamp and Lingo, two wonderful young ladies all moms would be happy to have their young daughters spend summer camp with.

Pennsylvania showed us why she totes the nickname Rocks-ylvania. Someone had continued to dump large amounts of stones underfoot for long stretches. During one of those sections, we navigated thirteen miles of trail paved with every conceivable shape of rock. Seldom were they smooth or flat. Instead, they protruded from the ground at all angles in irregular shapes, most often with a pointy side up. There was no place to set your feet securely, and when you did choose a surface, your foot would be contorted in ways it wasn't meant to bend. I found the best way to traverse these rock fields was to not think too hard about my course of direction, but rather choose a line, kind of like a downhill skier does through moguls, and go for it.

The black flies and mosquitoes posed more of a challenge than the rocks. DEET is my fragrance of choice for summer. My chemistry attracts the little biting demons more so than that of the average outdoor enthusiast. I will have swarms around me when the next person doesn't even notice any flying around. If I don't lather in repellent, I will become a buffet for all bloodthirsty insects for miles around. When I do get bit, the bites itch for days and sometimes weeks. So if I am unlucky enough to get several bites at once, it is pure misery for me.

On most days, I only needed to apply repellent once; occasionally, I needed a second dose around my head later in the day. On July 12—the peak of summer—I needed more than a touch-up. Five times I reapplied my DEET. I know this is not the healthiest choice, but it is the only thing that works for me deep in the woods.

———

I wonder what drives people to voluntarily do things that cause so much discomfort. I am sure the reason is different for everyone. At any one time, thru-hikers could go home. But the trail draws us back. As much as we enjoy our town days and the conveniences of our visits there, we strap on our boots, we throw on our heavy packs, and we take to the woods, not knowing what circumstances we will encounter.

We complain about the weather. We curse the insects. Our feet develop blisters, abrasions, and other issues. Our muscles hurt. We get hungry. We get lonely. Our gear falls apart. Yet, we keep going.

Hikers who are successful on the trail are not only certain types of people with the right physiques. That fact is made apparent by the data. I don't have the data to give you; the Appalachian Trail Conservancy might be able to draw up that spreadsheet. I just know from my own experience witnessing those who are on the trail. It's not necessarily your physical strength that will determine your success; it is more about what you have between your ears and within your heart. I have seen hikers as young as five years old and up to over eighty years old complete a thru-hike. The trail does not discriminate. Anyone who desires to follow those white blazes can do it.

Watching Shortcake venture out onto this journey after all she had gone through the previous few years made me proud of her. It was her idea, way back in 2015, to hike the A.T. It wasn't even something on my radar. I was just trying to get Batman's and my boys raised and through school without having a meltdown. When she suggested our thru-hike, I was game though; I was never one to turn down a physical challenge.

Shortcake being the one to initiate an Appalachian Trail thru-hike was ironic. We are complete opposites, as I mentioned before. And out of the two of us, one would not have thought such a proposal would have come from Shortcake, the quieter, less obnoxious, stay-in-her-own-lane kind of gal. But there we were, on one of America's national scenic long trails.

I had years of athletic training to fall back on. Shortcake, not so much. I wasn't tall, but I was several inches taller than Shortcake. Being vertically challenged on the trail has its own set of issues. Every obstacle is that much harder to overcome.

Shortcake had several friends, family members, and her two boys cheering her on. But she didn't have a special someone to confide in on those hard days that were too much to handle. She kept it all inside. All her troubles were held in silence. I vocalized most of my frustrations. We differ there also.

So why do we endure all this suffering? What is it about having a certain mental fortitude that drives people to do things that promise such discomfort? I don't know the answer to this either. Whatever the reason, whenever you witness someone going through a metamorphosis like I watched my dear friend experience, you can only be in awe.

The bloodthirsty insects drove both of us into our tents earlier than normal. As I sat protected by my tent's screen, I could hear fellow hikers whacking the little biters. Oh, the things we endure to commune with nature.

Our first night back in the woods swooned us into the arms of Mother Nature, helping us forget about the rocks that tore at our feet all day. We had enjoyed a wonderful stretch of glamping, but now it was time to get back to the real world. I enjoyed sleeping in my tent, don't get me wrong. I just didn't like having to set it up and pack it away every day. If money weren't an issue, I would have either paid someone to hike ahead and have my camp and supper ready or I would have stayed in as many hotels as I could. But since Batman didn't have deep pockets in his cape, I had to stay in the woods on my own strength if I wanted to hike another day. One reason we do things we don't want to do is so we can do things that we do want to do.

If there was a day to quit, July 12 would have been the day. Two nights in a row of bad sleep made hiking difficult. Add that to Pennsylvania rocks, a hurting knee, and temperatures to make the devil himself sweat, and you have a quitting recipe. Good thing I incorporated a few more ingredients to turn my frown upside down.

I couldn't do anything about the humidity, but I could tend to my knee and adjust my attitude. I hiked slower and more diligently and took a long break to rest my knee. Also, I enlisted the help of Vitamin I. For my attitude, I went to my happy place to help forget about the rocks and heat. Well, my second happy place. First place is Batman.

I had silly thoughts about Jason Statham. Instead of the summit sundaes he usually brought us, this time we imagined that at the end of that grueling day, he would be there giving massages to Shortcake and me. Hey, remember, a hiker's gotta do what she must.

We weren't the only ones who felt like quitting. At Windsor Furnace Shelter, an abandoned tent stood half erect, surrounded by gear. We felt a tad uneasy, stumbling onto the scene with the tent partially collapsed and items strewn around. We weren't sure if it was the location of a crime or if someone else was fed up with the cruelty of the trail. We were too hot and tired to worry about danger, so we went with the latter scenario because we felt the same.

Not only did we complete our scheduled miles, but we also arrived fifteen minutes earlier than planned. Just enough time for an imaginary mini rubdown. Shortcake checked the weather for the night and the next day. The temperature at 6:00pm was 85 degrees. No wonder I sweated so much and felt miserable. At one point during the day, I really thought I was sick with Lyme or some other condition. It was just my intolerance to heat. If it was 85 at 6:00pm, what was it at peak? I had perspired so much that by the time we were done for the day, there was nothing left of me except lips and toenails. The same was forecasted for the next day.

Another day of blistering temperatures and high humidity kept us wet. I wasn't sure I could take any more of that heat. I always used to say I loved the heat. Keep in mind, I am a Maine girl, and our summers rarely stretch the thermometer above 80 degrees. Those continuous mercury-pushing spells were more than this snow-girl could handle. I told Shortcake it was beach weather, not hiking weather. It was so hot, I needed a squeegee for my body. Now that's a sight that is hard to unsee. There are few words to describe the hot, slimy, dirty state of our bodies.

A.T. hikers are not playing with a full deck. I truly believe if a study was done on the brains of long-distance hikers, researchers would find their brains are not like the average Joe's. No right-minded person would willingly subject themselves to that kind of treatment and call it fun. Thank goodness our plans for the day only demanded 9.1 miles.

After the sweat bath and rocky hiking on Day 111, we welcomed the early finish on Day 112. Just as we set up our tents, the heavens opened and dumped buckets of cold mountain rain on us. Throwing the rest of our gear under cover, we dove in ourselves, then remained imprisoned in our tents as we were subjected to yet another thunderstorm.

We needed to hike almost 18 miles to keep on track to meet Batman. Good weather was forecasted so we thought the lofty mileage goal was doable. But as we all know, weathermen are paid to lie, and the rain started at 2:30pm. July 13 was summed up with three words: short, rain, and rocks. We ended the day early and the rain was still coming down when we set out on the morning of July 14.

To make matters even trickier, the trail was a complete jungle gym. With every mile we hiked north, the rocks became even more abundant. There was something for everyone—large boulder fields, oversized paver rocks set at jagged angles, and even a milder section that, although one hundred percent natural, resembled an ancient cobblestone road. All of which were wet, slippery, and treacherous to navigate. In 2015, this exact section had me on the brink of crazed. I had started crying because it went on and on. I stopped that nonsense, though, when I realized tears wouldn't help; so I laughed hysterically just to get through it.

This time, having a friend go through it with me also seemed to lessen the agony. We both struggled, but Shortcake with her tiny feet and shorter limbs seemed to struggle more than I. But as par, she didn't complain. I complained enough for the both of us. I don't know why I complained. I would rather be on a rugged trail than at home doing dishes or fighting traffic.

The difficulty of the terrain got to Shortcake also. After several hours of hiking and getting nowhere, she asked if we were almost there. I wasn't sure of our distance. She was convinced it couldn't be far. I let her continue hiking as I checked my GPS. We still had 2.7 miles to the shelter. It was pouring, and the trail was now a river. There was no way I was telling her the bad news. I hiked on without updating her, and she didn't ask again.

When we finally arrived, soaking wet from the rain, we claimed a spot and regained our dignity. Shortcake admitted to me that she had a mini internal breakdown. But just as I had given myself a pep talk in 2015, she told herself that it wasn't going to help to fall apart. I have officially deemed that part of the A.T. as the *Meltdown Stretch*.

In between raindrops, we erected our tents. At one point, I enjoyed a quick nature rinse. I had nothing to lose—my clothes were soaked anyway from sweat. I enjoyed the refreshing coolness of the water. I also filled my water bladders from the roof's run-off to be filtered later.

The rain never completely stopped, and with the high heat and humidity, my refreshing shower didn't last long—it soon felt more like a sauna. Soaked and hot, we relaxed in the shelter with a few other soggy souls. We ate, chatted, and then when sheer boredom overtook us, we retreated to our sweat boxes for an early night.

The common thread in winners is they do what needs to be done no matter what the situation. We may not have met the day's mileage goal for a second day in a row, but that was okay. We made it through another day and had a plan for the next.

Another rainy night. It started pouring again about 11:00pm and continued until early morning. It was a nice rain, the kind that drowns out all noise and lulls you to sleep. I was glad for that because when it did stop, I could hear the snoring from the shelter—the main reason I choose to tent!

Starting my morning as usual, I began packing up my sleep system and sleep clothes. Once they were securely inside their dry bags, naked as a newborn and just as wet and slimy from the humidity, I reached for my also-wet hiking clothes. They never dry overnight. That's just a fact. If you go to bed with wet clothes, they will be wet in the morning.

They were at the bottom of my tent in a plastic bag to keep my nighttime dry clothes and sleep system from getting wet. When I opened the bag of wet clothes, an overwhelming odor of ammonia filled the tent, bringing tears to my eyes. I knew it was not a good sign but forgot the exact reason one might smell like so.

I fumbled for the tent zipper, gasping for air as the ammonia choked my lungs. Thrusting my head out the screen and reaching to open the fly, I barely stayed conscious. Not caring I was naked, I inhaled several breaths before quickly grabbing the toxic bag of dirty laundry and tossing it outside.

Once I was packed, I mentioned what I had just experienced to Shortcake. A hiker from the shelter chimed in, saying it was because my body was burning up muscle due to my low-calorie intake.

Sometimes, it just doesn't pay to eat right. That week I had switched up my food bag and eliminated all junk food. I chose peanut butter, nuts, and dried fruits. Look where it got me! Smelling like a litter box. I thought the nutrient-dense food would sustain me better than my chips, candy bars, and jelly beans. Not a chance. Backpacking is hard work, and I guess calories are more important than what's actually in them. But both are important. So I went back to my original plan of eating whatever the heck I felt like consuming and carrying.

Shortcake and I stumbled and bumbled 12.4 miles over wet rocks, across the South's version of Knife Edge and over Bake Oven Knob (a fitting name that coincided with the week's weather). I broke a tent pole and lost my cat-hole shovel—a high-priced titanium mini shovel that could cut through roots and dig in the hardest soil. I think I know where it is and one day will go back to see if I can find it. A positive note, we were able to dry out our tents. The sun wasn't out, but it was windy and sometimes that is a better condition for drying things.

At the end of several grueling days, Batman was there to meet us. And just like that, we were off the trail and into air conditioning, with soft pillows for our heads and food for our tummies.

The world is our playground, and we had an all-day pass to unlimited climbing the next day. Batman joined us for the climb out of Lehigh Gap. We had short miles planned, so we took our time climbing and enjoying the view. We had spent so many days in the green tunnel of the forest that it was fun to be on the open rocks, high above the road below.

The trail was on a deforestation site caused by zinc smelting from 1898-1980. The area is now part of a superfund project to help the revegetation. Not sure what took place for that to happen, but its name says it cost a lot of money.

Despite the heat, we were all smiles. The previous day's storms had lowered the humidity, making the heat slightly more tolerable. Having a cool shower and hot food I am sure helped with the attitudes.

The fun trail with its rock scrambles and spectacular views were rewards for never giving up on a bad day. It's important to stay the course and push through the pain of rough days in life because eventually it will pass, and great times will be had.

My gear had been breaking down on me. First it was my poles. They had started showing signs of wear a month before. One tip had worn a quarter-inch more than the other. Now, after miles of Pennsylvania's rocks, both poles had lost their carbide tip so necessary for gripping.

Several weeks prior, my tent had decided to rip. I performed surgery with some Tenacious Tape® and the tear healed.

I damaged my Lifeproof case for my phone. Can you imagine that! Only I could destroy something indestructible. Gotta love the warranty. A new one came a few days later.

My boots started shredding. The left one anyway. You can tell which side I am stronger on. It was my left pole that also first showed wear.

Then I broke one of my tent poles. But since they were all connected by one cord, they all needed to be replaced. Good thing I was not tenting again until Friday. We were in glamping mode again, taking a small break from the trail.

My clothes were a challenge also. I wore out my tank top. No worries, I had a spare. My skort became too big—always a nice dilemma. A friend bought me the same one in a smaller size. That became too hot. Replaced it with shorts that gave me a terrible heat rash on my outer thighs.

We were so pleased with our efforts tackling the rocks, beating a storm, and getting in early, and we were ready to reap our reward of a relaxing evening in the hotel. That was spoiled by a power outage caused by the storm we had out-hiked. By the time we were able to check into the room, we had barely enough time to shower and get to bed for a full night's sleep.

Falling asleep was easy. We were all exhausted. Staying asleep was the issue. The hotel was having electrical problems and the fire alarm went off five times. By the third false alarm, we didn't even get up.

Despite the lack of sleep, we were up early and back on the trail. We had big miles planned—17.2 for the day.

9.5 miles were history, and we hadn't stopped once for a break. That was the longest stretch we had ever done without resting. Our bodies were becoming machines.

With our well-deserved lunch break done, we chatted with fellow hikers and then were back on the trail to finish our goal. Ice cream was next on our agenda. Near the end of the day, the trail brought us right to Zoe's Ice Cream. Here we had another well-deserved treat.

The biggest incentive for the day that kept us going through the heat and over the rough terrain was the New Jersey border. We finally said good-bye to Pennsylvania as we put the seventh state behind us.

While we were hiking, a day hiker met us coming from the opposite direction. She was excited about our journey and explained her desire to do the trail one day. Then she listed excuses of why she could not do it. Shortcake and I gave her tips on how to overcome each of her obstacles. But for each suggestion, she had a new excuse. We stopped offering guidance.

After she was gone, Shortcake and I discussed how someone who has an excuse for everything will never do a thru-hike, much less reach any other desired goal, even though they say they want to. Her thinking was wrong. She had an excuse for everything even when shown how to overcome it. It's a fact of life: You can have excuses, or you can have your dreams. But what you can't have is both.

BLACK BEAR TIP

You can have excuses or you can have your dreams,
but you cannot have both.

Day 118 Wednesday July 19
Zero

Day 119 Thursday July 20
Zero

Day 120 Friday July 21
Zero

20

It's About Me

I can't say enough concerning the importance of time off from the trail. I love being out in the woods and seeing everything nature has to offer. The physical and mental exertion makes me feel more alive than at any other time of my life. But even good things only stay good when done in moderation. For me, one week on the trail followed by a break is perfect. Two weeks is doable, and three weeks is way too long.

A mini hiatus was planned. Our start date and our entire schedule had been built around the event we were headed to.

The complete version of *Walking Home* initially was to debut in early spring, but the date was pushed out several times. We had adjusted our start date a couple times so we could go see it. But with the continued delays on the showing, we knew we had to get hiking if we wanted to reach Katahdin before the park closed. We would just make a marathon trip to Maine when the documentary finally screened. That time had arrived.

Trying to get the most out of our days, we were going to hike a few miles then head to Maine. But out of the blue, I suggested we take the day off and enjoy a zero at Shortcake's sister's house since it was on the way. The morning's weather forecast said the area would be experiencing a heatwave. I was kind of worried. What did they call the horrendous temperatures we had been hiking in? We decided a day off was well deserved, and family time was always a treat.

It was a smart decision. Shortcake reconnected with family while Batman and I tagged along. Usually, it was the other way around. They fed us, housed us, and waited on us hand and foot. A huge shout-out and big thank you to the Jordan family for letting us invite ourselves. You rock.

We left the next morning, continuing our travel up the eastern seaboard by car this time, not by our own two feet—that journey would continue in a couple days. Boothbay Harbor, Maine, the hometown of Ryan Leighton and Cody Mitchell, producers of the documentary, was our destination.

Good things are always worth waiting for. The premier of *Walking Home* originally was slated for October 2016. But as I told Ryan, "Masterpieces don't happen overnight." Then early spring was the goal, and that didn't happen. But finally, it was done and ready for the world to see.

A partial screening had taken place in 2016, a cliff-hanger leaving us all in suspense. That version is what so many hikers had viewed on YouTube, thus recognizing me on the trail and thankful to see that I made it.

It was a sold-out theatre for Ryan's hometown crowd in Boothbay. The photography and editing skills of Ryan and his co-producer, Cody Mitchell, brought the trail to life, not just by film, narrative, and music but also through heart and soul. He said it best when he explained it as threading a needle with multiple threads. "You can't push it; you have to let it come together."

After watching the documentary, I felt energized, just as I had way back in high school after watching the first *Rocky* movie. Instead of wanting to run up the steps in Philadelphia, I wanted to get back to the Appalachian Trail and hike.

It was so much fun to share this with my Batman, Shortcake, and three very special friends, Darnel, Linda, and Stacey, who drove all the way from Bangor. Throughout the hike with Shortcake, I tried extremely hard not to let the hike be about me, but these zero days were just that—all about me.

I had my fun in the sun on my first trek in 2015 all because Short-cake had sent me a text asking if I wanted to hike the A.T. If it wasn't for her, hike number one never would have taken place and I wouldn't be the person I am today. I wanted our 2017 experience to be focused on Shortcake and allowing her to get all she could out of the trail without my influence overshadowing her hike.

My intentions were so sincere and so pure. I will admit this was so difficult for me to do. I am a very outgoing individual, outspoken and driven. My rough edges have smoothed over the years, and I keep filing them down. I know humility is a character trait God wants us to perfect, but it is hard when you have such a vibrant personality and want to share everything you have, everything you know, and everything you do with everyone.

When Shortcake and I started 1,295.3 miles earlier, it was easy to hold to my goal and let her be the focus. We would use my previous knowledge to guide us in planning, but I thought I did a good job at staying in my lane and letting her discover for herself.

We enjoyed the honeymoon stage of sharing a great adventure. Everything was wonderful. It rained; so what, we were having fun. We were hungry; so what, we'd be in town soon. We couldn't find a flat place to tent; so what, we'd snuggle and laugh about it. We had to get up early or hike late; so what, we'd catch up on sleep another day. All was good.

Slowly that started to wear off. We were laughing less. We struggled more. Our conversations, sparse to begin with, decreased even more. Shortcake shared less and less with me. Of course, we had great moments and lots of simple moments, but the times of nothingness kept increasing, and we still had several hundred miles to go.

Loneliness gradually crept into my being. It seemed like Shortcake was withdrawing into a shell. We were hiking together, but alone. I coined that saying way before Covid. Our conversations were shallow. We ate separately and did most of our chores separately.

Since we were our own little group and we hiked so differently from most of the other hikers, we had developed bonds with only a small few, B.B. being one of them; but even she wasn't around. At times I felt like I was on a silent retreat.

I kept reminding myself it wasn't about me. That helped. Deep in my soul, I wanted this trip to be Shortcake's. I wanted her to get out of the journey what she needed to, in the way that was best for her, so I kept all that inside. Emotionally and mentally, it was pure torture for me. I will admit, it was difficult to keep that mindset to myself. But I did—most of the time.

July 19, 20, and 21 were about me, and as much as I tried to be humble, I basked in the limelight with all the gracefulness of a puppy walking on ice. Sometimes it is okay for things to be about yourself, kept in moderation of course. I know I struggle with this; Shortcake would probably say it was another one of my *issues.* Challenges make us better, and I still work on not being the center of attention, because no one likes a showoff.

I fall short in this task all the time. I know it is a character flaw, so I do work on it. But just the other day, Batman and I were chatting with a friend. We all were carrying on and teasing each other. My kind and thoughtful hubby, who rarely says anything negative about anyone, blurted out, "She is so arrogant!" He was referring to me. I was shocked at his truthfulness, and we all laughed. I guess I still need to file down those edges.

We were rested and well fed, so it was time to get serious again. We had slowly completed our zero-day chores over the last three days. Our resupply, laundry, and repacking were done. All we had left to do was continue resting and watch TV while we waited for the sun to go down. It felt great having nothing to do.

After watching the documentary, I couldn't wait to hit the trail for more fun and to continue testing my character and will. I had been one tough cookie two years ago. But in 2017, I seemed to be so wimpy. The combination of feeling like I was on an extended silent retreat and knowing I had nothing to prove was more than this crazy gal could handle. 2015 showed I could tackle whatever the trail threw at me and succeed. But in 2017, since I had options, I preferred the cushier selection.

Why is it we as a species tend to choose the path of least resistance? Since the dawn of man, we have been inventing and creating things to make life easier and, in many cases, do the work for us. One would think with all of life's amenities we would have more time to do what is important. But we don't. We fill that free time with even more errands, events, appointments, and other time-wasting tasks that keep us from the simple treasures life has to offer—faith, family, and friends.

I loved being on the trail, as tough as it was at times, because it was simple. All I had to worry about was shelter, food, and water. That left me time to focus on my faith, my friendships, and myself. Life wasn't cluttered out there. There was no drama except for the stuff we conjured up in our own heads. Was that what was happening to me?

BLACK BEAR TIP

It's okay to float your own boat once in a while as long
as you don't sink another's in the process.

Trail Log

Day 121 Saturday July 22
Time: 8:38am – 6:10pm
Mile: 1295.3 – 1308.6
Miles hiked: 13.3
Tented at mile 1308.6
Weather: Cloudy, hot, & balmy

Day 122 Sunday July 23
Time: 7:35am – 7:00pm
Mile: 1308.6 – 1325.0
Miles hiked: 16.4
Tented inside Gren Anderson Shelter
Weather: Cloudy, humid, & rain

Day 123 Monday July 24
Time: 10:47am – 7:00pm
Mile: 1325.0 – 1338.0
Miles hiked: 13.0
Tented at High Point Shelter
Weather: Cooler than lately, cloudy,
ended in rain

Day 124 Tuesday July 25
Time: 7:35am – 3:22pm
Mile: 1338.0 – 1350.4
Miles hiked: 12.4
Tenting at Pochuck Mountain Shelter
Weather: Cloudy & cooler

Day 125 Wednesday July 26
Time: 6:35am – 2:00pm
Mile: 1350.4 – 1362.1
Miles hiked: 11.7
Wawayanda State Park
Weather: Partly sunny & cooler

Day 126 Thursday July 27
Time: 7:55am – 5:40pm
Mile: 1362.1 – 1374.0
Miles hiked: 11.9
Tented at Wildcat Shelter
Weather: Cloudy, misty, & humid

Day 127 Friday July 28
Time: 7:30am – 6:18pm
Mile: 1374.0 – 1388.3
Miles hiked: 14.3
Tented at Fingerboard Shelter
Weather: Cloudy & hot

Day 128 Saturday July 29
Time: 6:42am – 4:45pm
Mile: 1388.3 – 1402.9
Miles hiked: 14.6
Stayed at the Deouls
Weather: Warm & nice sky

Day 129 Sunday July 30
Zero

21

A Visitor From Heaven

We were back in the woods after another wonderful stretch of glamping. From movie star (in my dreams) to hobo (reality). Amenities refreshed us, but a drawback of town days was that our hiking groove slipped. Every hiker develops his or her own routine for set up, take down, hiking, etc. When we go to town or slackpack, that routine is disrupted. On our days off, I tried hard to keep my routine as close as possible to my trail routine to prevent mishaps.

A mile into the hike, we stopped for a water break. Instantly, I felt something was missing. I didn't know what exactly, but I sensed I had left something behind. I quickly did a double check and realized the absent piece of gear was not just one item but two. I had forgotten my bandanas. I knew exactly where they were.

I had been out of sync packing up the night before and in the morning. Thank goodness I have a wonderful hubby. Never underestimate the powers of Batman. He hiked back down the incline we had just climbed, retrieved my bandanas, then returned, catching Shortcake and I, who continued hiking forward. He is amazing and I am blessed to have him.

Pennsylvania's finest spilled over into New Jersey. After a tiring hike over more rocks, Shortcake and I were ready to set up camp. Our campsite was waterless, and we were low on H2O. The water source, a stagnant pond skimmed over with scum, upset our stomachs just looking at it. We decided to conserve what we had for the night and in the morning fill up at the spring that the guidebook noted was three miles out.

Just as we were getting ready to retire to our own tents, it started raining. Colin, the hiker I had met at Pine Grove Furnace, was waiting for his lagging buddy to arrive. The two friends shared equipment. Doing this, hikers can split weight. But the downside is not having what you need when you need it. And in Colin's case, he had the tent but not the tent poles.

Good goes around. Hubby had helped me out, and I passed that good deed on. I let Colin hang out in my tent until the rest of his tent arrived. Hikers take care of each other out on the trail.

Regarding tents. I hoped mine would hold up. I had switched gear, since my other one had a broken pole. I didn't like the backup tent. It was heavy and the design was awkward. Of course, it had to rain on the night of its first use. Might as well put it to the full test.

The rocks continued to spew farther into New Jersey. I navigated them successfully, but they did tire my ankles more than I preferred. Shortcake, on the other hand, struggled more for foot placement. Between both of us, the rocks slowed us down considerably. Our long days exhausted us. Add wet conditions to the mix, and you have two angry hikers. As much as we searched for joy in the little things, sometimes we just couldn't see it.

On the second night of wetness after the movie screening zero days, we decided to set our tents up in the shelter. A rude and selfish act. It was after 7:00pm, and no one else was around. The weather forecast called for heavy rain. Not long after our tents were perched perfectly under the safety of the shelter, a solo hiker appeared. We apologized and offered to remove our little homes.

He wasn't fazed at the sight of our tents inside the shelter and said, "Great, then you won't mind when I set up mine." Sometimes you must bend the rules. It's taboo to set up one's tent in a shelter. But we didn't feel like getting wet, and the bugs had been horrendous. We didn't want to be eaten alive, either, if we stayed in the shelter. The New Jersey state bird should be the mosquito.

Night came, and the three us were snug as bugs in our own space, grateful we were not putting anyone out. But two hikers did arrive at 3:30am. We felt horrible. It was pouring out. We only had our screens up, which didn't take any more space than just our sleeping pads, so there was still room for both latecomers to squeeze in between Shortcake and Evac, the other hiker.

Sleeping in is a rare occasion for us on the trail, so we took advantage of the rain keeping us put. The rain plus the 3:30am arrival of the two other hikers had disturbed our slumber. Once the rain stopped, we packed up and headed out for an unusually late start, 10:47am.

Still rocky. It had been no bed of roses lately. I complained about everything. I tried hard to keep the joy in my heart, but all we did was hike, set up camp, and go to bed. Our pace was slow, and it seemed to take forever to cover what miles we did. The next day, we did it all over again. We talked very little. Not sure why. I think we were just tired. I even stopped taking pictures—and I usually take pics of everything. My phone was almost full, so I was limited on data storage; but even if I would have had space on my device, I didn't feel like taking pictures.

In April 2023, I referred to my notes. The guidebook and photos I had taken transported me right back to the hike, and I could remember almost everything about most days, including the feelings, the smells, and the essence. My journal and even my blog were limited in positivity for that stretch. I had little reference to recall what we did. But in what little I did record, I can feel the agony and turmoil during that stretch.

We ended the day in rain. Set up our tents in the rain, and had to do everything inside our tents. And that was another thing—I hated my tent. This backup tent was a shoddy design and the person who came up with it should have been slapped. I didn't even eat. I just wanted to go to bed and wait for it all to be over.

Somehow—and quickly—I needed to find why I wanted to remain out there, because too many more days and nights with horrible weather, bad gear, and a lost focus would send me home.

The rain stopped at some point but the droplets from the canopy danced off my tent all night. I do like sleeping in the rain. It blocks all noise, whether it's snoring, loud people, or forest noises. I can't hear animals lurking outside, scaring me half to death. The rain blocks all that out, and if there was a ferocious animal, it would be a quick death that I didn't know was coming. Instead of being nervous, I finally slept well.

The two large groups of hikers who were at the shelter quieted down quickly after dark, and I was soon asleep. My pity-party attitude helped, I'm sure. I only woke a few times to reposition and once to collect my thoughts.

I had a wonderful dream. Often, I wake up from dreams that feel too real to be a dream. Most of the time, they are of my mom, who passed away over 20 years ago. She is always smiling, healthy, and so happy. Sometimes she asks me to take a long walk with her. I always refuse and tell her I am not ready. Those dreams are a little freaky.

Most of the time, she just has a hug or piece of advice for me. I believe these are visits from heaven.

My dream that night was like that, only it wasn't Mom who came to visit and share wisdom. This time I saw a dear friend I used to teach with, and I coached with her husband. When I arrived at her house and went in, Sonny, her husband, was sitting on the couch. He was so happy and healthy in appearance. He radiated with a dazzling aura. I looked puzzled and said to my friend, "I am sorry, but I thought Sonny passed away." She didn't answer, but he did. He said to me, "Emily, you need to find the joy. It's there." And I woke right up.

I started the next day knowing my good friend had visited me from heaven that night. And that day I found the joy again. I took many more pictures of random things as I've always enjoyed doing. I didn't dread the dreary weather. And I didn't complain. I remembered life wasn't about me and neither was this hike. I had a warmth in my soul that only comes from knowing you are not alone in this world, no matter what your circumstances are.

One could not have asked for a better day to be on the trail. If only I would have heeded my own advice. Patience is the key. It seemed like I would get to a point where I could only handle so much yuck before I had a meltdown. Life—the trail—is still hard. If only I would have stopped, taken a deep breath, and hung on just little longer, because all things eventually changed.

My recent bout of negativity robbed me of the enjoyment surrounding me. I let the blinders of whoa-me block out all the good. Looking back, I know it was there; good is always present. We just need to be present.

But thanks to Sonny's visit, my joy was back, and in our short 11.7 miles we covered that next day, we saw everything. The trail was easy and gentle at times with no grade. At other times, it was a roller coaster with sharp ups and downs and rocky ascents. There were boardwalks, suspension bridges, and planked sections. We had road walks, meadows, marshes, and pastures. The only thing we didn't have was rain and bugs.

It is so easy to have an attitude of gratitude when all is well. It's another matter to keep the head in check when life causes frowns. It's those latter times I struggle with, and I need to remember to be patient because all struggles eventually end. The flip side is that all good things come to an end also. The good and bad are just like the weather in Maine. If you wait long enough, it will change.

Patience has never been one of my finer attributes, but the trail was teaching me its value. I do freak out less now and hardly ever panic. I still have my moments—Shortcake and Batman can attest to that—but life is about learning and growing to be the best that we possibly can be. If that means I need to struggle more, then so be it. It's through the pain and anguish that we grow the most.

I don't write all this to be preachy. I write it because I myself need to hear it. If I can help one person along with helping myself, then we both can grow together. On that perfect day as I hiked, I tried to remember the joy that was in my heart. I worked hard not to let anyone or any circumstance take it away. So when my smile started to dip, I took a breath and remembered to be patient, because *this too shall pass.*

We exited New Jersey and entered our ninth state.

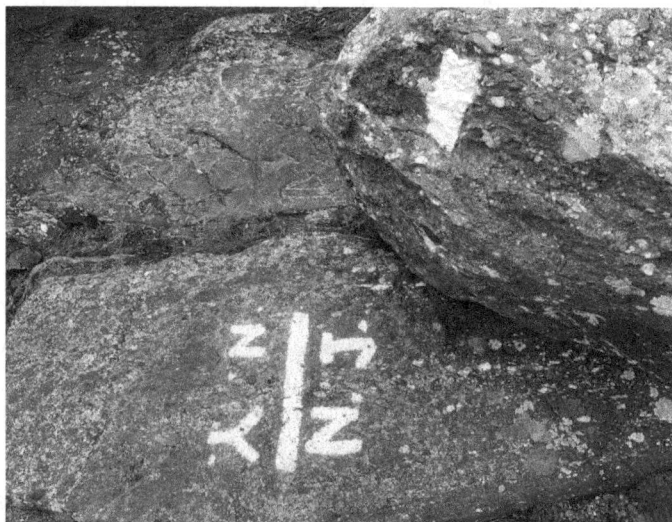

New York was fun. That was my interpretation. If you ask most other hikers, they will talk about how difficult it is. The state has lots of rocks but they're not like the relentless Pennsylvania stones. In New York, it's more like a jungle gym. We had our first rebar climb. I just love the climbing.

The climbs offered views as our reward, and the forests were clothed in much less undergrowth, exposing towering trees and a feeling of openness. The woods in the southern states are carpeted with varied plant life that encroached on and over the trail at times. It was freeing not to feel trapped.

New York is known as the deli state. Conveniently located to the trail are many sandwich shops, allowing hikers to munch their way through the miles of the Empire State. Also close to the trail is a creamery. What kept our feet moving on July 27, even though we were tired from all the fun yet challenging terrain, was ice cream. A half-mile road walk did not deter us from the reward of a hot caramel sundae.

By the time we arrived at the creamery, I didn't feel like filling up on a sweet creation. My taste buds wanted water and lots of it. While I loved the trails of New York, its water was not so favorable, and it was scarce. It was the worst-tasting water on the trail, and even after filtering it, a tinge of color remained. When you added a drink mix to mask the flavor, it only gave the concoction an even worse hue.

I splurged on seven bottles of water at a buck apiece. I am a water snob. The streams in New York have been stained the color of tea, with tannins that make the water taste very earthy and stale. Eweee. It won't hurt you, but I just don't like drinking it. The spigots at various places are no better. The city water tastes worse than the stuff we filtered on trail. Ice cream was not the cure for me that day; I had to have some good water. Besides, ice cream would have been disappointing unless Jason was serving me.

––––––

Rattlesnakes made for an interesting afternoon. A note on the trail warned us of their presence. The note was dated 7/22. We passed it on 7/27, and a snake was still in the same spot. As we were taking a photo of the warning, a second snake crossed the trail at the spot where we had stood two minutes earlier.

The next day, serpent sights continued, and we saw our first copperhead. At first glance, he looked like a giant one. Instead, it was a twisted mass of several snakes. We viewed from a safe distance. As we backed farther away, we noticed a second heap of muted orange and brown scales following the contour of a crack on a rock. Apparently, we had stumbled on a den of copperheads seeking shade from the afternoon summer heat. We were seeking the view on the other side of where those guys nested but thought it wise to wait for the next overlook.

snakes

Snakes, hard forest climbs under gigantic trees, and tough rock squeezes and scrambles filled our day. A nature's joyride. The trail resembled a roller coaster except that our descents did not build up energy to propel us up and over the next climb. We had to do it on our own, but the ride was just as exhilarating.

A pass through the Lemon Squeezer tested our strength and mental fortitude. A short section of trail inclines between two vertical rocks that inch closer together as a hiker progresses through the narrow channel. It is a tight traverse without carrying a load, and the size of your pack will determine if you need to remove it. For those who don't like confined spaces or are larger than the crevice, there is a blue-blazed work-around.

Inspecting the rocky area for any other resting snakes, Shortcake and I took turns making our way through the iconic structure. This was one time our small and short structures were an asset. What would have helped further is if Batman had been slackpacking us, but instead we had our full bags.

Each day, New York delivered treats. Either the trail provided fun and varied challenges or the wildlife thrilled us. Snakes always get your heart racing, but the deer bring a calmness to the heart. One day we saw two lambs and a doe feeding on the summer grasses, then we saw two does and one solo. They were so pretty. We never got tired of them.

We also saw the New York skyline from a ridgetop. That's as close to the city as I ever want to go. I am one of the few Americans who have no desire to visit the Big Apple. I really don't want to. But seeing it from a distance was cool, and it kept me immune to all the hustle and crowds of the big city.

We experienced our own mass of people with our hike up and over Bear Mountain. It's a tourist destination, and it was Saturday. Oh, my goodness! Our dealing with a nest of copperheads the day before was more pleasant than enduring the throngs of tourists who flooded the trail. One hiker was lucky I didn't throw him over the bridge. Short-cake and I were taking a picture of a wooden trail bridge, and he saw us waiting for others to pass over it. He all but pushed us out of the way to cross it. Then the black bear in me stirred, but I calmed her down. Lucky for him.

Despite the nasty water and a few rude hikers, New York delighted us. With joy back in my heart, little was irritating me. We were even rescued from the mayhem of Bear Mountain State Park by my friend Cathie. The timing was perfect. Ending our multi-day stint in the woods at a tourist trap had been a shock to our senses.

I had met Cathie through our son Patch, who played football with Cathie's son Derek at UMaine. Our sons both were kickers. Kickers and punters for football are like the outcasts of a family—the family must tolerate them, but no one really likes them unless they are needed. The group becomes close. That's how Cathie and I became friends. Much like a hiker's tramily (short for "trail family"), close-knit bonds are established by going through similar circumstances.

Cathie took us back to her house, where we joined her husband, Paul, and kids Derek and Danielle. We christened them as new trail angels. And they were the best ever. Providing us a ride, an inviting cool and dry place to wash up, and a place to sleep was wonderful enough. But that wasn't all.

Batman met us once he returned from his business trip to Germany, and the Deouls treated us to dinner at a pizza place. It was the yummiest gluten-free pizza I have ever had, and to this day remains #1.

We slept well that night, knowing we didn't have to get up early to beat the heat. A zero day with our friends was all that was on our agenda for the next day.

———

We went to bed with full tummies, clean skin and hair, in air-conditioning, and without snakes. Our new trail angels' generosity could have ended there, but it didn't. Breakfast was amazing! So much fresh fruit, pastries for Shortcake and Batman, and they had even researched gluten-free cereal and toast for me.

Lunch was another fiesta, and supper too was a banquet with steak and chicken, roasted baked potatoes with carrots and onions, summer squash with zucchini cubes, corn on the cob, and feta cheese. I think I had thirds of everything.

I am so grateful for all my friends, past, present, and future. Not just because they provided amenities for my hike, but for the love and support they have shown me. If you have one good friend, you are lucky. If you have two, you are blessed. I don't know how to categorize the number I have. Make sure you tell your friends you love them. They are truly a gift.

BLACK BEAR TIP

Always have an attitude of gratitude.

Day 130 Monday July 31
Time: 10:54am – 4;45pm
Mile: 1402.9 – 1410.2
Miles hiked: 7.3
Tented at Graymoor
Weather: Cloudy, hot

Day 131 Tuesday August 1
Time: 7:35am – 8:00pm
Mile: 1410.2 – 1429.0
Miles hiked: 18.8
Tented at RPH Shelter
Weather: Sunny & hot

Day 132 Wednesday August 2
Time: 8:09am – 1:50pm
Mile: 1429.0 – 1438.0
Miles hiked: 9.0
Tented at Morgan Stewart Shelter
Weather: So friggin' hot

Day 133 Thursday August 3
Time: 7:49am – 5:45pm
Mile: 1438.0 – 1454.6
Miles hiked: 16.6
Tented at Wiley Shelter
Weather: Hot & buggy

Day 134 Friday August 4
Time: 7:15am – 4:04pm
Mile: 1454.6 – 1467.3
Miles Hiked: 12.7
Stayed at the Jordans', Shortcake's
sister's family
Weather: Hot, cloudy, light rain,
thunder

Day 135 Saturday August 5
Zero

22

So Hot

I was feeling awful again and wondering if I would even be able to finish our short 7.6-mile day. I had felt great when we left the house. The rest and gold-star treatment at the Deouls' had me ready to take on the world. As we finished the hike through Bear Mountain State Park—which was much quieter on Monday—then continued through the Trailside Museum and Zoo, I began to feel ill and developed a headache.

Stopping every half hour or so to rest and drink did little to improve my state. Batman was hiking with us, and Paul Deoul lent a hand with vehicle shuttling. Batman retrieved the car and met us at the day's destination. He informed us the temperature was 103 degrees. So no, I wasn't sick; it was just hot! Each time the mercury reached triple digits, I became ill. Ugh!

---

130 days on trail, 1,400 miles hiked, 10 states completed, 1 tick bite, 1 set of broken poles and other miscellaneous gear mishaps, countless stumbles and non-injuring falls, several bodily pounds lost, many giggles and tears, a few scares and scars, and loneliness and friendships. Yet we still loved hiking the Appalachian Trail.

Each state gave us treasures to cling to despite all the negativity that we endured. New York was no exception with its tall forests, well-maintained trails, and delis. It is also home to the lowest elevation point on the trail. The bear enclosure at the Trailside Museum and Zoo is only at 177 feet of elevation. Mount Washington at 6,288 feet was the highest mountain left to climb on our trek, and we would end on Katahdin, at 13 feet shy of a mile high. That didn't sound like much effort still required.

If only we could have hiked the way the crow flies, but we couldn't. We were about 60 miles from New England, and it is said that when hikers reach New England, they have completed 80 percent of the distance but only 20 percent of the work. So when we left the comforts and fantastic hospitality of the Douels on that sweltering hot day, we didn't mind being only at 177 feet of elevation in the cool shade of the zoo's trees.

We finished the day at Graymoor Spiritual Life Center in New York. They allow hikers to camp on their grounds, which are complete with a pavilion, porta-potty, running water, electricity, and a huge baseball field to camp in. The peaceful setting was just the place to relax after a sweltering day on the trail.

Day 131 was another scorcher! The morning dragged on for hours as the miles added up slowly. We gave thanks for the sunny skies, but the heat was brutal. And to make matters worse, no matter where we resupplied on water, it tasted like chlorine or dirt—and often both at the same time.

One would think an 18.8-mile day would produce highlights, but that does not always happen. We hiked in my least-desirable setting, an overgrown forest with gnarly rocks. The long day went on and on and on. It was quite difficult and boring at the same time. I don't usually get bored. I can always find something to enjoy. But that day, finding joy was a little more difficult than usual.

I stand corrected—the sky was pretty.

We needed a catalyst to improve our mood. The Good Book says, "Ask and you shall receive." We came upon a brook crossing. This was one of the few streams that had water deep enough to require assistance in crossing. Shortcake veered to the right, choosing a shorter span where the shallow water ran over smooth rock. I suggested she take the crossing that had flat, dry stepping stones, but it was longer. She said, "No, I think I'll go this way."

I continued to the left and was across safely and dry in a matter of seconds. I looked right and saw Shortcake down, sitting in the stream and laughing.

How many times do we find ourselves in the same situation? Not that of crossing a stream but rather doing some task where we are offered advice from another who can see the whole picture. For whatever reason, we decline the advice only to find ourselves in over our head. It's at that point our character has a chance to shine through. Do we keep sinking deeper in our own mistake or admit our error, laugh at ourselves, accept help, and move on?

I'm not saying what Shortcake did was wrong; it just reminded me of how we sometimes operate in life. Not only did she laugh, but she also enjoyed the cool soak. It was the comic relief we needed to break the humdrum boredom of the trail on that terribly long hot day.

Wednesday, August 2, was another hot and miserably humid day. The day before, we had rocked out just under 19 miles, and then we suffered through just 9 miles the next day. We quit short of our destination and decided there was no shame in tapping out early. Our bodies spoke loud and clear to us, and when we didn't listen to them, they stopped performing.

We had pushed hard the previous day and then didn't sleep well that night. Despite the next day's low mileage, we still made our overall scheduled goal for those two days since we had done more the day before. Nothing lost except more sweat and calories.

A few days back, I had bought $7.00 worth of bottled water because New York's sources didn't agree with me. I just couldn't take any more awful water. At Morgan Stewart Shelter there is a ground pump. Ground pumps are a nice amenity at shelters and parks. Usually, the water is ice cold and crystal clear. But at this shelter, after I filled my hydration bag and hung it from a hook to filter, it looked like a catheter bag draped over the side of a patient's hospital bed. The yellowish-brown fluid did little to excite my desire to take a nice long swig.

Thankfully, my gravity-fed filter did its job, and by the time the collection bag was empty and the filtered water made its way to the clean side, the water was clear. But looks were deceiving. It still tasted horrible and upset my stomach no matter how I tried to mask the earthy taste with my flavor packets. Gross is gross and by any other name is still gross.

Tapping out worked in our favor. As we were setting up camp, the distant roll of thunder could be heard. The rain wasn't forecasted to arrive until after 6:00pm. We had time to get our gear situated and seek cover in the shelter with a few other hikers. The storm tap-danced around without much of a real threat for the longest time; then came the grand finale. If we would not have stopped hiking when we did, we would have been caught in the middle of it somewhere on the ridge ahead. We loved it when things worked out in our favor. Hikers 1, Weather 0 that day.

And B.B, who had stayed a week back at the Girl Scout camp, caught up to us.

We were dry, hydrated, fed, and even had time to take a baby-wipe bath before calling it a night. 16.6 miles were planned for the next day, and we needed all the rest we could get.

I was sounding like a broken record when it came to the weather and the bugs. All I seemed to do was complain about how hot, humid, and buggy it was. I decided I wasn't going to do that any longer.

I did well until I emerged from my tent in the morning. The screen was covered in mosquitos, and I began complaining before I even unzipped it. I needed to apply DEET before stepping out. "Oh, it's going to be one of those days," I said.

The terrain and footpath were quite nice. If only we could have enjoyed it more, but once again the heat and humidity had us dragging. And if we stopped too long to rest, I was a human buffet for all biters.

Part way through the day, we came to an Amtrak crossing. No station, just a crossing with a bench, like a bus stop, but for a train. It would have been so much fun to sit and wait for a ride that would hurl us into the Big Apple. That's the only way I would go to NYC—a quick trip in and out. In the beginning, we had thought we wanted to do this; but since we'd been on the trail, we decided a trip to the city would be way too overwhelming, especially for me. So we hiked on.

We didn't hike far. No need to head out of the way for food trucks when there was one 100 yards from the trail. We rested in the shade as Lou and Roseann cooked up some grub. We rehydrated on water and shakes. It was just the rest we needed before venturing into the open farmland under the heat of the afternoon sun.

The one-mile uphill walk through a hay field was painstakingly slow as we tromped on. Dilapidated farm equipment and structures dotted the landscape. I forced myself to take a few iconic photos of America's past.

It was a very long day of hiking. We arrived at the shelter area, set up our tents, collected water, and each went to our own bed to rest our weary bodies. All was well until the coyotes interrupted our sleep. Not once but twice they howled and yipped. The second time, it seemed like they were in the yard. We had visions of looking out our screens and seeing a canine's nose curiously checking us out. Thankfully that didn't happen. Only in our nighttime fears and my wild imagination do such things occur.

We finally made it to New England. Each day we closed in on Katahdin. Every step we had taken since we left Amicalola Falls so many weeks and miles ago was preparing us for what was about to come. Everyone worries about the White Mountains, but southern New England is no joke and Connecticut doesn't mess around. It woke us up. No more gentle slopes and touristy trails like New York and some of the southern states. We did some good climbs with rocks galore. It was fun and tiring at the same time.

We had hoped to arrive in town early enough for some perusing and munchies. The heat, terrain, and slippery rocks from another afternoon thundershower foiled that plan. Just as we were approaching the ice cream shop in Kent, Connecticut, our ride showed up to whisk us away for another day of rest. Batman was not the hero this time and neither was Jason Statham. Jay, Shortcake's brother-in-law, was our knight in shining armor and air-conditioning.

Gotta love family. Shortcake's family hosted us for a second time on this journey. They were superb. Once back at the Jordans' house, this time for more than just an overnight, we enjoyed a swim in the pool and pizza. The next day, we did the usual zero-day chores and rested.

Shortcake and I needed to resupply but our host, Shortcake's sister, Susanne, was napping, her husband was working, and the kids weren't around. Susanne's brand new car sat in the garage. We pondered how angry Sis might get if we helped ourselves to her set of shiny new wheels. Under normal circumstances, we knew she wouldn't have minded. But it was far from normal—the car was new, we hadn't driven in months, and we were in a city, not the backwoods. Our growling tummies and the need to do our chores before the day wasted away were too much of an influence. We found the keys and *stole* the car. We laughed and joked about being convicts and even took a photo of Shortcake driving without her hands on the wheel to tease Susanne. To make up for our thievery, Shortcake purchased groceries and I cooked a feast for all of us.

Thanks to the Jordans, we rested, we showered, we ate, and we did our chores all in the comforts of a home and air-conditioning. Another wonderful family contributed to the success of our hike. Shortcake and I were walking the miles and enduring the elements, but it's folks like the Jordans and the Deouls and so many others who impact a thru-hiker's journey in such a positive way and add to a thru-hiker's success.

BLACK BEAR TIP

Loosen up and learn to laugh at yourself.

Day 136 Sunday August 6
Time: 8:33am – 6:17pm
Mile: 1467.3 – 1481.0
Miles hiked: 13.7
Tented at Caesar Campsite
Weather: Partly cloudy, low humidity

Day 137 Monday August 7
Time: 7:00am – 3:15pm
Mile: 1481.0 – 1493.0
Miles hiked: 12.0
Stayed at Bearded Woods
Weather: Cool morning, drizzle, & rain

Day 138 Tuesday August 8
Time: 8:03am – 7:35pm
Mile: 1493.0 – 1507.7
Miles hiked: 14.7
Tented at Laurel Ridge Campsite
Weather: Cloudy, partly cloudy, sunny

Day 139 Wednesday August 9
Time: 7:33am – 5:15pm
Mile: 1507.7 – 1521.9
Miles hiked: 14.2
Tented at mile 1521.9
Weather: Sunny, mild, no bugs

Day 140 Thursday August 10
Time: 7:00am – 4:14pm
Mile: 1521.9 – 1534.1
Miles hiked: 12.2
Tented at N. Wilcox Mt. Shelter
Weather: Cloudy, hot & buggy

Day 141 Friday August 11
Time: 7:04am – 11:30am
Mile: 1534.1 – 1541.2
Miles hiked: 7.1
Stayed at Fairfield Inn, Holyoke, MA
Weather: Cloudy, partly sunny, warm

23

Pooh Happens

It was hard to leave the Jordans'. They are such a wonderful family, and their home was so cozy. But the white blazes called us forward. We packed our gear and loaded up the vehicle. Jay drove us back to the trailhead. Jessica, his daughter, accompanied us. We gave hugs and kisses and said good-byes to Shortcake's family, then Shortcake and I headed north once again.

The usual hot, sticky muck we had been hiking in for two months vanished that morning. The refreshing weather brightened our mood. I barely broke a sweat all day. Weeks before, Shortcake and I kept telling ourselves the weather would change in August. And it did. Even better, no bug spray was needed. First day since Pennsylvania I hadn't had to lather the DEET.

We also dubbed Connecticut as the all-or-nothing state. She was either completely flat or steeper than steep. We hiked five miles of flat. The first of those was along a dirt road next to a river; the last four were also along the river but on a flat trail. Then we had inclines that went right up and were even steeper on the way down.

Our strength had grown immensely since our first steps on the Appalachian Trail. It still took us several hours to all day to complete our daily goals, but instead of single-digit mileage being the norm, we averaged 12 to 15 miles a day. Seldom did we go above that, but we could when we needed to. And our packs no longer felt like a burden, even when fully loaded. While Connecticut threw a variety of stuff at us, we handled it like the experienced backpackers we were becoming.

On one section, we came across a wilderness school group who were rock climbing. Shortcake and I enjoyed watching the leader do his run. Dan scaled the steep ledge like a mountain goat. Thankfully, the A.T. did not also go that way. The scene brought back memories of when Shortcake and I had gone rock climbing in New Hampshire. It seems like all my crazy adventures have one thing in common—they are all Shortcake's ideas.

It was a long day of hiking. Even though we were stronger than we had been weeks ago, it still took a lot out of us to hike ten plus hours a day. It's like work. One hiker said it best: "All we do is punch in, hike, and punch out. Then do the same the next day." At least, with the cooler weather the joy was more easily found. Probably as we hiked north and the temps continued to drop and fall arrived, we would once again complain that it was too cold.

The respite at Shortcake's family's house, the cooler temps, and moderate trail had both of us chatting up a storm and carrying on like two junior high girls. These were the days I loved. I didn't feel like I was on a silent solo retreat. We joked and laughed our way through the miles. Lots of it would be good material to write about. But do you think I could remember it by the day's end? Stopping to write a note or stopping to record a voice memo would have broken up the mood and lessened the experience. My journaling and blogging while I hiked was only as detailed as my mind could recall.

We loved to take photos for a visual record, and that required a break in the action also. Yes, we wanted to capture that perfect sunset or that artistically framed landscape or that weird bug we had never seen before. We did all this so we could remember our experiences. But while we are trying to capture the present for future enjoyment, are we robbing ourselves of the present joy? How many times have we attended a sporting event, a celebration, a concert, or any other activity, and we are so wrapped up in taking photos that we miss the bigger picture? With cameras at our fingertips and our social media platforms competing for likes and reactions, we forget to appreciate what is right in front of us.

I am not saying we should never take the time to record and recall what we do. Heck, that's what this book is all about. But I do think we have to remember to be in the moment at times and it will be okay if you forget a conversation that would have been good material for a blog. It's okay not to capture every single second of a fiery sunset, or every meal we eat. It's okay to just be and let your soul soak up the essence of everything and everyone around you.

What in the world was happening to Shortcake and me? We were back to glamping. Two days on the trail after our zero, and we found ourselves back in the lap of hiker luxury. A little rain, and we scrambled for options to get out of the woods.

Our POD (plan of the day) was 14.7 miles. At mile 12, we were damp and had choices. We could call the local trail hostels. We could stealth camp illegally. Or we could hike in the rain up and over Mt. Prospect. The latter required a descent then a steep, slippery side trail to a shelter four miles away, getting us in about 7:00pm. The first option would have us dry and showered by 4:00pm. It was another no-brainer.

The first hostel option was full, so we settled for the Bearded Woods Hostel run by Hudson and Big Lou. Once there, we realized it wasn't a "settle for" by any chance. Wow! The place was charming and the owners so hospitable. I am glad we decided to get out of the rain. Our faith in hostels was redeemed.

Meals were served on the screened patio. The attention to detail was impeccable. Scattered Appalachian trinkets added a woodsy-trail vibe. I loved the license plates, one from each state the trail passes through.

Why is it when we have a bad experience, we tend to assume that anything else in that same field will result in the same outcome? Shortcake and I had some not-so-nice experiences at other establishments, so we avoided hostels like the plague. If we would not have bent our own rule of no more hostel stays, we would have missed this gem.

Hopefully, this would be a lesson learned for me to not be so set in my ways. It's easy for me to get a particular thing in my head and stick to it. It's difficult for me to be flexible. The trail had taught me to loosen up. Going with the flow helps to change my thinking for the better. Wish me luck on that one. Habits are hard to break.

Miles of smiles again on the trail. The day started with a fabulous breakfast at the hostel, then we were back at it for a later-than-normal start of 8:03am. Yeah, that's late for us with a 14-mile day planned. But we were rested, fed, clean, and, most importantly, dry, so all was good.

We crossed the 1,500 milestone. While we were snacking at that spot, another hiker joined us. We hadn't seen Nightcrawler since Fontana Dam. He was a funny character, loaded with ink and a quick wit. He was probably the only hiker who talked more and faster than me, and he liked cigars. I told him he looked like a bad boy. Upon first impressions, he is even a little scary—but he's all puppy dog inside.

We also met up with two other hikers, River and Single T, who we hadn't seen for a long time. Our hiking world pretty much consisted of just Shortcake, Batman, me, and occasionally B.B. So, it was a nice trail surprise to see familiar faces.

Sages Ravine was another surprise. It came at the end of the day, and its name says it all. We descended the steep green walls of the notch under the canopy of tall conifers. At the bottom, we followed a slow creek with cascades and pools. In a wetter season, I am sure it would have been perfect for a swim or soak. That wasn't the case on this day. And we were a little too tired and rushed to enjoy its full beauty.

After crossing the brook, we entered Massachusetts, our eleventh state. I really felt at home now. My four favorite professional sports teams hail from this state: the Red Sox, the Bruins, the Celtics, and the Pats.

The milestones were stacking up and the emotional roller coaster started to move. The end was in sight. Some days that seemed awesome, but other days it seemed the end was coming all too soon.

The next day was a reward for all the crap we had been through. The weather was fantastic. There were no biting insects. The views were incredible and frequent, and the hikers around us were fun. The trail offered challenging climbs with ridge walking; wooded, soft pine-needled carpet on the lows, and a touch of big walking. We never knew what was around the corner.

The only sad part was knowing we probably would not see our newest trail friends again. Kyle and Alex were two young fellows we had met a few nights prior while tenting at Caesar Campsite. They were already set up when we arrived. I was searching for the privy when I approached them as they sat comfy on their tarp. Noticing their heavy gear, which included a six-inch non-stick frying pan, I jokingly said to them, "Rookies!" I smiled and walked away.

For a few days we leapfrogged with them. Shortcake and I said they needed trail names. We just referred to them as *the boys*. When several of us hikers converged at Connecticut's highest peak, they were also there. I told them they needed a trail name. After some chit-chat and a change of conversation they referred to our first meeting and my calling them rookies. SHAZAM! Their trail name was born. From that point on, they became The Rookies.

Our last day of leapfrogging with The Rookies was sad. They were cool, and we enjoyed generational-gap differences. One of the greatest joys on the trail is meeting people from all walks of life at different stages in life going through their own set of challenges. The trail unites us all.

At the road, The Rookies left the trail. We tented close by and headed north without them the next day. It was another fabulous day to be on the trail. Nice weather and varied terrain kept our spirits high. The only challenge was finding good water sources. All the streams in the guidebook were dry except one. It emptied from a beaver pond, so I wasn't too interested in drinking it. We were able to get good water at a shelter, though. But that required a quarter-mile hike down a steep trail and then back up. It was good water, so it was well worth the trip.

The trail provided once again. This time for Stoop. Shortcake and I were taking a break after I collected the water. Another hiker came up, and we were chatting. He mentioned that he had broken one of his hiking poles he used to erect his tent. While at the shelter, I had noticed an abandoned hiking pole just lying inside. Stoop was unable to see it from his vantage point. I passed it to him and the smile on his face was priceless. You'd have thought he had just won the lottery.

Water wasn't the only challenge of the day. My personal issue was having to use the bathroom. Yup. It's something most people don't have to worry about in civilization and don't talk about either. On the trail, though, it can be a chore to use the bathroom. And bowel movements are a favorite topic of conversation. Hikers are fascinated with it.

We can't just go to the nearest bathroom and take care of business. If we are lucky, timing is right and we can hit a privy. Most times, we must dig a hole 200 feet off trail and 200 feet away from water.

A hiker's diet can be erratic, causing one's system to also be erratic. One day, it's loose stools; the next, you're plugged up tighter than a drum. The latter was my issue. I needed to go but couldn't. I tried relieving myself each time we passed a privy. But each time I made an effort, I thought I was going to blow a gasket straining so hard. So I hiked on.

With one mile left to hike, the urge came upon me so fast I said to myself, "Now is not the time!" We were in the middle of a climb. Each time I stepped up I had to use opposite muscles to keep from releasing my bowels. The challenge was harder than anything I had done to date. I knew a privy was ahead and I wanted to make it there. I did not feel like excavating a crater for the internal load I was carrying that was about to explode. But with each step up and even down, I could feel the turtling effect.

For those of you who do not know what the turtling effect is, I will explain. It's when you need to go pooh really bad and you are trying not to go, but it starts to make its way out anyway, then slips back in as you squeeze. Just like a turtle's head goes in and out of its shell. Those 1,500 miles made me stronger in more ways than I realized. Luckily, my strength prevailed. My gluteus maximus muscles proved to be great not just for climbing mountains, but also for keeping turtles in their shells. I made it to the outhouse just in time. Even on the trail, pooh happens.

Potty problems weren't the only issues I was suffering through. My phone was still giving trouble. I started with the newest iPhone at the time, but the battery life was not what it should have been. I relied on my phone for my GPS app, photos, notes, and updating my blog, none of which I could do without the device's battery rapidly losing a charge.

We had a nero day planned with Batman. He extracted us and drove us to a hotel about an hour from the trail. I needed to have an

Apple Genius look at my phone. That didn't happen, though, since I couldn't get it backed up. I just love tech problems.

If it's not one thing, it's another. The weather is too hot or it's too cold. The streams are flooded and mucky or they are dried up. The wind blows too hard or not enough to keep the bugs away. There are too many hikers, or we are lonely and haven't seen anyone for a while. We are hungry or we ate too much, or we ate the wrong thing, and our system is out of whack. On the trail, the list of our complaints exists just as it does in the synthetic world. But one thing remains constant: the trail and life will always be there.

We can keep on complaining, or we can choose to find joy in the little things, even in the challenges. Pooh happens more times than not. Sometimes it can pile up a little here and a little there, and left unchecked, it piles up high. Eventually it escapes, no matter how much we try to control the turtling. All we can do is try to find enough little things that bring us joy to overpower the pooh in our lives. The best way to do that is to not let the little irritations of life stew and fester. Deal with them before they get to the turtling phase. Because nobody likes it when pooh hits the fan.

BLACK BEAR TIP

Remember the past, plan for the future, but live in the present.

Day 142 Saturday August 12
Time: 9:30am – 3:00pm
Mile: 1541.2 – 1549.7
Miles hiked: 8.5
Tented at Berkshire Community Center
Weather: Cloudy, low humidity, nice

Day 143 Sunday August 13
Time: 7:42am – 3:15pm
Mile: 1549.7 – 1562.3
Miles hiked: 12.6
Tented at Cookie Lady's house
Weather: Cloudy start, sunny

Day 144 Monday August 14
Time: 7:18am – 4:15pm
Mile: 1562.3 – 1575.2
Miles hiked:12.9
Tented at mile 1575.2
Weather: Cloudy & nice

Day 145 Tuesday August 15
Time: 8:03am – 3:40pm
Mile: 1575.2 – 1585.9
Miles hiked: 10.7
Bunked at Bascom Lodge
Weather: Cloudy, drizzle, humid

Day 146 Wednesday August 16
Time: 6:54am – 5:11pm
Mile: 1585.9 – 1599.1
Miles hiked: 13.2
Tented at Seth Warner Shelter
Weather: Cloudy, breezy, warm

Day 147 Thursday August 17
Time: 6:54am – 3:55pm
Mile: 1599.1 – 1612.2
Miles hiked: 13.1
Tented at Melville Nauheim Shelter
Weather: Cool morning, partly sunny

Day 148 Friday August 18
Time: 5:40am – 1:25pm
Mile: 1612.2 – 1625.0
Miles hiked: 12.8
Sheltered at Kid Gore Shelter
Weather: Rain

Day 149 Saturday August 19
Time: 6:15am – 12;30pm
Mile: 1625.0 – 1633.2
Miles hiked: 8.2
Tented at Mile 1633.2
Weather: Cloudy & nice

Day 150 Sunday August 20
Time: 6:17am – 4:54pm
Mile: 1633.2 – 1650.7
Miles hiked: 17.5
Bed at Green Mountain House
Weather: Partly sunny & perfect

24

Black Bear Uncaged

We took advantage of sleeping in and breakfast at the hotel. The hour drive back to the trail combined with a late start limited the number of miles we could do. That was okay. We still had fun, and getting done early allowed us time to chill. Too often we arrived late to camp and all we had time to do was set up our tent and go to bed.

Batman had been around, helping us for the weekend, and giving us the luxury of a hotel, slackpacking, and restaurants. Since his assistance depended on the road crossings, this also meant that we were limited in how far we could go each day. That was still okay. Sometimes the short days were the best days.

Massachusetts, a.k.a. Massa-ROOTs-etts began showing us why she is called that. Each state has its own characteristics and challenges, and I think a rooty trail is the worst of those. The rocks of Pennsylvania are more tolerable than roots. The narrow woody structures interfere with balance. Their gnarly, twisted shapes swallow up feet and ankles. And if they are wet, they are as slick as oil on plastic.

The rooty snake pit of a trail didn't stop us from getting our miles in for the day; only 8.5 miles were scheduled. We liked to do between 12-14. But with two nero days in a row, we needed to pick up the pace. Katahdin wouldn't stay open, waiting for us to get there.

We ended our day at the Cookie Lady's House. She owns a working farm 100 yards from the trail. Hikers who stop by are often treated to cookies. We stopped by, and she gave us a basket of homemade treats to share. I can't eat them, but Shortcake and Batman did. With our afternoon snack devoured, Shortcake and I continued, and Batman drove ahead to meet us at the end of our day.

Our planned miles for the day carried us 3 miles past the Cookie Lady's home. Batman met us there and took us back to the farmhouse. Not only did the Cookie Lady provide tasty homemade cookies, she also allowed hikers to camp. We relaxed in her yard, cooked, and ate our trail food at her picnic table, then fell asleep in our tents.

The next day we slackpacked a few more miles before Batman needed to return home for another fun-filled work week while Shortcake and I played *real* hiker, fending for ourselves. We had enjoyed the lighter packs for three days. Then as usual, once we had our fully loaded monkeys back on our backs, we had to start the day with an incline. Lucky for us we were now fit as a fiddle and the heavy loads barely slowed us down as we glided up and over that first ascent.

We spent most of the day hiking—as we did every day. Shortcake and I didn't always talk, and sometimes we went for long durations without a word spoken. During those silent times when my brain was free to wander, I came up with some of the strangest thoughts, mostly in the form of questions. On Day 144, August 14, I gave my blog followers a break from the usual day-to-day trail update and posted those thought-provoking questions. They gave a glimpse inside my brain. Here are some of the important subjects I pondered on those silent days.

1. Can snakes move backwards?
2. Is time relative or constant?
3. Do aliens really exist?
4. What is the name of those little orange lizards with black spots? (Since there was no one to answer me, I provided my own answer: "Lizard!")

5. How many times is it normal to fart in a day? And above what number should one seek medical attention?

6. Why does it seem that coyotes like to poop on a log or rock?

7. Is it safe to drink water from a stream that has large amounts of foam if you filter it?

8. Why does poison ivy exist?

9. Why is it there are so many tent sites along the trail during the day, but none when it comes time to needing one?

10. If beer is made with wheat, barley, or hops and those ingredients are broken down into simple sugars, then the yeast eats that, is there still gluten in the beer?

11. How many medium-sized helium birthday balloons would it take to float my 35-pound pack above me as I hike?

12. If I am lying on my air mattress during a thunderstorm, am I safe from a lightning strike?

13. Are those government communication towers used to talk with aliens?

14. If deer could talk, what would they say about us humans?

15. Why is the hair on my head falling out but hair is growing uncontrollably in other places?

These are just some of the crazy thoughts that kept me entertained when nothing important was going on. I seldom walked in complete silence. Even when no one was talking or around, my mind was always flooded with noise. It was entertaining yet exhausting at the same time.

It's just as I read the humidity factor: 94 percent. That guaranteed that none of our gear would have had a chance to dry out.

Our 6:00am alarm was ignored as the rain pounding on our tents rang louder. We were not about to start the day wet. At least, I wasn't going to. But poor Shortcake was unknowingly sleeping in a puddle. She was unaware of this fact because the two inches of elevation provided by her air mattress kept her afloat, but most of her gear had been soaked.

It rained just long enough to drench the trail. The weather forecast for the day was promising, with temps in the mid-70s. A respite from the heat. Then I read the humidity factor: 94 percent. That guaranteed that none of our gear would have had a chance to dry out.

Even with the drizzly morning and soggy trail, it was a fun day of hiking. We finally had a climb over 3,000 feet, the first since leaving Virginia. Our day ended at Mt. Greylock, Massachusetts's highest peak at 3,491 feet of elevation. We rented a bunk at the Bascom Lodge near the summit.

Several other hikers stopped in for their dinner. Others continued, but for a moment, it looked like a hiker reunion as we all gathered around the picnic tables and exchanged trail tales.

While we cooked our hiker meals, the sun burned through the overcast sky just enough and, combined with a light breeze, dried our gear. Once our chores were done, Shortcake and I headed inside for a shower and clean bunks while our new hiking friends headed north to the next shelter.

Bascom Lodge provided another glamping experience as we trudged our way north. One of the joys backpacking offers is the freedom to pitch a tent almost wherever and whenever you please. But having to set up camp every single night is also one of the biggest drawbacks. When nice accommodations are available, it's a treat.

The next day began with a descent from 3,491 feet to 660 feet. I despise downhills. They are so painful for my knees and feet, and by the end of that descent—the longest one in weeks—they were screaming at me for a rest. Shortcake's feet were also hurting. She suffered in silence, but I could tell by her gait that she was aching. I also noticed she was doubling up her socks. This added extra cushion for the bottoms of her feet.

Our rest was short. Then Shortcake and I ascended back up to 2,229 feet. It was a day of big ups, big downs, and smaller PUDS thrown in to keep things interesting.

The best part of the day, though, was that we ticked off another state as we left Massachusetts and said hello to Ver-mud. I mean, Vermont. The state has rightly earned her nickname of "Vermud" because of, well, all the mud. There was a huge mud pit right at the border to welcome us in.

With every negative there is a positive. All the mud meant the ground was wetter and the water sources were more plentiful and better. The water no longer looked like ready-made iced tea.

Vermont is also known for the Green Mountains and it's obvious why. They are so lush and green, cool, and shady. Sometimes a little too much. Even on a sunny day, we walked in dark conditions.

––––––

Vermont was so close to home. Even though I enjoyed hiking the Appalachian Trail, I was missing home more and more with each step. In 2015, I don't think I was homesick. Sure, I missed everyone and my pets, but I didn't long to be home. I don't know why this time was so different. Was it because my dad was ill? Was it because I was so tired? Was it because there were too many silent-retreat days even though I was with a partner? It baffled me. But I was ready to go home, and if something happened that prevented us from finishing, I was mentally okay with that.

Before I knew it, though, I would be sad that the journey would be over. Burning the emotional candle at both ends was taking place full-flame. The time for mixed emotions had already started, and I would flip-flop with them the rest of the way to Katahdin. I needed to remember to be present in the moment. Home would be there when I returned, as well as my family and friends, God willing. But if I fretted about not being home or spent all my time catching up on the latest Facebook posts, then I wasn't being on the trail. That just didn't make any sense at all.

––––––

A new state brought on new vigor. That first full day in Vermont, I hiked ahead of Shortcake most of the day. Usually, Shortcake hiked in front, allowing her to experience sights and sounds first, since this was take two for me. But I needed to stretch my legs. The trail was pleasant and easy in terms of elevation, even though it was steadily climbing. I enjoyed hiking fast. It got my heart going and energized me. I got that natural high from the endorphins released from exercise. It's a free and a natural drug.

The little extra zip in my pace and length in my stride seemed to boost my spirits. The chemical reaction taking place helped to overcome the mental yo-yoing I was feeling. Maybe all I needed was to hike in a way that met my needs a little more. In the beginning, I was so focused on doing what I could for Shortcake's needs that I forgot to do what Black Bear needed.

I would sprint—my version of hiking faster—for a while, then stop and take a rest, allowing Shortcake to catch up. She was never far behind, sometimes less than a minute. But it was just enough exertion for me to stretch my legs and get the heart pumping. I don't know if that is what had me feeling better or if it was a coincidence, but one thing was for certain, it was a great day for me.

We arrived at Kid Gore Shelter, our destination, early enough to enjoy a leisurely evening. By 7:45pm we had completed our chores and retired to our tents. Bad weather was forecasted. We hate packing up when it's wet out, so we had an earlier than normal start planned again. Sleep was one eye-wink away, when it was rudely interrupted by several hikers arriving at the shelter.

There are always latecomers at the shelters. Most are considerate of others already asleep. Not that crew. One guy saw my food bag hanging in the shelter from the pre-strung mouse-safe lines and went wild. He was throwing obscenities and accusations so loudly the next mountaintop could hear. He couldn't believe someone would hang their food bag in a shelter and was going to remove it.

I admit, I was wrong. Food bags get hung in a tree or locked in a bear locker, not in a shelter. But to our defense, no one had been in the shelter, and it was late.

WELL, first, he didn't have to be so loud and obnoxious. Second, you don't touch another hiker's gear, and thirdly, you don't mess around with Black Bear. I am very nice most of the time. I don't get too riled up or show aggression often, and I am rarely purposely rude to others. But I noticed that as I traveled north on the Appalachian Trail, my good nature or tolerance for stupidity and inconsiderate behavior headed south.

Black Bear uncaged. I stormed out of my tent, yelling at him not to touch my food bag. My words were quite colorful, and he was taken aback by my little 5-foot-3 mighty stature. He tried to back himself up, but I let him have it with all my vocal strength. All the while, Shortcake quietly appeared and removed her pack from the shelter as silently, discreetly, and cutely as a dormouse.

Fearing he would throw my food bag into the woods, I returned to my tent with it. After my exit, he carried on about it to his friends, who seemed less amused by him. I marched myself right back up to him and let him have some more of my wrath. He was your typical know-it-all expert who has a story for everything and could not care less about what you have to say. But that night, he heard what I had to say whether he liked it or not. Not sure if it was a good thing, but it felt good to put him in his place. So much for turning my cheek. I guess I still need to work on that.

The latecomers continued their inconsiderate behavior until 10:00pm. They had no regard for the hikers trying to sleep in tents surrounding the shelter. I agree, the food bag I hung in the shelter was inappropriate and dangerous. But the guy's attitude was all wrong. If he would have politely asked for its owner to remove it, I would have done so without hesitation. But their loud conversation and pot smoking was way out of line. We all were sharing the space and its only right to keep your actions in check, especially when it's that late. Ironically, no one in the shelter hung their food bags in a tree.

Even though it had rained on us most of the day, I had a great day, knowing I didn't let them walk all over us. It wasn't the "turn the other cheek" behavior I should have chosen, but since they lacked proper etiquette, I thought I should deliver a good lesson.

Full of rage, I couldn't fall asleep. I slowly calmed myself down like I had learned to do with the onset of panic attacks. I eventually was sleepy enough to doze off.

That didn't last long. Nature had other ideas. In 2015 in the 100-Mile Wilderness, I had unknowingly set up my tent on a moose path. I was almost trampled during the night. To this day, I am still amazed the giant mammal didn't trip on my guide-line. This time, I apparently set up my tent on a turkey-trot trail. First, I heard one lone biped hop close to my abode. Then silence. Then I heard the call of a bird. Next, there was a stampede right past my tent. All I could envision were those raptors in Jurassic Park running by. My heart raced. Then silence again. Another call from the lead turkey, and then another stampede.

This went on countless times. After the second heart-fluttering alarm, it became comical. I fell asleep laughing at turkeys and stewing over what I could do in the morning as payback to the shelter crew.

I don't like to be vindictive, but they were the ones who had unleashed the Bear. I settled on playing "Good Morning," a song by Mandisa, on my phone and shining my headlamp into the shelter. I turned the volume up to max and held it up close to the shelter as I walked by. It was 5:50am. I had several other devious things I wanted to do, but my angel side prevented me from going that far.

———

We passed a few ponds, and the elevation was a gentle descent from 2,855 feet down to 2,230 feet over 8.2 miles. But the mud was horrible. Several times I thought poor Shortcake was going to lose her footwear as she misjudged her step, causing one boot to land into deeper than expected mud. "SCHMUCK!" could be heard loud and clear as she pulled herself free from the slimy sludge.

Our short day ended next to a stream where we washed our shoes then dried them in the afternoon sun. Batman met us for hiking and resupplying since it was another weekend. Gotta love Saturdays and Sundays. We were able to glamp on trail, complete with camp chairs and real food.

The next morning was cool and crisp. We started with an easy climb to the top of Stratton Mountain. The only view was from the fire tower. Shortcake and Batman conquered it. I made it up the first flight. When I rounded the landing to continue upward, the wind caught my chest and I said, "NOPE! That's high enough for me." I kept trying to climb the towers and I kept chickening out. It was cloudy anyway, so I didn't miss anything.

After our climb up and over Stratton, the rest of the day was pretty level. We were grateful, since we had 17.5 miles for the day. We only agreed to do that many miles because Batman slacked us and we were staying at Green Mountain House Hiker Hostel in Manchester Center, Vermont. Its caretaker, Duffy, is one of the nicest guys you'll meet. The place felt like home. So much so that we took a zero day.

Our week had been full of challenging terrain and boredom, loss of tempers and joys, good weather and bad. A zero day was well deserved, and Green Mountain House Hostel was the perfect place to calm our spirit, clean our bodies, and refresh everything for the next stint.

BLACK BEAR TIP

Be nice to the Bears; you never know what will uncage their fury.

Trail Log

Day 151 Monday August 21
Zero

Day 152 Tuesday August 22
Time: 7:34am – 4:54pm
Mile: 1650.7 – 1665.5
Miles hiked: 14.8
Sheltered at Lost Pond Shelter
Weather: Cloudy, evening T-storm

Day 153 Wednesday August 23
Time: 6:15am – 5:15pm
Mile: 1665.5 – 1580.4
Miles hiked: 14.9
Tented at Minerva Hinchey Shelter
Weather: Cloudy & nice

Day 154 Thursday August 24
Time: 6:15am – 9:11pm
Mile: 1680.4 – 1700.8
Miles hiked: 20.4
Tented at Rutland, VT
Weather: Partly cloudy, cooler, needed a
layer when stopped

Day 155 Friday August 25
Time: 7:40am – 5:20pm
Mile: 1700.8 – 1715.3
Miles hiked: 14.5
Tented at Chateauguay Rd
Weather: Nice

Day 156 Saturday August 26
Time: 6:16am – 5:00pm
Mile: 1715.3 – 1730.7
Miles hiked: 15.4
Element Hotel in Lebanon
Weather: Nice

Day 157 Sunday August 27
Time: 7:34am – 5:45pm
Mile: 1730.7 – 1748.4
Miles hiked: 17.7
Hotel Element Lebanon
Weather: Perfect & cooler

Day 158 Monday August 28

Time: 10:01am – 2:16pm
Mile: 1748.4 – 1756.0
Miles hiked: 7.6
Element Hotel Lebanon
Weather: Perfect & cooler

Day 159 Tuesday August 29
Time: 7:20am – 5:20pm
Mile: 1756.0 – 1770.9
Miles hiked 14.9
Tented at Smarts Mt. Campsite
Weather: Cloudy & cool

25

The Missing Days

So, where's the eclipse? We were supposed to see it. I always miss astrological events. The last one I remember seeing was when I was in elementary school in the 70s. I surprise myself that I can remember that far back. Shortcake and I were on a zero day and Google informed me an eclipse was to take place. Nothing happened. All we saw was sunshine all day. Go figure.

Our zero day flew by, just like always. If we weren't chasing the calendar to get to Katahdin, I would have preferred to stay another day to rest. But when we received reports from other hiker friends up ahead saying that it was 37 degrees on Mt. Washington, extra zeros were a luxury we couldn't afford. We'd had good food, good friends, and rest. That had to curb our desires for another week to ten days. Besides, too much time at an awesome hostel might make it too hard to get back to the trail.

The end was in clearer view though. Nothing could keep us from reaching our goal, not even the comforts and hospitality offered by Duffy at the Green Mountain House. There will always be obstacles on the way to our goals. Those obstacles aren't always bad things either. They can be anything that keeps us from reaching whatever it is we are striving for. In my case, I had to decide if I wanted the accomplishment of doing two complete A.T. thru-hikes or if I wanted to rest and relax more. All I knew was I hadn't come that far, through that much suck, to quit. I could rest later. There was still more to see and more to do with Shortcake and Batman.

————

As much as we wanted to chill at the hostel, we didn't. But it was a good thing we had a zero day. It gave us a chance to rest up for a day of peak bagging. We left the hostel fully loaded and climbed up and over four different mountains in under fifteen miles. We flew over Bromley, Styles, Peru, and our favorite of the day, Baker Peak. Baker was the lowest at only 2,635 feet elevation, but it offered the best view after we scaled its ledgy spine. It was a perfect spot to rest before our final 2-mile push to the shelter.

We decided to stay in the shelter due to the forecasted thunderstorms. Thunderstorms had chased us from Georgia to Maine and didn't seem to want to leave us alone. When we arrived at the shelter, two young section hikers were hanging out and playing cards. They were new graduates from college. Smarties, a mathematician and a premed student. Soon after our arrival, a young couple hiking south joined us. It was a tight squeeze, but we made do.

I waited to set up my gear until they set up theirs. I like to sleep with my head at the opposite end of others. Germs, eweee. That didn't last long. The young girl's feet smelled horrible. I couldn't handle it, even after she stuffed them inside her sleeping bag. So I flipped around and kept my face toward Shortcake's. I never have good experiences in shelters, but I keep trying. It's insanity to do the same thing expecting different results.

The storm came just as we finished dinner. Great timing again. It didn't last long. I was glad. I was worried for the group of college orientation students tenting nearby. We all survived the night and were ready to take on the trail by morning.

Jennifer, a writer friend, lost 23,000 words of a manuscript she was working on when Word deleted it. When I heard that, my heart sank; losing what you worked so hard to compose is a writer's worst nightmare, even more so than receiving rejection letters. I couldn't imagine what she was going through. Luckily, she was able to restore back to a previous version, so not all was lost.

I too had been laboring on my own writing that I had neglected. Weeks had passed since I last worked on this memoir. I jumped back in, picking up my notes to continue crafting this book.

As I hiked, I took loads of photos, I kept a small field-guide paper journal with bullet notes, I wrote scribbled notes in my paper guidebook, and I kept a detailed blog. When I immersed myself back into my writing, I discovered ten days were missing from my blog. That's when I truly knew what my friend Jennifer was going through. In my blog posts, I had elaborated on my bullet notes and scribbles. But I couldn't account for ten days of my hike except with what existed in photos and hen-scratching.

As I deciphered my field guide, trying desperately to recall the sights, sounds, smells, and feelings of those missing days, my anxiety began to rise like yeast in a ball of dough. I felt discouragement seep in and start to rob me of the joy I get from writing. I quickly snapped out of my doom and gloom and pushed that discouragement back. I told myself, "I got this!"

There are forces beyond our control that want to steal the joy from our hearts. They want us to feel unworthy. They want us to fail. They want us to give up. They want us to stop using our talents for good. Most of the time those forces are masked as discouragement, defeat, or some unsurmountable obstacle. But when we recognize that we can control how we respond to those negative situations, we can overcome them and succeed at what it is we want to accomplish.

We can't do this alone, though. We might think we can, but when we put our trust in the Lord, it will be much easier to do. He gives us our talents, but His adversaries try to strip us of the joy in using those gifts for good, and they will pull out all the stops to keep us on a dark and unlit path. If we let discouragement push out the good and fill us with despair, we're helping those adversaries.

The route we initially mapped out might change, but we will still be able to get to our destination. Jennifer needed to add a little more time to her route. I eliminated a few details from mine, and you will need to alter your journey from time to time. But the story will continue as long as we keep moving forward.

My photo library, bullet notes, and scribbles in my guidebook tell a monotonous tale spanning 120 miles over ten days. We climbed mountains, we tented, we stayed at a hotel, I slept terrible, the weather was cooling off with each step north. We saw interesting and weird sights in the woods. We met nice hikers. We met rude hikers. Batman met us. We slacked. We crossed into New Hampshire, our 13th state. We did a 20-miler. Shortcake received a care package that lifted her spirits. My notes detailed nothing and only sparked vague memories of those missing days.

I pored over my notes several times, trying to refresh those ten days. I was ready to give up. I decided to take a break. When I came back, I scanned my blog posts and discovered they were out of order. Rejoicing that my detailed posts had been recovered, I began reading them to fill in the blanks for this chapter. But guess what? Very little lit up in my brain.

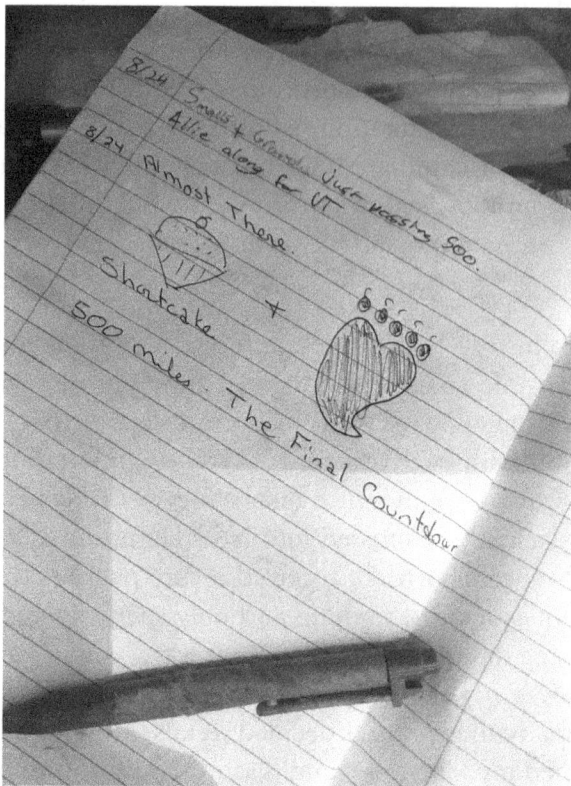

Usually when I review all my notes, read my blog post, and match that up with the photos I took that day, all my senses collide and I am right back on the trail, remembering every twig, root, memory, and feeling. But not this time. Those ten daily posts could have stayed lost, because they did little to spark my memory of the hike.

But they did ignite the pain. Two bullet points from my notebook shot straight through my heart. No notes, photos, or blog post reminders were needed to bring me back to that point in time.

* Bruce called. Dad is in the hospital
* Called Becky. Dad had a heart attack

Then as I read the missing blog post, scantly recalling the details of that section, one paragraph snapped me right back to that day on the trail as quickly as Jeannie nodded her head to move from one place to another in *I Dream of Jeannie*.

I stopped to check cell service since down below I had none and wanted to let Batman know we were good. When I checked my messages, I had one from home informing me about my dad's health. I spent several minutes talking with my family. It was really hard being so far from home with Dad having such health challenges. He has damage to his heart and another heart attack was not what he needed. The only thing that helped me was as always, prayer and knowing what good hands he is in with my sister Becky and brother Buddy. With the news of Dad, I hiked on, barely remembering the miles under my boots.

BLACK BEAR TIP

Use fear, discouragement, defeat, and other obstacles as stepping stones to better and greater things.

Day 160 Wednesday August 30
Time: 6:5am – 5:30pm
Mile: 1770.9 – 1783.8
Miles hiked: 12.9
Tented at Ore Hill Campsite
Weather: Perfect, sunny, blue sky

Day 161 Thursday August 31
Time: 6:11am – 7:26pm
Mile: 1783.8 – 1800.4
Miles hiked: 16.6
Tented inside woods at NH-112
Weather: Cloudy & cool

Day 162 Friday September 1
Time: 10:45am – 5:10pm
Mile: 1800.4 – 1807.9
Miles hiked: 7.5
Tented at Eliza Brook Shelter
Weather: Cloudy & cool

Day 163 Saturday September 2
Time: 7:05am – 5:16pm
Mile: 1807.9 – 1816.7
Miles hiked: 8.8
Hampton Inn
Weather: Cold windy start, ended warm & sunny

Day 164 Sunday September 3
Zero

26

Bad News

New Hampshire treated us kindly with sunny, clear skies and temps perfect for hiking. We had nothing to complain about. The rugged trail kept our attention on the path, but too often my mind wandered to Maine. Not just because that was our destination, but that was where Dad was. I was his little girl—a 51-year-old little girl—and he was my rock. We fought like bighorn mountain sheep, each one just as hard-headed as the other, but we were just right for each other. We were each other's biggest fan and would also put each other in their place as needed.

Our relationship was much like the trail in New Hampshire, long descents, tough climbs with spectacular views. Just like the day we climbed Smarts Mountain. We went down, then we went right back up Cube Mountain, with views wide and far. Mountain peaks after mountain peaks looked like never-ending waves on the ocean.

We had trail magic. The first was from Jane. She was waiting to pick up her son and his friend who were also hiking, and she decided to hand out food and beverages as she sat at the trailhead. Lucky us.

Hikers we saw earlier in the day told us about Carl, the omelet guy, who set up a kitchen in the woods right on the A.T. and was making any sized omelet a hiker desired.

The record was a 30-egger. Shortcake and I each had an omelet ten times smaller than the record. We arrived at 4:30pm and he shut down at 5:00pm. We just made it. Earlier, I didn't think we were going to. I contemplated going ahead to snag a couple egg creations for Shortcake and myself. But I didn't want to leave her for my own selfish reasons. I chose to hike like we usually did. Then, we not only made it in time to have omelets, we also had the trail magic I mentioned earlier. Things always work out, especially when decisions are made with the heart.

———

We entered the White Mountains on Day 161 of our hike with an ascent of Mt. Moosilauke.

With 360-degree views, it was our first big climb since the South. It is a tough climb and should be memorable. I do remember the climb from 2015 and my notes for 2017 say that Shortcake and I were bad asses, doing 16.6 miles that included a 3,500-foot climb over Moosilauke at 4,800 feet and then a descent to 1,870 feet. My notes claim,

> It was incredible!!! Again, our initial plan was to stop south of the summit at a shelter. At noon we arrived there and decided since it was so nice and early, we would push up and over Mt. Moosilauke. In order to do it though I needed to cook some lunch.
>
> We were stretching our food and I was out of snacks. The only food I had left in my bag required cooking. Since I hike slightly faster, Shortcake set out after she consumed her calorie-deficient lunch. Mine wasn't much better, but it's all we had. Once I was done, I followed her up the trail, eventually catching up to her over an hour later. We weren't sure if we were crazy fools or just bad asses. Only time would tell. We figured the worst-

case scenario was that we'd arrive at the other shelter by 7:00pm. Plenty of time to set up camp, eat, and get to bed before dark.

Huh, we didn't figure in all the possible factors like, overcrowding. We climbed the beastly peak in the wind and cold and made it to our goal, only to find the shelter full. No room in the inn or surrounding area to tent for us. Thank goodness we had hiked the distance by 5:00pm. Two hours better than our worst case. That gave us plenty of time to hike the 1.6 miles to the road and hope to stealth on flatter ground. So we thought.

It was a grueling 1.6 miles of treacherous rocky descent that took us two and half hours to complete. We did safely arrive at a tent site. But we had to set up with our headlamps. We were tired, exhausted, and felt an overwhelming feeling of accomplishment.

We learned today that it is so important to have a plan A, a plan B and even a plan C. It doesn't mean you are copping out or being soft. It's a sign of having smarts. Sometimes there is a time for craziness, sometimes for being a bad ass, and other times maybe just a time to rest. Tonight, we were bad asses!

One thing I do recall about that day is the descent and where we tented. That stands out as memorable. The other thing I remember is when Bruce called me. No trail names to lighten the spirit.

"Em, you need to call home."

I remember the soft ground of the trail. I remember the pain in my sister's voice when I called her, letting me know that Dad wasn't doing well, but not to worry, he *should* be okay. I remember letting Sharon know what was going on but trying to play it cool. We couldn't go home; we were so close to the finish line. But my dad was dying, and I was on the trail.

In 2015, I was prepared for this. I even had a chat with Dad before I left. We agreed, if something should happen to him while I was hiking, I would stay on trail in fear that if I returned home, I wouldn't go back and complete my hike. He wanted my success as much as I did. We joked that if he did die, he wouldn't know if I was at his funeral or not. My siblings would know and would kill me if I didn't come home, but he wouldn't know. Now, that joke was too real.

I was torn. I had already done a successful thru-hike. I had nothing to prove. I wanted to go home but I didn't want to fail Sharon.

After our bad-ass summit and descent of Mt. Moosilauke, Short-cake and I decided to shut off our usual 5:30am alarm and sleep in. I didn't even remember the last time on trail we had done so. It was a cool, quiet night making sleep easy after such a hard workout, and it felt nice to lie in my cozy sleeping bag without the worry of having to get up and out for an early start.

We had low miles planned. We knew we would be pushing our limits to go for another big day after what we had done the day before. On some days, single digits were enough. Low miles don't mean easy, though. Mt. Wolf was in our way, and she was no joke. Everyone talks about the big summits, but sometimes it's the overlooked ones that give the most trouble. It was a cloudy, cool hike that felt longer than our marathon descent the day before. Being the troopers we were, we did what needed to be done without complaints.

We set up camp and chatted with fellow hikers as the temps dropped. After supper, we all retired early to our own tents to rest up for the big climb of South and North Kinsman Mountains. Every day now held a challenging climb and sub-double-digit mileage became the norm. But with those climbs, our work was rewarded with incredible views. I looked forward to those climbs. The work was half the fun. It's in the times of challenge that we grow, and with each step forward and up, I felt my strength grow as well as my confidence. Not only was that rewarding, but the best part of all was that the harder I worked, the more I got to eat.

Our luck at hitting popular destinations on a Saturday was terrible. I think the whole world was climbing up the mountain while we were trying to get off it. If time were more on our side, I would have avoided all popular destinations on weekends and holidays.

We worked hard to get to the top of South Kinsman. With the summit to ourselves, we indulged in the grandeur of the view. It was amazing. The mountain profiles rolled into the distance like storm waves across an endless ocean as the semi-hazy horizon blended the faint peaks into the emptiness of the sky.

We enjoyed a quick snack while the wind whipped and whirled, cooling us to the point we needed to add an extra layer of warmth. With snacks consumed, we headed toward the north peak. As we did so, we passed multiple hikers on their way up. We were dressed in layers, and they were scantily clad in shorts and tank tops. Oh, did they have a surprise waiting for them.

There were so many hikers. All I wanted to do was get off the mountain and out of the woods. Hiking on a Saturday is bad enough. Combine that with a Labor Day Saturday, and it was more than I could handle. We spent most of our time in the woods, seeing very few people, and then, SHAZAM!—instant crowd overload because it's a holiday weekend.

Everything was too overwhelming. I was secretly in pain for so many reasons, from my feet and legs—a new symptom that was disrupting my sleep more and more—to wondering why Shortcake would go silent, to worrying about my dad. In photos from those days, I seemed happy, but I can tell there was a hollowness behind my eyes where joy once filled.

———

Batman hiked in to meet us. He was the only day hiker I was glad to see.

We hiked out not a second too soon, and he whisked us away to town. We decided since bad weather was forecasted, we'd finally take a much needed zero.

The crowded mountain should have been a telltale sign for us. The holiday weekend with bad weather made it impossible for us to lock down a last-minute reservation. We had to drive over an hour from the trail to find accommodations. We finally secured a room and were soon settled in for the night.

We were not thrilled to have to travel so far from the trail to find a room and to have to take an unplanned zero due to weather, with the clock ticking and weather changing. Fall was approaching and so was Baxter's closure date. But things always seem to work out, even though in the midst of trying times we don't have the vision to see the full picture.

Because of those issues, I was in cell service and received contact from home that my dad was still not doing well. He was still in the hospital from his health issues a couple weeks before, and my siblings thought I should come home. There is a time to hike and a time to tend to priorities. So that's what we did. Shortcake, Batman, and I packed up our gear and headed north to Maine.

BLACK BEAR TIP

Always have a backup plan.

Days 165 – 177
Sunday September 4 – Saturday September 16
Zeroed in Maine

27

Dad

When I received news about Dad's condition, it was too late to drive the five hours home. The three of us decided to sleep at the hotel rather than risk a dark, rainy drive through the mountains and backwoods. Not knowing what was in store for the next several days, I asked Shortcake if she wanted to stay on the trail and I would meet up with her on the trail after I went home. She decided to take a hiatus and go to Maine with Batman and me.

I don't remember much of the drive. It was my time to be silent. I was trail exhausted for all the reasons mentioned in previous chapters. Even with Sonny's visit from heaven to encourage me and the fact we were now in New Hampshire and soon to enter Maine—the most spectacular part of the trail—I was worn out. Now I had the fear of what state I would find Dad in.

The car rolled past fields and forests just beginning to show the change of seasons. In between bouts of deep sleep and being jostled awake by the vehicle's movement, my mind raced with horrible flashbacks of when my mom had died 24 years earlier.

It was a normal day, brisk, but a nice February day in Maine. I don't remember the date without looking at a calendar, but I do know it was Ash Wednesday. For Christians, it is a holy day of prayer and fasting, marking the first day of Lent—the season of penitence before Easter.

I was teaching at the time. Bruce was working in Guam. My mom was scheduled to have a lung biopsy. She had something growing in her good lung. She was in remission from lung cancer, but her healthy lung decided to be a Petri dish for some unknown growth. I was running behind and put off calling her to wish her luck.

As I drove up the interstate to school, I passed an iconic stand of white birch and recalled all the times we had passed those trees headed home from whatever place we went to. Mom loved those trees. Wishing I had taken the time to call her—we didn't have cell phones back then—I reassured myself she would be fine, and I would pop over to see her after work.

I was in the middle of Physical Education class when a co-worker entered the gym to inform me I had a phone call. I didn't think much of it, even though it was during class. Usually, the secretary took messages and gave them to us after class. But when I heard my uncle's voice on the other end, I drew a blank. Why was Uncle Buster calling me at work? He has never called me. Then he asked if I could pick up my sister and sister-in-law and bring them to the hospital.

I don't know if I was in shock or denial, but the three of us drove the 45 minutes to St. Joseph Hospital, talking and wondering what was wrong. I don't know if they *knew,* but I certainly didn't know the full situation. My uncle hadn't given any details. He just asked me to gather my sisters and come down.

My aunt and uncle met us at the elevator and led the way to my mom's room. Deep in my heart, I knew it wasn't good, but since no one had said anything yet, I was hoping for some sort of life. What I saw when I entered the room dropped me to the floor.

There she lay on the hospital bed with the side rails up. In my horror, I flippantly thought to myself, *Why does she need those? She isn't going anyplace.* One arm untucked from the sheet, slightly leaning away from her as her palm lay lifeless open to the ceiling as if she were reaching for some invisible hand. She was ashen gray, and multiple tubes protruded from her mouth and seemed to be choking her instead of providing life-sustaining support. Other family members were around her bed, just staring as we walked into the room.

I couldn't handle what I saw. I fell to the floor crying. My father picked me up, but instead of consoling me, he gripped me firmly and told me to get a hold of myself. I choked back vomit. There was my mom—dead! And I wasn't allowed to cry? This was not the time to be the infantry First Sergeant-father who raised me. I needed a tender hand, but none was given. I didn't even consider what he was going through until years later, looking back. He too probably wanted to implode but couldn't, for his kids' sake.

Why didn't I call? I didn't get to say good-bye. I didn't even get to know her. There were seven of us kids. I don't recall much of what I was like in my younger years, but as a teen, well, I was terrible. Mom and I fought often, all my fault. Looking back, she was awesome. As a young, newly married woman, I was just beginning to love her for the amazing woman she was. But now that relationship was cut off at the knees. How could I go on? Why didn't someone prepare us for what we were going to see? Why wasn't I allowed to cry?

Dad was at Eastern Maine Medical Center, thankfully a different hospital than the one where Mom had died. It was on the way home, so we were able to go there first. I was scared out of my mind as we approached the parking lot and entered the front lobby, even though this time my family had updated me on his condition. All I could picture was my mom and how she lay with tubes and wires sticking out of her.

Sharon initially was going to stay in the vehicle, thinking this was a family moment. I assured her she was family and my dad loved her dearly too and would want to see her. The three of us entered his room, and as we did, Dad looked up. He was sitting on his bed. I did not cry this time, but Dad did. He sobbed when he saw us, but not for his condition and not because he was happy to see us—he was. I don't remember everything he muttered through snot bubbling from his nose, but I do remember he said, "You two need to go back and finish the hike!" Looking at me, he added, "You need to help Sharon reach the end."

Dad was our biggest cheerleader and enjoyed following our journey. He kept a map of our progress and looked forward to my phone calls home to tell of the latest trail happenings. When he saw us, he was so afraid we would not go back and finish. We had to promise him we would do just that.

―――

Dad had always hated hospitals. I think they reminded him too much of being in a MASH while serving in the Army. He needed to spend the night to stabilize, and if his numbers were still good in the morning, they would release him. And they were. My brother and sister brought him home late the next morning.

Shortcake, Batman, and I spent our morning at home doing what we always do on a zero day, tending to hiking chores such as laundry, food, and gear checking. Since we were home, I decided to switch out whatever I could with warmer choices.

We spent the afternoon visiting Dad at his house, just a few miles away. Then we returned home to make our plans to return to the trail. Dad was in great spirits and seemed to have dodged the invitation to go be with Mom. We decided to head back to New Hampshire to step back into the Whites for more hiking adventure and honor our promise to Dad to finish what we started.

Shortcake had been great. She tagged along with me off trail while I tended to family affairs, knowing each day we zeroed delayed our journey to Katahdin even more and possibly made it more complicated.

If there is one thing I've learned, things happen for a reason. I am just glad the weather drove us out of the woods. If not, we would have been on a stretch of trail that would have been impossible to easily escape from. I did not want to take the chance of not being able to say good-bye this time. But all seemed well; we got to see Dad, and we got to rest.

―――

My phone rang. It was late. I was half dazed and not completely aware of where I was—long-distance hiking does that to a person. Sleeping in a different spot almost every night can be confusing. My brother, on the other end of the call, asked me to come up to his house.

He and my sister share our childhood home with our dad. From that call until eleven days later, my timeline and details are a mystery. All that remains is a general sense of what went on, who did what and where, with a few scenes burned into my memory.

When I arrived, Dad was sitting in his bedroom chair as restless as a student who'd been caught cheating and was waiting outside the principal's office. I stroked his hair and hugged him gently to help soothe his nerves. He argued and pleaded with us about going to the hospital. He finally conceded, and we called the ambulance. Amber, red, and golden lights cut through the darkness in the driveway as we led the first responders through the old Victorian home.

I had never seen Dad so frantic. So scared. His eyes were worried. He tried to be strong but failed as his nervousness spilled out as tears. My strong dad, the infantry First Sergeant of 20 years who insisted we be strong in every aspect of our lives, was crumbling with every breath he took.

My sister climbed in the ambulance to accompany Dad on the short 8-mile trip to our local hospital. My brother and I followed. Once there, he was admitted, and we began making phone calls to the rest of our siblings, who all showed up at different times. All but our oldest brother, who was in New Hampshire with his wife who was having double knee replacement. When it rains it pours.

A battery of tests was done, and more tests. Then wait. Wait. Wait. And wait some more. My siblings and I took turns being with Dad. We all wanted to be in there with him, but the room was small, and we didn't want to overwhelm him or get in the way of the staff.

Finally! Results! Another heart attack! Years ago, Dad had bypass surgery and recovered well. At times, one wouldn't even know he had heart issues. But in January before this hike, Dad's heart was slowly failing as he suffered from several minor infarctions. He was in great shape for his age, and his body was strong and able to recover from each one. But this time his meds could not keep up with all the little heart attacks that currently plagued him. The doctor informed him they could prescribe more meds to help lessen the chance of another one.

I don't remember who Dad told first, that is irrelevant, but he let us know he was tired. He was tired of taking meds. He was tired of not feeling well. He was tired of being out of breath. He was tired of being tired. But most of all, he said he was tired of being without Mom.

He requested all medication be stopped. The doctors and nurses explained to him over and over what that meant. He would die. They explained it to us. We knew. But it was Dad's call, not ours. And when he made that choice, a peace fell over him. When it was my turn to be with him, as tears filled his eyes again, he looked at me and said, "I just want to go home. I don't want to die here."

<hr />

My sister and I consulted with the physician to see if we could take him home, but the doctor said the tussling for transport would be too much and he wouldn't make it the few miles to his house. We didn't let Dad know this. We comforted him and told him we would see what we could do about getting him home, and he never asked again.

All medication was stopped except for an IV drip to administer pain meds as he wished, and he was moved from the ER to a room that had an adjoining private room for family to gather. "Comfort-care" is what they call it. A gentle term that means the waiting period before you die. We asked the cold question, "How long does he have?" The standard response was given: "Two days to two weeks. Everyone is different." I hoped for the latter. I wasn't ready to lose my last parent.

Calls were made to more family and friends, and over the next week, the doors to his room revolved with visitors coming to say good-bye to a great man. He wasn't perfect. He had some big issues, but he was still a great man. He was able to say good-bye and so were all of us. It was hard knowing that any second he would be gone; but at the same time, it was beautiful.

Stories once forgotten were retold. A broken family came together, even if only briefly. Pain filled the hearts of those around, but laughter also cut in as tales from the past lightened the mood. Dad said he saw Mom, and later he saw Jesus. We knew he was toggling between this world and the other. It was a cloudy day, and at one moment Dad lifted his hand toward the window. His eyes were streaked red with lines of anguish. We thought he was reaching for heaven. But instead, he barely mumbled something about bombs.

You see, my dad was a Vietnam and Korean veteran, and he NEV-ER talked about the war. He buried those memories. But on his dying bed, decades from the battlefield, some escaped. The clouds in the sky reminded him of the war. He thought he was being bombed. My heart ached. We all knew Dad suffered immensely in silence when he came back from the wars. I was too little to know anything, but growing up, we all knew not to ask about his tours.

We will never know what we ask our men and women to endure when we send them off from the safety of our shores to unknown territories to do God knows what. There is no medicine to cure what takes place there, and there is no potion to hide the pain; and no matter how hard the person works to stuff it away, it eventually surfaces.

———

The nursing staff, trained to tell when life is about to end, let us know it would be soon. We all gathered around his bed. As much as he wanted to be in the arms of his loving wife at the feet of our Lord, he fought to the very end. His heart weak from attacks, his body scarred from seen and unseen battles, he lay still in his bed as his chest heaved for the last time. That's when my whole world changed.

BLACK BEAR TIP

Love your family and friends with all your heart
and tell them daily that you love them.

Trail Log

Day 178 Sunday September 17
Time: 2:41pm – 5:45pm
Mile: 1816.7 – 1819.4
Miles hiked: 2.7
Tented at Liberty Springs Campsite
Weather: Cloudy & hot

Day 179 Monday September 18
Time: 7:05am – 5:25pm
Mile: 1819.4 – 1827.0
Miles hiked: 7.6
Tented at Garfield Shelter & Tent Site
Weather: Cloudy & warm

Day 180 Tuesday September 19
Time: 6:15am – 6:30am
Mile: 1827.0 – 1836.8
Miles hiked: 9.8
Stealthed after Zealand Hut
Weather: Partly cloudy, humid & warm

Day 181 Wednesday September 20
Time: 6:15am – 11:30am
Mile: 1836.8 – 1844.5
Miles hiked: 7.7
Tented near mile 1844.5
Weather: Cloudy & warm, beautiful fall
day

Day 182 Thursday September 21
Time: 6:00am – 2:30pm
Mile: 1844.5 – 1850.8
Miles hiked: 6.3
Tented Mizpah / Nauman Campsite
Weather: Mostly cloudy

Day 183 Friday September 22
Time: 3:49am – 5:35pm
Mile: 1850.8 – 1862.6
Miles hiked: 11.8
Madison Hut
Weather: Sunny

Day 184 Saturday September 23
Time: 8:00am – 5:40pm
Mile: 1862.6 – 1870.4
Miles hiked: 7.8
Rented a Ski Condo in Attitash, NH
Weather: Sunny & warm, 80s

28

Life Goes On

We spent another week at home, doing what families do when a loved one dies. Shortcake was there by my side the whole way. Most of the time she was in the background, house-sitting, pet-sitting, doing dishes, or anything else that needed to be done while our family gathered the pieces and planned the funeral. She never once fretted about getting back to the trail.

On September 17, we climbed into the car and headed back to Franconia Notch, New Hampshire, where Batman had extracted us that rainy evening. With the long drive back, we didn't step foot on the trail that day until 2:41pm. We hiked a short 2.7 miles. But in the Whites, less than three miles is still a workout, especially after two weeks off.

Saying good-bye to my dad had been agonizing. I knew he was in a better place, a place of freedom—free from pain, free from loneliness, free from heartaches, free from stress, free from disease, and free from wars a lifetime ago that haunted him till he died. But that thought didn't fill the emptiness within me. Tears randomly flooded my eyes and overflowed down my face as we hiked, reigniting the pain caused by his absence.

Despite my sadness though, it was nice to be back on trail. The leaves were beginning their colorful transformation, and the evening air no longer held the day's humidity. The trail was tough, rocky, and steep. Its difficulty helped to keep my mind off losing Dad. At least I didn't have to be alone in my tent that first night back in the woods. Batman hiked in with us.

I looked forward to finishing our journey, and I was glad it was fall. It's my favorite time of year, and I expected our passage through New Hampshire and Maine to be just beautiful.

The 2.7-mile hike the day before was more than just a warm-up back to the trail. Reentry into some of New Hampshire's toughest terrain and several days without hiking did a number on our daily mileage average. We were content with 7.6 miles on our first full day back.

I love the ruggedness of the trail. Pushing myself to do difficult things is a high for me. The harder, the better. Sometimes I pay for it in the end, but during the challenge, I soar. I may not be fast and agile, but I feel great doing it. It's during times of stretching ourselves when we see growth, no matter in what area of life we are pushing ourselves.

I soared mentally and physically over 4,000- and 5,000plus-footers which included Mounts Liberty Springs (4,283), Little Haystack (4,800), Lincoln (5,089), Layfayette (5,263), and Garfield (4,458).

My emotions and feet navigated the rocky terrain. If it wasn't for the challenge of the trail keeping me focused on the task at hand, I would have been a sobbing fool. I was completely engrossed in the hike, and my feelings were flip-flopping from one extreme to the other as the trail allowed.

I finally snapped out of another one of my pity parties when I realized Shortcake was hurting too. Our two-week hiatus had been more of a break than she bargained for. I could tell something was not quite right, so I asked how she was doing (as I did most days). She isn't like me; I wear my feelings and ailments on my sleeve. One never has to wonder what's going on in my world. It's usually obvious. I'm an open book most of the time. Not Shortcake. She's locked tighter than Fort Knox. But that day, she confessed, "My lower half feels like it is in a coma." I can usually pick up on subtle cues, but that day I was so wrapped up in my own pain of losing Dad I hadn't noticed earlier how much discomfort my friend was in. My heartache was more than I could have ever imagined. Once I got my focus off me and projected onto Shortcake, I felt a relief. My pain seemed minor.

It's funny how that works. We get into our own little situations big or small and they seem to drown us in misery. But as soon as we look outside of our tears and put that energy toward another person with love, our pain subsides and even vanishes for a while. It's so much easier to wallow in our own self-pity, but it's more rewarding and less painful if we can rise above that to reach out to help another. It doesn't make our pain go away; it'll still be there, but it doesn't seem to hurt as much. God designed us this way. Second Corinthians 1:4-5 tells us God encourages us so we may be able to encourage others, because in His divine wisdom, He knew that when we do so, our own afflictions are lifted.

The muscle memory in our legs sprang back nicely. The New Hampshire terrain was a challenge, and our bodies felt it, but we carried on as if we hadn't even stopped. What we were most grateful for was the unseasonably pleasant fall weather.

It was much warmer than we had expected, and we were not complaining. We gladly sweated through our layers. While home, we had switched out our summer-weight clothing for our winter gear. It was mid-September in New England, which meant weather could be as temperamental as a two-year old, and we would be hiking at elevations seldom below 2,000 feet. Who knew it would be unseasonably warm in the White Mountains of New Hampshire in September?

While our legs adjusted fine to life back on the trail, the miles of long, steep descents had my feet screaming and begging for rests more frequently than normal. It was my turn for sore feet. I just kept reminding myself I was having fun.

Batman hiked south to meet us. I so cherished the fact that he had vacation and could hike along with us. At times, he would hike in with us and camp, then the next morning hike back out to leapfrog the Batmobile ahead and hike in from the other direction. It was so reassuring to see his smiling face greeting us. We also knew that meant the end of the day was close at hand.

No tears for Dad on Day 180, despite that I couldn't stop singing the song "You Raise Me Up" by Celtic Women, one of Dad's favorite songs. It's a beautiful piece that brings peace to my heart and usually tears, even on a good day. But maybe that's why my eyes were dry instead of stinging wet. The lyrics helped me remember the good, which helped ease the pain.

Another reason the floodgates closed that day was that I tried not to cry. It was a chore to focus on the positive, but it was worth the effort. When I started to dwell on the negatives of Dad's passing, my spirits would dip. So I tried to remember the good times. In fact, I started thinking of one new item each day about Dad that I was grateful for, and when a negative thought tried to enter my brain, I'd think of what I was grateful for to take its place. I learned quickly that replacing the bad thoughts with good thoughts was a better way to get through this difficult time.

Another bright and early start. A 5:00am wake-up call is not what Shortcake preferred, but in order to accomplish our daily mileage goals we often had to do things we didn't necessarily want to do. Me, well, I love mornings! I can't wait to see what the day has in store for me, whether it's out in the woods, at home, or at work. Pair a great morning with my hubby and nice weather, and the excitement to emerge from my tent early was made even easier.

Even if the night is filled with sleeplessness, mornings are still a gift not to be wasted. Getting up early is just one way to get the most out of that gift. And the trail's treasure the next day was a gentle, smooth, and practically incline-free walk.

Even the final descent into Crawford Notch was nothing to complain about. It didn't get any easier than that in New Hampshire.

Our early morning start and easy trail guaranteed an early arrival at our destination. This gave us time to hang out at the AMC (Appalachian Mountain Club) lodge to finalize our traverse of the Presidential Range. It was a warm, beautiful, sunny day but we preferred the comforts of being inside, sitting at a table.

Once our plans were finalized and reservations made for Madison Hut, we left the coziness of the lodge's lounge and headed back to the trail. We needed one more quick stop at a gift shop just up the road to feast on ice cream. We never passed up an opportunity for such novel treats. Despite our small size, Shortcake and I could pack away the food.

The AMC and gift shop were only a short distance from the trailhead. It wasn't long until we were back to hiking mode. We decided instead of cranking out a few more miles we would camp just off the road, saving the climb of Webster Cliffs for the morning. Good weather was in the forecast, and I knew from my 2015 hike that a challenging trail with great views was ahead. We didn't want to miss any of it due to a setting sun.

The only drawback of rising before the sun was that we needed to go to bed early. But that didn't happen. Shortcake, Batman, and I weren't ready for bed until just before the sun dipped behind the mountain peak, clothing us in darkness. Our headlamps guided our last chores as each one of us finished our nightly routines.

The early morning start again involved the use of our headlamps. It was beginning to be the norm. Early fall meant fewer daylight hours available for hiking. The sun woke up shortly after we had boots on the trail and before the trail turned tricky. It wasn't long before we could tuck our lights away and enjoy the rugged climb of Webster Cliffs, on Mt. Webster.

We completed a mere 6.3 miles in 8.5 hours. The only way to describe our pace that day was slow. I am not sure if it was due to the challenging trail or because there was so much to photograph. Either way, it made for a long day, even if we did finish by early afternoon.

The views along Webster Cliffs and Mt. Jackson were stunning. We even glimpsed the notorious Mt. Washington. As we climbed, the trail offered views below, and we watched our vehicle become smaller and smaller. Eventually we could no longer see it as we hiked on. We instead gazed on the view in front of us, letting that view pull us forward to the next day's hike—The Presidential Range.

The never-ending panoramas, though, were not my favorite sighting. It was the alpine bog. It amazes me that a mud pit can exist at such elevations. We were grateful for the planks that carried us over the three-foot-deep mudholes. They were even dry from the drought. I probably would have lost my pole if it had been a rainy spell.

We arrived at Mizpah Hut just in time to receive offerings of leftover soup—all we could eat. With the purchase of our thru-hiker punch card, we could have one free soup and one baked good at any of the huts. We were thrilled when the caretaker offered us unlimited quantities.

We weren't spending the night in the hut. Instead, we were camping on the tent platforms close by. The huts are pricey and not a luxury we could afford to do more than once. We were saving that splurge for after our traverse of the tallest mountain in New England, where some of the world's worst weather has been recorded.

Bedtime was scheduled even sooner. We had most of the Presidential Range to traverse, an 11.8-mile hike with most of it above tree line and mostly above 5,000 feet. Mt. Washington is halfway across, at 6,288 feet. We started early, very early.

———

Heading out under the cover of darkness, we thought there wouldn't be much to slow us down in the camera department. We were wrong. The stars were bountiful as they twinkled above, and the glow of our headlamps created new ways to view nature. Our cameras were on overdrive.

Hiking above tree line in the darkness was eerie and exhilarating at the same time. Even though we could not see the openness, we could feel the vastness. After we'd hiked two hours in the dark, the soft glow of the sun started to carve shapes into the horizon. The dark silhouettes morphed from black giants in the distance to gray, artistic sculptures blanketed in a pink glow.

As the sun rose above the mountains, it turned into a golden ball that blinded us if we so much as dared to look in its direction. Every second the scene changed, like a chameleon moving across varied terrain. It took us a long time to hike with the morning sun. The brilliant light show captivated us, slowing us down as we attempted to record every different hue that presented itself over the horizon. That was one morning worth the very early start.

We reached the midpoint of our hike before the tourists flooded Mt. Washington. It was busy, but not crazy. We snapped our summit photos, had a break at the welcome center, then headed for Madison Hut, almost 6 more miles away.

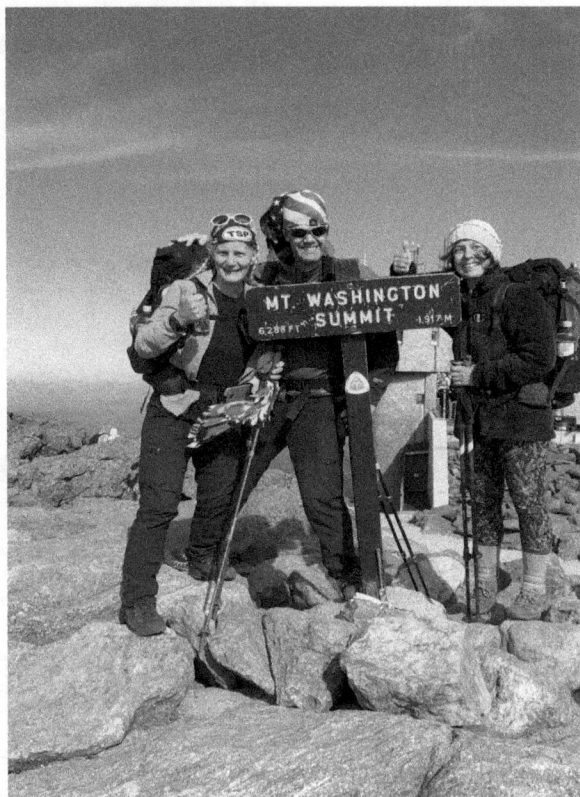

Soon after we left Mt. Washington, Shortcake's feet told her they had had enough! The only problem was, we weren't done. We had no choice but to continue. Like a trooper, she kept hiking one painful step at a time. We had to get to Madison Hut. We had reservations which were nonrefundable, and at $140 per person, with no place to camp above tree line, we had no choice but to hike on. That we did.

Eventually we sent Batman ahead to let the hut know we were definitely coming. We didn't want them to let the other guests eat our portions of dinner. We always had our guts' best interests as a priority.

My knees joined in the pain party along with Shortcake's. The hut, a mere dot at Mt. Madison's base, finally came into sight below us.

An oasis, teasing us with how close she appeared to be compared to the distance we actually still had to traverse. A half hour later, we both limped into the hut.

Thirteen and a half hours of pure rock torture! Hikers who complain about the rocks in Pennsylvania clearly have never hiked in New England. But in New England, you are rewarded with open mountaintops that have views stretching as far as one can imagine.

So, I exaggerated a little. Yes, the rocks were numerous and a little tiresome, but with the right attitude, they can be fun. Just like anything. You can dwell on the hard or you can focus on the fun. I chose fun. The rocks make a giant jungle gym, and the trail was my playground. But thirteen miles of them can be daunting. Even with the difficulty, it was a nice change from the closed-in forest. I enjoyed gliding over them as we hiked on.

The hours added up, and we didn't have too many miles to show for the time we had spent on the trail. Our lack of progress wasn't only due to the rocks; it was also because of our endless photo shoot.

We wasted no time claiming our bunks as we removed the burdens of our packs and rested before dinner. With a warm meal in our bellies and a roof over our heads, our pain waned, at least mine did. Shortcake was quiet again, so my guess was that she still hurt.

It was a gloriously exhausting yet rewarding day. We safely and victoriously traversed most of the Presidentials in one day, taking the time to enjoy its many profiles. We were blessed with clear skies and warm weather, something not every hiker gets to experience on those summits. It was one of those days we thought would never end. Our strength and courage grew a little greater that day.

––––––

Wow! What a first week back on trail. It was hard, but you don't get views like we had unless you work for them. And that we did! With the summit of Mt. Madison, the White Mountains—the Presidentials of New Hampshire—would be done. We successfully and painfully completed them on Day 184, Saturday, September 23. Those mountains were one of my biggest concerns returning to the trail. Weather can have an attitude in that region, and I wasn't looking forward to having a quarrel. Our late start getting to the trail in March while we waited for the screening of *Walking Home*, then going home to see it, and then a two-week hiatus to say good-bye to Dad had us hiking in the fall when weather in New England at its best is even more unpredictable.

We skipped our pre-sunrise awakening the next morning since we had a roof over our head and someone else cooking breakfast. Our stomachs dictated our actions on most days, and that day was one of them. Capturing a sunrise on top of Madison would have been glorious, but we settled for views through the windows of the hut.

I had my fill of oatmeal loaded with nuts, dried fruit, and brown sugar. It was a treat, and I didn't have to filter extra water to cook or clean. That's why we happily paid the big bucks to stay there.

With our tummies full, packs packed, and good weather forecasted, we headed up to summit Mt. Madison. In 2015, Madison was my favorite Presidential peak. Unlike Washington, it was quiet. That wasn't the case in 2017. It was another Saturday, and people were out taking advantage of the incredible fall weather.

The climb up involved half a mile of rock scrambling from Madison Hut to the peak, short in distance but not in the time it took to hike it. I thrive on terrain like that. I am not as quick as I once was, but it was still a thrill for me, and with over 3,800 miles of backpacking under my boots, my fear of heights was lessening.

After we enjoyed a brief stay at the crowded summit, we headed down one of the rockiest descents above tree line on the whole Appalachian Trail, excluding Katahdin. Batman took off ahead. He was much stronger and faster than Shortcake and me. He arrived at Pinkham Notch long before us, giving him time to hitch a ride back to Crawford Notch to fetch our vehicle.

The Presidentials may have been done, but the challenges continued. A zero day would have been wonderful, but no time for that. The Wildcats were next. In 2015, I was relieved to have successfully and safely traversed the Presidential Range only to be slapped in the face by the Wildcats. Neither myself nor my hiking buddies, Maps and Moxie, had heard any mention of the Wildcats and their difficulty. They knocked us on our butts. I was looking forward to them this time. They may have been hard, but they were also amazing.

BLACK BEAR TIP

Share your highs and lows, because when joys are shared, they are multiplied, and when pain is shared, it is divided.

Day 185 Sunday September 24
Time: 8:18am – 4:40pm
Mile: 1870.4 – 1876.3
Miles hiked: 5.9
Stayed at Carter Hut
Weather: Incredibly awesome

Day 186 Monday September 25
Time: 7:00am – 4:40pm
Mile: 1876.3 – 1883.5
Miles hiked: 7.2
Tented at Imp Shelter and Tent Site
Weather: Cloudy & hot

Day 187 Tuesday September 26
Time: 6:00am – 1:40pm
Mile: 1883.5 – 1891.6
Miles hiked: 8.1
Hotel in Gorham, NH
Weather: Hot & hot

Day 188 Wednesday September 27
Time: 6:15am – 5:12pm
Mile: 1891.6 – 1903.3
Miles hiked: 11.7
Stayed in Gentian Shelter
Weather: Hot, 90s & sunny

Day 189 Thursday September 28
Time: 6:13am – 5:18pm
Mile: 1903.3 – 1912.9
Miles hiked: 9.6
Tented in Goose Shelter
Weather: Sunny & hot

29

Good-Bye New Hampshire, Hello Maine

After hiking ahead of us leaving Mt. Madison, Batman had scored big time in finding us a room. It wasn't any run-of-the-mill motel or hotel. It was some kind of condo/time share/resort. We had a three-bedroom, two-bath crib spread out on three levels. The only drawback was that we didn't have enough time to enjoy all the amenities.

We needed to finish New Hampshire, and in order to do that, we had to tackle the Wildcats. Most hikers talk smack about how hard the Presidentials are, and you hear very little of the Wildcats. But in my opinion, they are way more aggressive than anything else on the A.T. I don't know if that was because by the time we reached them, we were exhausted from all the other miles, or because they really were that difficult.

Batman hiked across the feline-named peaks with us, from Wildcat E through Wildcat A, with the exception of Wildcat B, since the A.T. didn't summit that peak. He needed to head back out to leapfrog the car again. Batman sure did earn his trail name.

From one of the peaks, a tiny, hazy ridgeline could be detected if you squinted and used your imagination a tad. It was Maine—about a four- or five-day hike away. Woo-hoo!

After Batman left, Shortcake and I made a .9-mile treacherous rocky descent waaayyy down to a pond below where we would spend the night. We were hoping for a work-for-stay at the last hut in New Hampshire.

The huts in New Hampshire are self-sustained, fully-operated bunkhouses with running water and electricity. The cost is pricey due to the nature of what it takes to operate them. It's a hiker's luxury to be able to stay at such a place while hiking in such remote areas. Each night the huts offer a few lucky thru-hikers an opportunity to do a work-for-stay.

We asked if there was a possibility for Shortcake and me to do chores in exchange for sleeping on the floor. Our hearts sank when the caretaker said no. But without even taking a break, he added that no work was needed but we could still sleep inside. We were lucky to be able to stay at Carter Hut free—as a no-work work-for-stay.

Our emotions roller-coasted just like the terrain we covered that day. They sank low when he said no, then skyrocketed when he finished his sentence with a yes. We were thrilled! We found tasks to do anyway. We washed dishes and wiped down the tables. It was the best night's sleep I had in quite some time.

The climb out of Carter Hut was just as steep as the descent ending the previous day, and the rest of the day was filled with rocky ups and downs as well. Hiking was all the trickier as the humidity settled on the rocks, making them one slippery step away from an injury. At least the thunderstorms that were predicted never formed. That probably would have been terrifying.

Another day with less than ten miles. It's normal to have your miles shortened when you reach New Hampshire and Maine, due to the difficult terrain. It's to be expected. But with our setback of going home for two weeks, the calendar was slipping away, and our short-mileage days worried me. We needed to finish on time. Baxter State Park, home to Katahdin in Maine, the northern terminus of the Appalachian Trail, closes October 15. It was September 25, and based on my 2015 schedule, we were behind the eight ball, and it was all my fault.

Somewhere soon we need to make up miles. That was extremely stressful for me. I worried about the logistics a little too much, and Shortcake didn't seem to worry about them enough. Somewhere we needed to meet in the middle.

The nice benefit of low miles, though, was that sometimes we arrived early, which meant, hopefully, more rest. On those rare occasions when we were not hiking from sun-up to sun-down, I liked to rest in my home away from home and do nothing.

I love to take naps, and I so looked forward to being able to nap midday some place along the trail. That never happened in 2015, and so far, it hadn't taken place for me yet in 2017. At our speed, there was no time for extended breaks if we wanted to reach our goal. Just like zero days, naps were a luxury we could no longer afford. They would have to wait until I got home or until *Happy Hiking: Third Time is a Charm*.

Gorham, New Hampshire, is a quaint, hiker-friendly town. It has just what trail folk need without being overly crowded. There are hostels, several motels, eateries, and resupply stores. We chose a room at the Royalty Inn instead of a hostel. By this time, I had enough of sharing sleeping quarters and bathrooms with strangers. I preferred my own space.

Batman was with us again. He wanted to cross into Maine. He wasn't able to do it on my first thru-hike due to a last-minute change of plans. When we reached Grafton Notch in Maine, he would hike back to retrieve our car once again.

The hike out of Gorham was a 3,000-foot descent over six miles. The last two miles were sweet, which meant most of the down was squeezed into four miles. The end may have been a cakewalk, but the morning was not. I was tired and sore. To make matters worse, the numbness in my hand and arm had grown worse. It used to trouble me only at night, interrupting my sleep. Since the hike out from Madison, the numbness had been happening during the day to the point that I was unable to grip my pole. I hoped it was just an overuse injury and would eventually heal once we were off trail. Until then, I rested it as much as I could by using only one stick.

Despite my increasing ailments and the hole left in my heart from Dad's passing, I still found joy on the trail. I saw it every day. Sometimes it was in the smells, sometimes in the trail's character, other times in the animals, sights, and people. On this day, it was the sky, a mixed palate of colors.

Shortcake had one more birthday greeting to find and send. This time it was for her brother-in-law, Jay. Earlier in the hike, she had found a mylar birthday balloon caught on a branch, and she snapped a photo to send to her sister. She had artfully created birthday wishes from food and other items to send to each of her boys on their birth dates. This time, the trail provided the medium again for her artistry. This time, with rocks. She spelled out Jay's name and snapped the photo to send later. When she was done, I changed the *a* in *Jay* to *o* and spelled *joy*.

For late September, the weather was wonderful, even at times a little too hot. The views were stunning, and the trail continued to strengthen us. It was easy to forget about my pain when the surroundings were so beautiful. And even if the aches cried out louder, I still counted it all joy.

———

We finally had our first easy day since entering New Hampshire. First, we climbed Mt. Hayes at only 2,555 feet, then down a little, then back up to Cascade Mountain at 2,642 feet. Our bodies were conditioned, and it was just another day in the park.

The heat was not as forgiving. It was in the 90s. Enough already! It was fall. Where were the cool, crisp temperatures? Water was scarce, which made the day even more difficult. We were in conservation mode and running slightly dehydrated.

We stayed inside the shelter that night. We usually tented, but with the soaring temps and not a soul in sight, we decided to spread out instead of spending a sweltering night in our enclosed and airless cocoons. The shelter had a rare view overlooking the valley. We fell asleep to the pastel colors of a sunset framed by wispy clouds and accented with an almost-full moon, dreaming of Maine, our fourteenth and last state—only 4.7 miles away.

———

New Hampshire ushered us out gracefully with one last summit, Mt. Success, a fitting name for our accomplishments. It was a windy undertaking, with sweeping views. We were beyond ecstatic to reach the Maine border.

The huge milestone—thirteen states down, one to go—called for a celebration. We invited Captain Morgan to the festivities at the border sign, along with cookies, gluten-free of course.

New Hampshire gave us a run for our boots that we survived and recovered from, thanks to a nice exit. Then Maine met us at her door-step with a huge entrance fee. She didn't fool around. If one wanted access, they had to earn it. She was rough. She was tough. And she was rugged right from the get-go, with steep climbs involving hand scrambles, iron rebar holds, and one very long log ladder that seemed to reach heaven.

And let's not forget the dipping temperatures. I had to ask for it the day before, didn't I? We went from the 90s to temps forecasted to dip below freezing at night. Welcome to Maine. It was amazing!

But we made it. Shortcake and I were finally in Maine. There was nothing to stop us now except maybe our own death. We were not the same persons who set foot on the trail so many months ago. We were hardened and softened in so many ways. Our bodies were strong, but we were tired. We were preferring to sleep indoors rather than on the ground. But our wills were still strong. Our friendship grew and slipped and grew some more. We were worn, yet we still yearned for those last miles that would eventually bring us to Katahdin—our goal. There were still almost 300 miles to go, but those seemed insignificant to what we had already done. It was just a matter of continuing to move forward, one mile at a time.

BLACK BEAR TIP

Count it all joy.

Trail Log

Day 190 Friday September 29
Time: 6:11am – 7:00pm
Mile: 1912.9 – 1922.6
Miles hiked: 9.7
Tented at Grafton Notch
Weather: Below freezing start, overcast,
cool

Day 191 Saturday September 30
Time: 6:18am – 3:31pm
Mile: 1922.6 – 1932.9
Miles hiked: 10.3
Tented at East B Hill Road
Weather: Sunny & cool - perfect

Day 192 Sunday October 1
Time: 6:11am – 3:30am
Mile: 1932.9 – 1943.0
Miles hiked: 10.1
Tented at South Arm Road
Weather: Cool start, warm ending

Day 193 Monday October 2
Time: 6:05am – 6:00pm
Mile: 1943.0 – 1956.4
Miles hiked: 13.4
Tented just after Route17
Weather: Crispy morning, warm,
beautiful fall day

Day 194 Tuesday October 3
Time: 6:15am – 5:00pm
Mile: 1956.4 – 1971.2
Miles hiked: 14.8
Tented in Piazza Shelter
Weather: Cold start, clear blue skies,
cool

Day 195 Wednesday October 4
Time: 6:17am – 4:00pm
Mile: 1971.2 – 1982.9
Miles hiked: 11.7
Tented on old road next to Oberton
Stream
Weather: Hot &windy

Day 196 Thursday October 5
Time: 6:22am – 3:34pm
Mile: 1982.9 – 1994.3
Miles hiked: 11.4
Tented at Crocker Cirque Campsite
Weather: Awesome - sunny and cool

30

Cat Fight

Always be careful what you wish for. For two days we had been dying in the heat and were begging for cooler temps. We got them. Details are important though—with my request, I had forgotten to specify my temperature preference.

In life we often want this or that, and when we receive it or achieve it, we wonder why we ever wanted it in the first place. Grass is seldom greener on the other side of the fence; it only looks that way. Once you step over the fence to grab the lushness of what you thought was better, you realize it was just the light tricking you. It's not long before you come to your senses and then appreciate what you had.

In my case, it was the warm weather. According to the calendar, it was early fall; but fall usually comes earlier to New England than to the rest of the east coast. It's my favorite time of year, when the air is supposed to be fresh and crisp with low humidity, making it perfect conditions for hiking. We had sent our summer gear home, but we had been having unseasonably warm and even hot days. We were suffering through the heat. I pleaded for cooler temps.

Overnights and the first hour or two in the mornings were much cooler. That made for great sleeping. But to go from the 90s to below freezing in 24 hours was a shock. We needed to change our routine slightly to compensate for the fall temps we were asking for on those

90-degree days. We got what we wanted, but did it have to be so drastic?

———

The cooler temps were much appreciated as we traversed the *funnest* (I know that isn't a word, but it is *funner* to use) mile on the whole Appalachian Trail. The iconic section at mile 1914.5 to 1915.6 (in 2017) is known as Mahoosuc Notch. It is deemed the most difficult or most fun mile on the Appalachian Trail. It's all in your perspective.

In the Notch, hikers must navigate over, under, and around huge boulders that have fallen or were carved out when the ravine was formed. It took us two hours and fifty-eight minutes to traverse this one mile of pure hiker misery or heaven. I loved it. It was a giant jungle gym for this little monkey. Shortcake even seemed to enjoy it. Such obstacles were even more of a challenge for her.

After we made it through safely, Batman hiked out ahead of us. Hiking wasn't the only chore for him. He needed to hitch a ride from Grafton State Park back to Gorham, New Hampshire, to retrieve our car. Then return to Grafton, where Shortcake and I would be waiting for him. Payback is going to be hard when Batman decides it's his turn to adventure and I will be the support.

Shortcake and I arrived at the trailhead just as the sun set. We set up our tents and had supper. It was well after dark before Batman arrived with the car and our resupply for the next stretch. Once we gathered from the Batmobile what we needed, we all retired for the evening. Another day done.

Maine was so pretty! I am not sure if it was my favorite state because it's home, because it was the last state of our hike, or because it was just truly amazing! It was lush and green. The woods varied from evergreens to deciduous and a mixture where the stands met. The path meandered through a green tunnel then played peekaboo with the sky as hikers climbed to a summit. Once above tree line, hikers basked in the sun, close to heaven, as they hiked. Maine's peaks were breathtaking. No matter which direction we looked, we were almost guaranteed to see a body of water or several bodies of water, endless trees, and far-off peaks to be climbed. What we seldom saw were signs of civilization.

Leaving a summit, hikers started their descent playing peekaboo again before they disappeared back into the forest. Even the trail itself varied from carpeted with soft pine needles and other fir tree spills to rocks that put Pennsylvania to shame, mud pits that rivaled Vermont, and roots that resembled snake pits that must have overflowed from Massachusetts. The climbs seemed to go on and on, and the drops were bottomless.

Maine was hard work on its own, but doing it after hiking New Hampshire was exhausting. I felt like I aged 20 years. My body ached all over. But we kept going.

It was easy for me to forget about all the yuck. The unseasonably hot weather. The grueling effort we were putting in day in and day out. My broken heart. The loneliness of hiking with my dear friend who was so withdrawn. None of that mattered when I was surrounded by all the beauty of the Maine wilderness.

I loved all that Maine had to offer, but the summits were most amazing. It could get a tad claustrophobic in the forest, so when we reached the openness of a peak, we stretched out and took it all in. Unfortunately, we spent little time at the top. It was either too cold or too windy. Down south we were chased off open balds by incoming storms. Up north, it was too cold—I had to ask for it, didn't I? Or it was too windy. At least there were no bugs.

———

Batman wasn't with us when we departed from Grafton Notch. He needed to leapfrog the vehicle to meet us at the end of the day. That meant we could slackpack. Woo-hoo! We loved that. We hadn't had a day off since returning to the trail after Dad's death three weeks before. The next best thing to a zero day is a slackpacking day.

When we reached Andover's East B Hill Road at the end of our day, Batman shuttled us into the sleepy little town for a hot meal at The Little Red Hen. The diner had exceptional food, and it was our lucky day. Timing had us there on Saturday for their AYCE Italian buffet. Afterward, we headed back to our tents at the trailhead for another brisk night in the Maine woods.

There are so many reasons to love October. One of my favorites is the fresh air. It's not stuffy, yet not so cold the lungs ache. That cool October air also creates a fog over bodies of water that is hypnotizing to watch.

Another reason I enjoy October is because of the clear blue skies so often seen that time of year. It's the perfect backdrop for nature's beauty. Even a dead tree has character when set against the vast emptiness of the blue canvas. It's a gentle reminder that even in death there is beauty.

The first day of October was a primo start to my favorite month. There was nothing negative about the day. The morning was cool and refreshing with a gentle climb. The trail was blanketed in crispy, crunchy leaves reminding me of when I was a child and we'd play in them.

It also had me thinking of Dad. Not so much in pain at his loss but rather gratefulness for the dad I had. Fall was our time together, whether he was taking me to the field to kick around soccer balls on a Sunday afternoon after church or going to a soccer game to watch me play or going to camp to sight our rifles for the upcoming deer season and shoot a bird or two. I'd be lying if I said there were no tears, but being back on the trail at that time of year was also very healing for me.

––––––

In the afternoon we had a tough, steep, and rocky climb. Thank goodness we were slackpacking. But as I have said before, I love the hard stuff too. In many spots, the ascent was aided by wonderfully crafted stone steps, ladders, and rebar rungs.

The nicest surprise of the day was a picnic table. None of the campsites or shelters we stayed at in New Hampshire or Maine so far had a picnic table. It was true rustic camping. At a campsite in the middle of nowhere, we came across a table. Unfortunately, we had just had our break 150 yards back. That seemed to be typical of trail life, though. We would hike and hike, hoping to find a nice spot to stop and eventually gave up, settling for something less desirable. Then after our break, we'd hike a little bit farther and voilà, there would be the best place.

How many times does that happen in real life? We desire something but lose patience and settle for something less because we don't have the strength, willpower, faith, or compelling reason to hold out. Sometimes there is no choice, or the circumstances really do prevent us from continuing, but it's those other times when we give up and don't persevere that cause regret. Holding out for a better resting spot isn't a deal-breaker, but next time I feel like stopping an activity, project, or assignment because *I don't feel like it*, I'll think twice and push on. I hope you do also.

––––––

We were able to slackpack another day. We loved doing that. It is a totally different experience hiking with an empty pack compared to hiking with a 37-pound monkey on your back. Serious thru-hikers who consider themselves purists think slackpacking is cheating, just like yellow blazing, skipping parts of the trail. I think those people secretly wish they had a Batman of their own.

For me, if your feet connect with the ground from Springer Mountain, Georgia, to Katahdin, Maine, following the designated Appalachian Trail for that year, then you are a thru-hiker, end of debate. It doesn't matter if your pack weighs ounces or mega pounds. I do feel if you skip a spot, yellow blaze, aqua blaze, or anything besides white blaze, then you are not a traditional thru-hiker, the key word being *traditional*. There is nothing wrong with taking alternate routes if that's what you want to do.

Everyone experiences the trail in their own way. It was just a pet peeve when I'd hear hikers say they hiked the A.T., then find out they skipped a large section because it was too hard, or they skipped a set of mountains because it was too cold. My favorite excuse was, "I jumped ahead to be with my bubble because I couldn't keep up."

There is no prize or reward for thru-hiking. But there is the satisfaction and pride that goes with completing something that only 25 percent of the people who attempt it accomplish. And someone saying they thru-hiked the trail when they didn't negates the effort of those who did. Just saying.

———

October 2 was another incredible fall day. It was a roller-coaster kind of day, but the hike was not too hard. We had a little bit of everything. There were ups, downs, hardwoods, primitive mossy evergreens, exposed rocky ledge peaks, and closed-in forests. Batman leapfrogged ahead and hiked back in to meet us as he usually did. This time he brought bad news. Nothing horrible, though.

He had forgotten to record his vacation request in the books, so he was scheduled for an out-of-town meeting. That meant we had to change our plans on the fly. After a quick meltdown, I gathered my wits. Oh well, sometimes plans change. I have learned to roll with it out there. Life is too short to worry about what you can't control. Being flexible is way less stressful.

We enjoyed our slackpacking while we had it. Shortcake and I would be left to our own devices. We could handle it; after all, we were now very accomplished thru-hikers. Sure, we loved the conveniences of modern amenities, but we were also quite at home without them in the wild. Life was grand.

————

We were enjoying the hike. It was a 13.4-mile day, and I knew what was coming at the end. It's not always good to know what's up ahead, and this was one of those times. I wished it was dark. I kept it to myself. I didn't want to burden Shortcake. It wasn't terrible; I just knew the ending climb was steep and difficult. It wasn't dangerous or scary either, just hard and long.

Some things are better left unshared. Shortcake soon found out for herself. We both were glad to reach Route 17 and the car. It was in a large parking lot with a scenic view overlooking the Rangeley lakes region—a spot called Height of Land.

Once there, we had just enough time to resupply from the Batmobile, hike a mile farther to a stealth site, and set up our tents by sunset. Another long yet successful day on the Appalachian Trail.

We had big miles planned, compared to recent days. It was nice to build our daily average back up. Even with full packs, we hiked the easy-peasy terrain with less strain and completing more miles. Yes, we needed to enjoy ourselves but we also wanted to get 'er done. That's a poor attitude to have for such an amazing journey, but I was so tired emotionally and physically. I assumed Shortcake felt the same, but I wasn't sure—she wasn't sharing her feelings. To be honest, I didn't share my thoughts about just wanting it done, either.

Based on what I did in 2015 compared to our current hiking strength, I estimated our summit date to be October 20—17 days away. We were starting to get requests from friends asking to join us. We were secretly glad it didn't work out. Having friends who were not seasoned backpackers tag along would have thrown a wrench into our mojo. We were barely hanging on ourselves. For quite some time, it had been just the three of us. We had lost any hiking bubble we had, which wasn't much. Most others had hiked far ahead or had flip-flopped. There were only a few other hikers we had seen consistently who were still out there. At that point in the game, we were fine with just our trio.

Maine never seems to get old. I've lived there all my life, well, since I was 4. I don't remember anyplace else. I never tire of its beauty. On Day 194, we passed lots of ponds. At one, about mid-morning, the vibrant sun danced on the water's ripples like diamonds on a trampoline. It took me forever to hike the shoreline. I was enveloped by its performance. I could have called it a day and stayed there in the quietness of the shore, captivated by the jewels shimmering on the surface. But Katahdin was calling.

Then at day's end as we were heading to the shelter, there was a solo leaf lying on a plank. Void of its normal chlorophyll, it revealed the hidden hues of tangerine and rust. It was as if someone had put it there as a welcome mat.

There is so much beauty in the world and most of the time we are too busy to notice it. Sometimes it's huge, like a sunrise or sunset; and other times, it's small as a lonely leaf. But no matter the size, it is there for us to enjoy if we just take the time. Since my two thru-hikes, I have embraced that short saying, *Enjoy the Little Things*. We seldom have grandiose happenings, but if we look for them, there are little things all around us everywhere and every day. And a ton of little things can add up to a big thing.

It was another lovely hike in Maine. The morning started out warmer than the past few. It was a sweat-through-your-clothes kind of day, then we'd freeze when we stopped because the wind stripped any warmth we generated. That meant lots of time spent adding and removing layers, depending on the intensity of the hike.

It was another one of those tedious tasks we performed. Dress warm to start, or dress cool and tough it out until the heart produces an internal furnace. I didn't like to tough it out, so I dressed warm in the morning; then about fifteen minutes into the hike, I needed to begin the de-layering process. On a warm day like that day, I shed clothes soon. But it was gusty all day, so the layers went back on when we took our breaks. I coined the term in 2015 for this action: *the runway fashion show of hiking*.

Saddleback Mountain, The Horn, and Saddleback Junior were on the day's agenda.

It was spectacular. We were above tree line for most of the day, dipping in and out of the evergreens as we traversed the peaks. The open ledge walking of Maine's mountains is so enjoyable. It's almost like being on pavement. Not that I want it to be asphalt; it's just that the smoother surface allows me to concentrate less on where I place my feet, which allows me to look around. There is always something interesting to see when I don't have to look at where my feet are landing.

Such as a UFO. Oh, it was just a weird cloud.

I was having a great time. The weather was amazing for fall hiking. No bugs and no rain. I hiked in front. I usually took the back and let Shortcake lead, but I needed to stretch my legs. All the tough ascents had my quads and hamstrings tightening. At least once a week or so, I'd take the front. It gave me a chance to lengthen my stride, since my gait was a little bit longer than Shortcake's. It hurt me to modify my hiking style for too long. So I was lead dog for a while, but I always kept her in eye or ear range—so I thought.

Most of the day, Shortcake was extra quiet. This wasn't unusual, but I sensed something was different. When we stopped for breaks, I tried striking up conversations. Words from her were short and to the point and kind of rude, with no explanation. So I let her be. I just figured she needed quiet time and didn't need an annoying, chatty friend trying to fix things.

So I continued the routine of hiking slightly ahead, then resting. Shortcake would show up shortly after, sometimes less than a minute after I stopped. I was never that far ahead. Few words were spoken, but not because of a lack of trying on my part. Most of the time we sat in silence, together but alone.

After a morning of being ignored, I did hike on for the rest of the afternoon. I figured if I was going to be *alone*, I might as well be alone. That way I could enjoy the day without wondering what was wrong, what I had done or not done. I tried asking what was up, but got no answer. I was tired of being ignored and not knowing why. I never wanted the trip to be over as much as I wanted it done at that very moment! Hiking ahead was not the right thing to do, but I did it anyway. I needed to get right in my mind before I said something that I couldn't take back, and I didn't want to ruin our friendship over one bad day.

I arrived at the day's destination by 4:00pm. It was a wonderful flat spot on an old leaf-littered woods road next to a stream. I relaxed and scoped out the setting, taking in the fresh fall air and the accomplishment of a hard hike on one of Maine's beautiful, iconic sections.

My tent was almost erected when Shortcake arrived. I was so glad to see her. Even though I was a tad perturbed by her earlier behavior, I was still worried. It had been almost an hour before she finally showed up. I was anxious to see how she was doing, hoping the alone time had done her some good as it had for me.

Since I was feeling great physically, I wanted to assist with her day's-end chores. She'd been acting differently since that morning, and since she wasn't sharing her reasons, my only thought was that she was tired and sore and could use a helping hand.

I started toward the trail where she was exiting, and she was livid! She did not want to speak with me. I wasn't going to take the silent treatment any longer. When I tried to explain my side all she did was yell, **"No, NO, NO!"**

She was so upset with me because I had hiked ahead. Sure, that wasn't the best thing to do, but I tried several times to talk with her and find out what was wrong. I had chosen to hike on rather than blowing up.

Instead of staying and talking things out, she hiked on. I had no idea where or how far she went. She made it perfectly clear she wanted to be left alone.

I was flabbergasted! A wonderful day of hiking was tainted by a lack of communication. Earlier in the day, she had not shared with me what was bothering her. That frustrated me. Then my hiking ahead and not expressing my feelings sent her overboard.

After I finished setting up my tent, I sat down and cried until I was too exhausted to cry any more. I didn't know what to do. Should I pack up and meet her? But it was getting dark. Should I text her? But there was no service. Would she be okay? Little did she know this was the section where Inchworm, a hiker in 2014, went missing and her remains were found two years later.

Would I be okay if I went after her? I chose to stay put. In case I didn't catch up to her, I didn't want to be setting up in the dark alone. So I sat there in my tent, trying to fall asleep and worrying about my friend as more tears streamed down my face. I cried for Shortcake. I cried for my dad. I cried for my family; I missed my boys so much. I wanted Batman back. I cried because I wanted to quit. Tears and snot soaked my sleeping bag as I cried myself to sleep.

The next morning I set out alone, wondering when I'd meet up with Shortcake. Sleep had been nonexistent; I couldn't stop worrying about my friend. I had mixed emotions. I was scared for her well-being, and I was mad she had separated. That wasn't wise for either her safety or mine.

Mixed emotions can be very draining. It's confusing. I was glad an hour or so into the hike when I saw her fresh wet footprint on a board along with a dry tent spot. Then I only had to expend energy on one emotion, anger. I fumed until I caught up to her. I noticed her up ahead, but I was too stubborn to let her know I was there. I stopped before I thought she saw me.

We were about to climb, and I didn't want to deal with our issue while trying to tackle a 700-foot incline. Once Shortcake was out of sight, I continued. I caught up to her taking a break at the summit of Lone Mountain. I had to chuckle to myself when I saw the name of the summit—it was fitting for the situation.

We hashed out our disagreement, but I didn't feel Shortcake was over being upset. At least, we talked. Communication is so important to healthy relationships. My friends are too important to me for any animosity or grudges. I was thankful that we talked some more at our next break, and just like that, all was good.

Summiting Sugarloaf, a popular ski resort, was not on the agenda for the day. We were thrilled the trail side-skirted the peak. The trail had been easy all day even though it was mostly uphill. When we arrived at the junction of the Appalachian Trail and the trail to the summit of Sugarloaf, the path to the mountain peak went abruptly up. It looked like a rocky nightmare. With smiles on our faces and happy feet we continued on the A.T. without giving Sugarloaf peak a second thought.

The day's hike ended with an impressive descent to South Branch Carrabassett River. The names of Maine's lakes, ponds, roads, and summits can be so confusing. I think every river has a South Branch, East Branch, North Branch, and West Branch name. Then many of the peaks have something similar, such as the Goose Eyes. And there are too many Trout Ponds and No Name Ponds to keep track of. But this day, I only had to remember South Branch for the Carrabassett River. The trail down was steep and exposed to the valley below. At times the cliff to our left was completely bare of trees as the trail carved its way to the river below.

We arrived at our campsite early enough to enjoy some down time. After our chores were done, the chilly air drove us inside our tents. Just as we were often driven off summits by weather, we were often driven into our tents by weather or bugs.

We didn't mind. We both were tired. The early morning starts combined with nineteen straight days of hiking and an emotional explosion were wearing on us. But we pushed on.

BLACK BEAR TIP

Communicate. Communicate early. Communicate politely.
Communicate lovingly. Communicate often.

Trail Log

Day 197 Friday October 6
Time: 7:15am – 7:15pm
Mile: 1994.3 – 2006.7
Miles hiked: 12.4
Tented at Horn's Pond Lean-to
Weather: Slight drizzle, cloudy, cool

Day 198 Saturday October 7
Time: 7:04am – 6:20pm
Mile: 2006.7 – 2019.5
Miles hiked: 12.8
Tented at East Flagstaff Tent Pads
Weather: Cloudy, warm, cool on the peaks

Day 199 Sunday October 8
Time: 6:10am – 4:54pm
Mile: 2019.5 – 2034.6
Miles hiked: 15.1
Tented at Pierce Pond Lean-to
Weather: Cloudy, rain, cloudy, warm

Day 200 Monday October 9
Time: 5:00am – 9:40am
Mile: 2034.6 – 2038.6
Miles hiked: 4.0
Logdominium at Northern Outdoors
Weather: Crispy morning – cloudy, humid, damp

Day 201 Tuesday October 10
Time: 6:15am – 6:15pm
Mile: 2038.6 – 2053.3
Miles hiked: 14.7
Tented at Bald Mountain Brook Lean-to
Weather: Sunny & windy

Day 202 Wednesday October 11
Time: 6:22am – 4:50pm
Mile: 2053.3 – 2066.3
Miles hiked: 13.0
Tented at Horseshoe Canyon Lean-to
Weather: Sunny, warm, cool when stopped

Day 203 Thursday October 12
Time: 6:11am – 4:00pm
Mile: 2066.3 – 2078.6
Miles hiked: 12.3
Tented at Leeman Brook Lean-to
Weather: Freezing start, sunny, cool

31

Racking Up the Milestones

We didn't need to begin quite so early since we would arrive at our rendezvous spot before Batman, making Day 197, Friday, the first morning start in a long time without a headlamp. Too bad I didn't get a full night's sleep, though. It baffled me how I could be so exhausted yet couldn't fall asleep until the night was almost over. Guess it was no big deal I overslept. One extra hour in a horizontal position is always welcomed.

For someone who claims to be positive, I sure did gripe about a bunch of stuff. I really do lean toward the positive side of life. I wonder if I was actually complaining or I just liked to talk, think, converse, and communicate. And that I was just stating the facts or happenings for the day. Yeah, we'll go with that.

I hadn't complained, I mean *noted,* much about it since the first week on the trail, but my right hip and leg had been causing me great pain at night. It didn't bother me too much while I was up and active, but as soon as I reclined for the night, the pain flared up. That alone was bad enough, but my right arm and hand were also giving me trouble.

I am not one to pop pills or hit the bottle to ease aches and pains, but on the trail, I had a steady diet of ibuprofen, acetaminophen, and sodium naproxen. This medication was only enough to lessen the pain. With all the discomfort though, the biggest challenge for me to overcome was the sleep deprivation the pain caused.

My body wasn't healing overnight like it usually would. My exhaustion was beyond normal. At times I felt like I was in a coma, not aware of my surroundings. I was on autopilot, doing the same thing every day, then repeating. Sure, there were lots of times of joy. How could life get any better? I was living the simple life on a grand adventure with my bestie. But I was wearing out, and if my previous estimate was correct, we still had fifteen more days of hiking.

Shortcake had her own set of symptoms to deal with. I knew her feet gave her pain with each step, and she had quiet pains she never shared, though I knew they were there. But months of aches, pains, and sleepiness did not stop us. We passed the 2,000-mile mark on Day 197, Friday October 6.

When I was a kid, I went to the horse races with my dad. From far up in the grandstand, I always chose the horses who looked like winners. The ones that trotted with pride, heads held high. The ones who were strong and whose muscles twinged as their coats glistened in the sun got my bet—if I could have bet.

I doubt that anyone at Amicalola Falls looking from afar when Shortcake and I started would have laid down any money on us reaching Katahdin. If they did place a bet, it surely would have been against our success. We were two middle-aged empty-nesters, one with some backpacking experience, the other with none. Neither of us were in the best of shape, and we certainly didn't trot up the trail like winners. Who would have *thunk* we would make it that far?

The problem with judging a horse by its size, color, and shape or by judging anyone by their outwardly appearance is that you can't see the person within. You don't know what drives them to excel in the face of adversity. You don't know the passion that pumps the heart to keep going when everything is against them. And you don't know the soul of the person, that keeps them on track. And that's how it was for Shortcake and me. We may not have looked the part in the beginning, but for anyone who had dared to bet on us, they could now laugh all the way to the bank.

We never doubted ourselves. At times, we may have questioned why on earth we were subjecting ourselves to such misery. We then would remember our *why* and push through. As long as we kept our goal in front of us and visioned it, we could keep going. When we let the aches, pains, and challenges take a grip, we'd get discouraged. It was then we knew we had to grab our goal again and dangle it out front.

One comical way we kept the dream alive was to say Jason Statham was meeting us with ice cream. That always motivated us. It had been weeks since we used that little trick. For the last hurdle of the day, we dusted off our go-to motivator and pictured the handsome, buff actor sitting on top of Katahdin with our favorite flavors, one in each hand. It was silly. It was fun. And it worked.

Second day in a row I didn't hear my alarm. I think Shortcake enjoyed it. She didn't serve as a backup alarm and let me sleep. It wasn't like me to oversleep. I was so very tired. My body was shutting down. Every day I chatted with my body parts when they held a tantrum. I told them they couldn't quit yet. We weren't done. I promised them spa treatments after the journey was completed. I guess the last two nights my motivational chats were ignored, and my bag of bones stole an extra hour of sleep from the hiking day.

The extra sleep was needed though. We had a roller-coaster hike planned. We hiked up and over Bigelow Peaks. There are several peaks making up Bigelow Mountain, one of them being Avery Peak. It is named in honor of Myron Avery, who had the vision for the Appalachian Trail.

The peaks were covered in mysterious clouds most of the morning. We prefer the splendid views at the top of summits after a climb, but that day we thoroughly enjoyed the artistic beauty found in the misty blankets.

The clouds gracefully changed as the wind blew them over the contour of the mountains. Sporadically, holes appeared in the cloud cover, exposing the brilliant fall colors below us. This was leaf peeping at its best, and there was no traffic to contend with.

Thanks to skipping my 5:00am wake-up call, we finished in darkness again. I much prefer packing up in the dark over setting up camp by headlamp. With the former, we know what the area looks like. But ending in the dark is much harder. I assigned Batman and Shortcake to set backup alarms. I didn't want a hat trick of sleeping in.

We completed fifteen miles even though the rocks and roots were damp and slick, with occasional snake-pit root sections. We also had rain, the first since returning to the trail after our two-week hiatus in Maine, and even that only lasted a short time midday. We managed to dry off before dark when the temps dropped. We were so blessed with incredible weather.

Peak foliage set the autumn trees ablaze with vibrant colors. Seeing it from within the canopy, I felt like we were in a kaleidoscope. Every hundred yards or so, the trail palette changed. We saw fresh greens and yellows, then we'd turn a corner and it would be oranges and reds. Farther up the trail, it would be muted browns and burgundies. Then back to yellows and greens, and the prism would spin again. It was magnificent. Just another reason fall was my favorite season.

Pierce Pond Lean-to was our destination. The structure sat overlooking Pierce Pond and facing west. We thought about sleeping inside to enjoy the view, but it was too nice of an evening. We arrived early enough to set up outside, leaving the shelter for latecomers. We had been leapfrogging with fellow hikers Foxy, Mantis, and Kit-Kat for several days, and we were sure they'd stroll in after dark.

We claimed spots at the edge of the pond, in front of the lean-to but far enough away as not to hinder the view from inside the structure. It was a beautiful evening. We enjoyed our meals as we watched the setting sun. We also planned an extra-early day—and there could not be any oversleeping. We wanted to be first in line at the river crossing the next day.

———

The hike from Pierce Pond to Caratunk, Maine, was rocky, rooty, and covered with damp leaves. Despite that, it was easy and enjoyable. We meandered along streams most of the way. I love water and never tire of seeing, hearing, and feeling it. There's just something about it I find healing. And I seemed to have needed lots of healing, spiritually, physically, and mentally.

I am strong willed in all areas, but even I get overwhelmed. When I reach the breaking point and can't rely on my inner strength, it's then I remember I can't do it alone. The beauty in nature reminds me of God, and He is my true strength. Water is one of those cues that help me to stay focused on Him.

We were the first ones to reach the Kennebec River. Great! That meant we didn't have to wait in line. We only had to wait for the canoe guide to start the shuttle service. The Appalachian Trail Conservancy hires a registered guide to shuttle hikers across this treacherous water crossing, and October 9 marked the last day for shuttles across this wide river.

Most of the time the river snakes lazily along Route 201, but the depth of the water can rise rapidly and without warning when the hydro company releases water through the dam upriver to generate power. This is good for rafters but not good for hikers. In fact, people have died trying to swim this section.

We arrived before the shuttle service started at 9:00am, giving us time to enjoy the riverbank and have more snacks. We liked any chance to eat. Promptly at 9:00am, Rob, our canoe guide and a friendly chap who obviously loved his job, ferried us to the other shore.

Once the three of us had our boat ride, we continued hiking half a mile to US Route 201, where Batman had parked the Batmobile. Then it was a short 3-mile ride to Northern Outdoors. We arrived way too early for check-in. I wasn't concerned about that. We had chores to do and had access to the laundry room, the main lodge, and the restaurant. What else did we need? Jason and some ice cream maybe?

Timing was everything. Just as we went our separate ways to do chores, it started raining. Thank goodness, we had powered through a 4:00am wake-up. Our early start had earned us first-in-line shuttles, a longer nero day, and a day's hike without getting wet. As much as I like the healing powers of water, the drenching downpour would not have been enjoyable on the trail. Instead, we sought the benefits of hot hydrotherapy as we soaked in the establishment's outdoor hot tub, sipping hot chocolates with a little Irish cream kick.

Batman put us back on trail the next morning then left for another business trip, this time to Canada. We would see him again at the pizza drop north of Monson, a day's hike from the beginning of the 100-Mile Wilderness.

Our hike out of Caratunk was easy, beautiful, and just perfect. The sun was shining. The air was crisp, and the trail offered many colorful sights, from the bright autumn leaves creating a mosaic canopy to the muted colors of the ones that fell and littered the path, creating carpets for us to trod on. A handful of the fuzzy white hickory tussock moth caterpillars crept along the aging fall leaves, looking for just the right one to snack on. Tufts of bright green mosses created a patchwork amongst the thinner layers of dropped leaves. Even my snack of jelly beans provided a rainbow of colors to tantalize our imagination.

———

The nero day followed by easy hiking was just what we needed to lift our spirits and our mojo to carry us through the next section, and one of my favorite hikes was just ahead. Our second day out, we summited Moxie Bald. At only 2,629 feet, it was an easy and delightful climb.

If I have one vice in this world, it's my addiction to Moxie, a carbonated beverage popular among Mainers. Moxie is flavored with gentian root extract, which is very bitter. It's one of those tastes you either love or despise. I am of the prior. Moxie was first produced around 1876 as a medicine called "Moxie Nerve Food." It became one of the first mass-produced soft drinks. The brand shortened the name to just "Moxie," which means audacity, adventurousness, boldness, and daring—the perfect moniker for a drink with such pizzazz.

I wanted to crack open a can of the fuzzy, distinctively different drink at the summit, but I was too lazy to carry it in my pack. I at least was wearing an orange shirt, the signature color for Moxie.

In 2015, I almost took Moxie as my trail name. I am so glad I didn't, because I met a wonderful fellow hiker who was much more deserving of such a name. She and her hiking buddy, Maps, continue to be a special part of my life. Whether I am drinking it, climbing it, or hanging out with friends named it, I just can't get enough Moxie.

Caratunk to Monson is one of my all-time favorite sections. It's remote and a pleasant hike after tackling some of Maine's toughest sections. The forests were beautiful with low climbs that still offered views. I also enjoyed the water fords.

A ford is when hikers must cross a stream without a bridge of some sort. Maine seldom erects bridges over the waterways. The snowmelt and spring run-offs would just destroy bridges, so hikers must walk through the water. It requires the removal of footwear if you want to keep them dry. With any luck, depending on the depths and flow of the current, hikers might be able to rock-hop to the other side. Sometimes there is a rope to assist the hiker through a swiftly moving current. As we moved out of the High Peaks area of Maine to lower elevations, water crossings were becoming an everyday occurrence and would continue so, even several a day.

I didn't mind the fords. Instead of dreading the task as a time suck-er, I looked at it as a chance to soak my tired feet in the cool waters. But I will admit, when you are trying to make the miles, having to take your shoes and socks off several times a day cut into your mph. For this reason, many hikers just walk right though without undressing their feet.

It is also a nice change of pace. I try hard to look at the glass as half full, but as I add years to my youth, I am discovering that not everyone appreciates my positivity. In fact, sometimes it has caused disagree-ments. That I don't understand and never will. How can someone be upset with me for being too positive? I won't let that discourage me though. I will always have a full glass. Even when its empty of liquid, it will be full of air.

We entered the last major section of the Appalachian Trail and probably the most logistically challenging for most thru-hikers—the 100-Mile Wilderness—on October 12, Day 203. Most thru-hikers stop in Monson, Maine, for one last chance of civilization, rest, and resupply. The 100-Mile Wilderness begins here. After Monson, there are no stores or amenities easily reached until hikers exit the wilderness.

Hikers must carry all their food for the trek through the most remote wilderness of the Appalachian Trail, plus carry another two days or 20 miles worth to get them from the end of the 100 miles, through Baxter, and up and down Katahdin. There is one small off-grid store at the exit of the 100-Mile Wilderness, but their goods are slim pickings, depending on how busy they have been with other tourists.

With advances in technology and increased private services, hikers can schedule shuttles and food drops through the 100-Mile Wilderness. It is remote, but it is also heavily trafficked by the logging industry and other outdoor enthusiasts besides hikers. Dirt roads cut through the wilderness, making access to the Appalachian Trail easy for anyone who can read a map and follow locals' directions.

Hikers usually schedule their shuttles and/or food drops while in Monson. Shortcake and I had Batman, so we skipped Monson and continued hiking across Route 15. We would resupply the next day from the Batmobile at a predetermined location easily reached by back roads.

Another week of hiking was in the books. Maine's High Peak summits were enjoyed. We crossed over the 2,000-mile mark; safely navigated the canoe shuttle, making it to Caratunk; then enjoyed a stroll past Monson as we entered the 100-Mile Wilderness. We truly were on autopilot as we racked up the milestones with each step forward.

BLACK BEAR TIP

Keep moving forward! You eventually will make it to your goal.

Trail Log

Day 204 Friday October 13
Time: 6:47am – 4:00pm
Mile: 2078.6 – 2089.5
Miles hiked: 10.9
Tented at Long Pond Stream
Weather: Freezing in morning, sunny,
cool

Day 205 Saturday October 14
Time: 6:04am – 6:48pm
Mile: 2089.5 – 2105.6
Miles hiked: 16.1
Tented at Gulf Hagas parking lot
Weather: Cool & sunny

Day 206 Sunday October 15
Time: 5:55am – 4:21pm
Mile: 2105.6 – 2120.0
Miles hiked: 14.4
Tented at Logan Brook Road
Weather: Cool & cloudy

Day 207 Monday October 16
Time: 5:03am – 3:10pm
Mile: 2120.0 – 2138.0
Miles hiked: 18.0
Tented at Antlers Campsite
Weather: Crispy morning, sunny, cool

Day 208 Tuesday October 17
Time: 5:13am – 5:40pm
Mile: 2138.0 – 2157.2
Miles hiked: 19.2
Tented at Pollywog Stream
Weather: Sunny & windy

Day 209 Wednesday October 18
Time: 5:22am – 4:30pm
Mile: 2157.2 – 2174.7
Miles hiked: 17.5
Tented at Abol Pines State
Campground
Weather: Sunny, warm, cool when
stopped

Day 210 Thursday October 19
Time: 5:05am – 11:20am
Mile: 2174.7 – 2184.6
Miles hiked: 9.9
Tented at Katahdin Stream
Campground
Weather: Freezing start, sunny, cool

Day 21 Friday October 20
Time: 5:00am – 3:45pm
Mile: 2184.6 – 2189.8 plus 5.2 back
down
Miles hiked: 10.4
Slept at home
Weather: Cloudy start, sunny, cool,
WINDY

32

Katahdin

Temperatures were consistently getting cooler and below-freezing overnight temps were the norm. It was a nice relief. Cold nights made for great sleeping, and with the aid of air-activated hand warmers, packing up in the chilly mornings was manageable.

The cooler weather was a result of the almost cloudless skies. The stark blue canvas backdrop behind the kaleidoscope of trees made for beautiful days of hiking in the Maine woods. Being surrounded by such beauty helped us forget all the yuck we had endured together and in the silence of our own hearts. It was easy to get into the zone and crank out the miles.

It was maybe a little too easy. We were so focused that I almost lost my Shortcake. I stopped to de-layer, and while I did, I noticed there was cell service, so I contacted Batman to confirm our meet-up location and approximate time. After I was done, I continued to catch up to Shortcake. I usually did so within a short time.

Since our little cat fight and miscommunication, I no longer hiked ahead. When I felt the need to stretch or hike faster with longer strides, I would pause briefly to tend to miscellaneous needs or take a mini break. This would create distance between us. Then I would stretch at my own pace and catch up.

But after my call to Batman, it seemed to take longer than normal to catch Shortcake. I assumed my timeout was longer than I had thought. So I hiked faster and harder to close the distance to her. Wow! She must have kicked it into high gear! So I sped up even more, almost running. Still no Shortcake in sight!

It was well past our regular break time, and I had already gone by several spots that would have been ideal for a break. I was concerned. I should have reached her by then, and I knew she would not have resisted the temptation to rest at one of those ideal spots. I decided to sit and take a break. With my *sprinting*, I needed rest and food before I could continue. While I was sitting on a root in the middle of the trail, I thought I heard something, but the crows were squawking so I dismissed it.

Now I had a dilemma, do I go back or continue forward? My decision was made for me. Way, way off in the distance, I heard a faint, "Blaaaccckkk Beeeaaarrr, wheeere arrre yooouuu?" Shortcake had taken a wrong turn. I had passed her and didn't know it. She knew I was in front of her because she saw me, but due to the mossy forest and roller-coaster terrain, I did not hear her calling out for the last couple of hours. That was a little scary.

It's comical, now that we are both safe. She was in the zone and missed a turn. I was zoomed in on catching her as fast as I could, not knowing I was ahead. I wasn't paying any attention to the sounds of the forest. Then she was cruising trying to catch up to me. There's always something new on the trail to overcome. So now, instead of playing *Marcoooo Poloooo*, we play *Blaack Beeaar, where are youuuuuu?*

We ended our first full day in the 100-Mile Wilderness at what we have dubbed "The Pizza Drop." In 2015, Batman delivered pizza there to my hiking buddies and me via an unmarked trail for Barren Ledges. Then we delivered pizza at the same place for our exchange student from Germany, our honorary *third* son, Aaron, who came back to visit and hiked the 100-Mile Wilderness. We have continued to deliver pizza there to other hikers as well as to our son Patch when he hiked in 2022.

Batman was not there when Shortcake and I arrived, so we set up camp and waited for him. We didn't mind that he was late. After all, you can't bite the hand that feeds you. He was delivering pizza.

With tummies full and another cool night, we would be off to Gulf Hagas the next day with less than full packs. Slackpacking again. Slackpacking in the 100-Mile Wilderness, what a treat. Shortcake and I had it so good with Batman's help. Don't think for one minute we didn't have what it took to do that without his assistance. We've already proven that we did. But it sure was nice to shed weight when we could.

Maine has interesting and redundant names for their peaks, as I mentioned earlier. Sometimes a mountain may have a wide base with several distinct peaks. In this case, the summits all use the same name with add-ons such as South Crocker and North Crocker, or Bigelow Mountain Horn, Bigelow Mountain Avery Peak, Bigelow West Peak, or Goose Eye East, West and North Peaks. My favorite names of peaks were a set in the 100-Mile Wilderness: Fourth Mountain, Third Mountain, and poor Three and a Half Mountain, that didn't even get a summit sign.

I amused myself and Shortcake with trying to figure out how they came up with such names. I could picture old-timers sitting around a logging or hunting camp, trying to give directions to a fellow harvester or hunter. I gave my best impression of a Maine accent as I ad-libbed a complete conversation of how a certain mountain range was named. This would entertain me for hours.

Nature also entertained me, as it usually did. Wonderfully crafted pitcher plants sat waiting for their next meal before the cool temps killed off any last surviving insects. Red spruce trees, adorned with mini cones, looked as if someone had just finished trimming their Christmas tree.

After almost thirteen hours of hiking, we arrived in the dark. As was his normal routine, Batman had leapfrogged the car and our gear ahead, then hiked south to meet us. We camped in the parking lot of Gulf Hagas, a very popular hiking spot. Batman told us when he arrived the place had been packed. By the time we got there, all the visitors had left except one car. Since the parking lot was almost vacant, we decided to set up in the parking lot to make things quicker and easier for us in the morning. We didn't take up any extra space as we set up our tents between the vehicle and the tree line, only taking up what space anyone would normally need to access their car. Besides, we were heading out before sunrise and the gate didn't even open until 6:00am.

Some people thought we were crazy to keep the schedule we had been on. Early morning starts, hiking all day with little rest, then hiking until dark on most days. But we were focused, and it was the little treasures like the anomalies of the spruce tree that feed our desire to keep pushing to our goal of Katahdin.

The mountain usually closed October 15, but since the year was unseasonably warm and dry, Baxter State Park stayed open until October 22. It was a blessing. Under normal circumstances, we would not have been able to finish our thru-hike. Our late start back in March, combined with taking time off for the movie and then the long two weeks for my dad, had us way behind the eight-ball. But with the great weather and the closure date pushed out, nothing could stop us.

You never know what you will see in the woods. A plastic Dalmatian sat on a large rock above the trail like a gargoyle, keeping watch over the forest. He was not easily spotted. Haha, no pun intended. But he was not hidden either. Neither Shortcake nor Batman saw him. A few yards from the dog's post, I had a flashback, as I so often did. I remembered he was there, so I knew to look up. There he sat, just as vigilant in 2017 as he was in 2015.

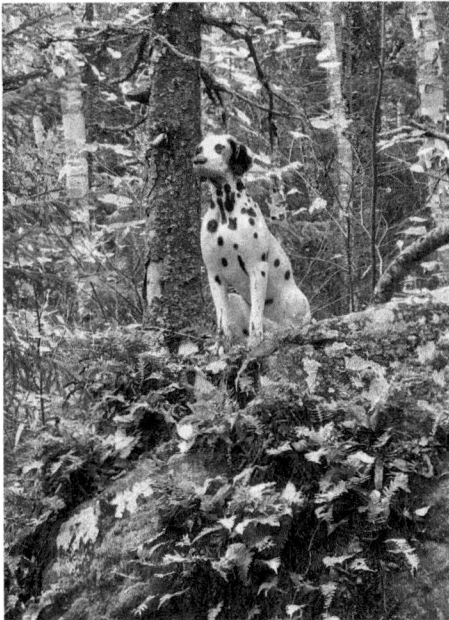

I am not one for non-natural items to be left in the woods. I take to heart the Leave No Trace principles, and I don't like seeing man-made stuff left on the trail. But even I found a little joy in this. The dog's placement was inconspicuous and only would be spotted by an observant visitor to that part of the wilderness.

We were supposed to see our first view of Katahdin at some point in the 100-Mile Wilderness, but Mother Nature kept that first glimpse from us. We crossed over the flat peak of White Cap Mountain and didn't even bother to tread out to the view. The mountain was socked in with fog. That was the least of our worries. The wind whipped and howled around us, giving me another flashback to when Shortcake and I traversed the open balds of Big and Little Hump in hurricane winds. I was grateful it was easy terrain. Hiking in that wind on a steep mountain incline would not have been fun.

We arrived at our destination, a dirt road far from civilization but not out of Batman's scope, successfully completing our second full day in the 100-Mile Wilderness.

There was absolutely nothing to complain about. The sun shined, the air was crisp and cool, and the terrain was kind to us. It wasn't all flat, but it was pretty darn sweet. Days like that were why I gritted through all the other yuck. One day of heaven wipes away all the other days of hell.

The day before, we had a choice to make. Since Batman's return, we had been slackpacking, but if we wanted to continue with such luxury through the remainder of the 100-Mile Wilderness, we had to do an 18-mile day, followed by a 19.2-miler, finishing with a 17.5-mile day—no matter what the weather was or what the terrain was. If we could do that, we would be able to summit on our present ETA, the date I had predicted way back that we might summit.

We chose to go for it! With a 4:00am alarm, we were up, packed, and ready to rock and roll by 5:03am. The day was gorgeous, and we easily did our miles, finishing early in the afternoon. We camped at Antlers Campsite on Jo-Mary Lake, among tall slender pines, on ground carpeted with pine needles. It would have been perfect except for the wind howling and blowing again.

We ended the evening with a wonderful meal and hot cider. We retired early, and our heads were on our pillows by 5:15pm. We needed to rest hard and fast so we could tackle the next day's 19-miler.

We were given a mixture of surprises that next day. The smooth, leaf-covered trail made us feel like we were in heaven. Then we had rocky sections to remind us we were still here on Earth. And then, we finally were treated to our first view of Katahdin. It was that view that made us realize why the Penobscot Indigenous people named the mountain Katahdin. It means, *the Greatest One.*

There wasn't much of a trail to the lake's edge, but I knew in my heart that from the shore I'd be able to see the crown jewel of Maine, Katahdin. I led Shortcake to the lake shore over the not-so-safe path. Once there, we had to make our way across a few large boulders to gain a clear line of sight. I hoisted myself up onto a large rock and inched as close to the far edge as possible without falling in. I couldn't get close enough to the mountain. I just sat there in awe of her. The hike had been so long and often extremely painful, mentally and physically. While I sat there, I was for a moment pain free.

This was by far the most treasured gift of the day, but there were more to follow. We walked around beautiful Nahmakanta Lake. It's a long, narrow lake, and the trail follows the southern shore. At one point, we left the edge of the lake and climbed up through a rugged, forested gorge. Once at the top, we were offered another view of Katahdin way off in the distance.

Another wonder of the day was a spectacular display of courtship by a spruce partridge. He was strutting his stuff right in the middle of the trail for two fair ladies sitting in the branches. He was not bothered by our voyeurism. In fact, at one time I thought he was dancing for us also.

The last surprise was almost as great as the first view of Katahdin. When we arrived at our destination with not much time before the sun set, we saw our tents already erected. THANKS, BATMAN, YOU ROCK! A 19.2-mile day, and we didn't even have to set up our own tents.

Our last day in the 100-Mile Wilderness was an easy hike. We left bright and early after our 4:00am wake-up call. We packed up the car and enjoyed yet another day of slacking. Batman drove 25 miles on the dirt road to get back to pavement. He had errands to do and a food run that would take him into Millinocket.

After another long dirt-road drive, he arrived at the state campground by Abol Bridge, where the 100-Mile Wilderness exits. He once again had our tents set up. Every hiker should have a Batman. I couldn't imagine what that type of service would cost if you were to hire it out. Smiles on our faces was all the compensation he needed, though.

The trail hovered around 1,100 feet of elevation with one little bump as we easily hiked up Rainbow Ledges to 1,500 feet. The flat plateau of its peak was dotted with various-sized rocks, bushes, and short trees. It resembled a garden jungle gym waiting to be explored and played upon.

Maine does fabulous work on their trails. In numerous spots, trail builders have constructed incredible stone pavers, stone steps, and even log ladders. It's just lovely, and very much appreciated. A huge shout-out to the men and women who volunteer their time to do such laborious work. But nothing compares to the natural beauty the trail exhibits with her flora, fauna, and bedrock that naturally occur up and down the trail.

It was a blessed day from the start. Soon after the sun appeared, there was debris lying on a rock in the form of a cross. It was tiny and easily overlooked, but my keen eye spotted it. I felt it was a sign just for me. While the past several days had been going well, I still wanted this hike to be over. I was so tired of everything. I was beginning to be annoyed by little things. Through no fault of hers, I felt myself wanting to snap at Shortcake. But when I glanced down and saw the cross, a soft voice whispered in my head, "All is well." It was a true sign from above. Wow! My heart filled with warmth instantly.

————

All our days are a gift, but it was reassuring to see that little sign. We take so much for granted in life, with all the hustle and bustle it brings. Sometimes we need gentle reminders of just how blessed we are.

Life isn't all that great at times. Sometimes it's downright horrible. When it's good, we carry on and enjoy the moment, not wanting for anything. But when it's bad, we wish for a better life or, in some cases, no life at all. We cannot rely on our own strength; we are too weak. We must call on God, even if we feel at times that He has abandoned us. We gain strength when we surrender and turn to our Creator to help us through the difficult times. This would be easier to do if we also gave Him credit for the good times instead of ignoring where our blessings come from. God isn't a tool we put on the shelf and only bring down when we need it. He is our friend, with whom we share the good and the bad, just like we want to do with any friend—except He will never hurt or leave us.

With all the goodness around me that day, I was still feeling lonely and down. The twig cross was just what I needed to get me out of my slump. I am glad I was open to receive it.

We ended the day at the famous Golden Road at Abol Bridge. So many iconic photos of Katahdin have been taken there, including my own. It was a clear day, and not a cloud hindered the view of our goal. It would have been a great day to summit, but we were still a day away from taking on The Greatest One.

On our last day of regular hiking we completed a 9.9-mile stroll through one of the easiest and most scenic spots on the entire Appalachian Trail. We knew this section would be a breeze to complete, but we chose to get up at our usual early time so we could enjoy an afternoon of R&R on the other end, before our summit hike the next day.

We headed out once again guided by our lamps, meandering along the river, where we watched the sunrise as it burned off the morning mist. There was so much water. Rivers, streams, ponds, small tributaries, and waterfalls led us through the forest. What a way to end this great adventure.

The trail opened up to a beautiful area where the water was calm on the upstream side, almost stagnant, then it flowed thunderously over the smooth ledge and emptied downstream to a pool with a beach. We could see a trail across the shallow, ledgy water at the top of the falls, but we were hesitant to cross because the flow was so fast and the rocks were mossy. The water was no more than a couple inches deep, and we really wanted to access the beach for our morning snack. But we decided to munch on our food before tackling the crossing.

With our calories devoured, we also needed a potty break before making the risky top-of-the-falls water crossing. I hiked back down the trail from the direction we had come to do my duties far from the water source. As I did, I noticed the trail actually continued in a different direction and not across the falls. We had noticed the double white blaze that denoted a turn, so we had turned. Unlike other states that offset their double blazes in the direction of the upcoming turn, Maine doesn't. When we saw the double, we turned. We were not fazed by the crossing because Maine also has few bridges across water, so we thought it was just another ford. In reality, the trail went straight and the turn we thought was the trail was just a side trail to see the waterfall. A little confusing. Wow, that could have been bad!

I had another blessing reminder. No one else could see it, or they didn't notice it the way I did. I love it when the sun shines down through the trees in a majestic way. To me it looks like the arms of God reaching out to hug me. He sure was giving me signs that all was well and to remember my why of why I was out there and not let the petty stuff get in the way.

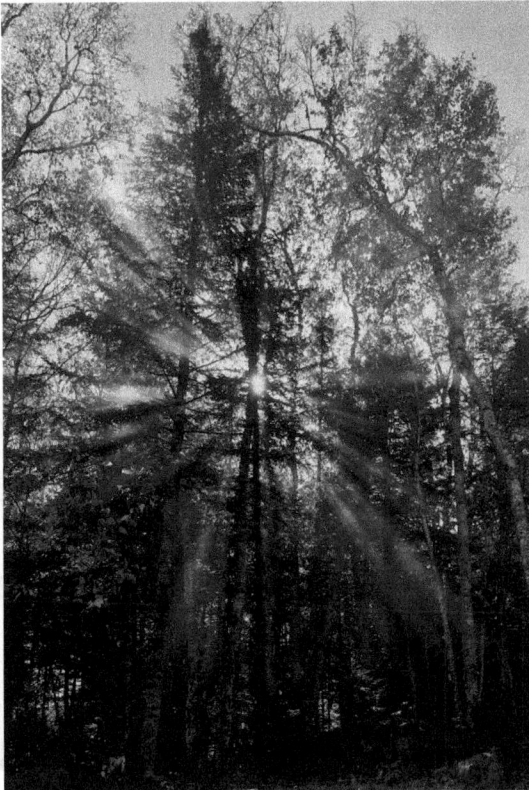

We made it to Katahdin Stream Campground by 11:20am, with plenty of time to set up camp and enjoy our last evening in the woods. Most hikers stay at the Birches, two tenths of a mile from the trail. It is for thru-hikers only. We opted to reserve a campsite at Katahdin Stream. The A.T. goes right through Katahdin Stream Campground, so we didn't have to do any extra steps.

We had a wonderful afternoon just chilling around a fire. I even cooked us hamburgers and rice, thanks to Batman, who brought us real food. It was my last gourmet trail cooking for the journey. I had made lots of tasty meals on the trail back in the beginning but gave it up for a lighter pack and when I didn't feel like hot food in hot weather. But our last night on trail deserved something special.

I couldn't believe we were almost done! It had been a very long 7 months, and we were finally down to our last night in the woods. I had mixed emotions. I loved it out there, but I wanted to rest. My body had gone on strike weeks ago. And I wanted to get home to finish grieving for my dad. Not that that ever ends, but there were things I needed to do. I was glad we were summiting the next day. I couldn't wait to climb Katahdin once again. I love that mountain!

We kept to our early schedule of waking up before the sun did. Headlamps pierced the darkness one white blaze at a time. We made it to the first opening in the forest, but not quite to the tree line. The blank canopy of the night faded away from pink to tangerine to light blue over the distant mountain range we had spent the last several days hiking.

Less than half an hour later, we made it to the challenging, nerve-racking, and exposed rock scramble of the Hunt Trail, which is the trail the A.T. follows to the northern terminus on top of Katahdin. It's like traversing Mahoosuc Notch, only vertical. There we stowed our poles. Hands, feet, knees, and any other point of contact was needed to make the climb. One wouldn't fall off the mountain, but a wrong step or mis-handhold could send one down in a nasty tumble.

We climbed the rocky spine up, up, and up until we crested the upper, flatter spot. We passed the junction for the Abol Trail, the one we would descend. Then it was on to the tablelands, a relatively flat plateau completely exposed with a slight grade. Nothing but pink granite rocks, worn of any lichen by years of hikers treading on them, marked the trail with the iconic painted white blaze every several yards. The stones on the mountain varied in size from pebbles to five-gallon-bucket-sized ones, with occasional large rogue ones that looked out of place.

The almost cloudless sky provided no relief from the sun. If it wasn't for the fact that we needed several layers to thwart the buffeting wind, we would have fried. The way we were dressed looked like we were hiking in the Artic, but we were far from cold. Shortcake even stowed her signature cupcake hat in fear of losing it to the mountain's gale winds. It was any wonder she could see where she was going; her warm brunette locks tousled about her crown untamed as Mother Nature gave her an up, down, and sideways hairdo.

Batman scurried ahead to capture the ending with his iPhone. Shortcake was in the lead by a few steps. We had begun our journey in that order, and we would end our journey in the same manner. As we made our way to the weatherworn summit sign, I slowed my pace and eventually stopped, giving my friend space to claim the prize however she was so moved. She hung back about a yard, taking in the sign and her accomplishments before approaching it. Surrendering herself to the sign, she rested her upper torso on the right side of the wooden structure. Her windblown hair hid her face as she nestled her head on the structure. It was as if the sign was comforting her.

I approached on the left, mirroring her posture as I reached out and attempted to tuck her wayward locks away from her face. I then gave a sisterly tap on her nose and a that-a-girl pat on the shoulder before extending my hand open to receive hers. She reached over, and we held hands as our tired bodies seemed to revive with life from the sign. We stood there for what seemed like a lifetime as the wind howled around us, flapping the straps of our packs and everything else that was dangling free.

Five and a half hours. That's how long it took us to climb to Baxter Peak, Maine's tallest and grandest mountain, on top of Katahdin.

Emotions were high, ranging from pure joy to sadness. We were ecstatic that we had accomplished such a quest, and we were glad it was almost over. We still had to climb down. But we were also sad because it was over.

———

No cleverly crafted words could summarize that day. On March 20, 2017, two middle-aged women set out on a journey that was four years in the making. A year before that, such a quest was not even on either of our radars. Odds were not in our favor. But there we were, standing on top of Katahdin, the northern terminus for the Appalachian Trail, seven months after our first steps.

We saw one solo hiker who came from the Saddle Trail and cruised past the summit sign, then hiked away via the Knife Edge Trail without even stopping. Then a duo of college-age girls summited, but also didn't stay long. Except for those three other hikers, the mountain was quiet except for the roar of the wind. We cherished our solitude at 5,268 feet. It is a rare experience to have clear skies on top of the mountain, and then to have it all to oneself is even more rare.

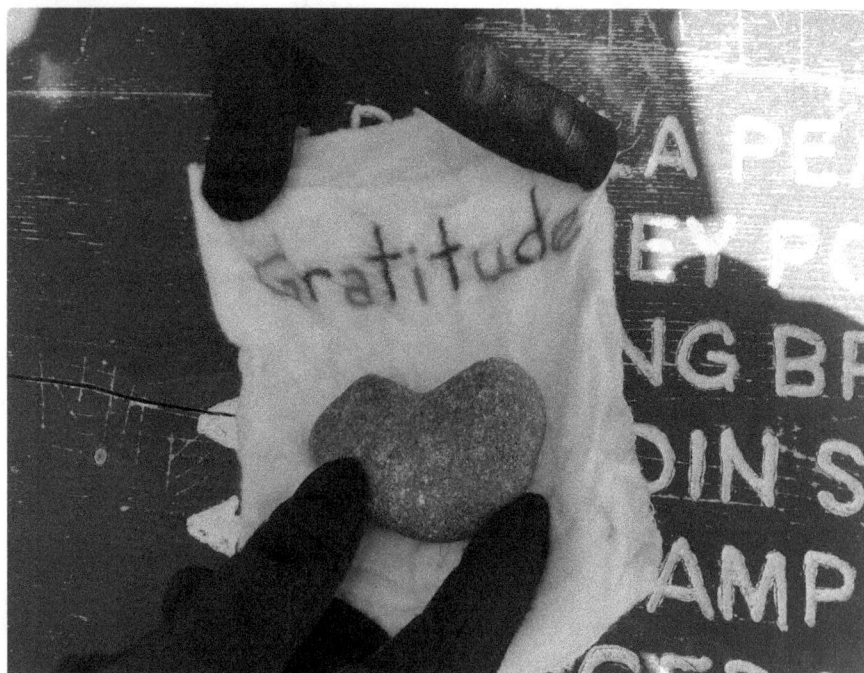

Before leaving, we did as most hikers do when they bag a summit, and that was to pose with the sign. We did individual photos as well as group photos. I also pulled out the little stone I had been carrying since Day 1, a heart-shaped stone in a little cloth bag with the word *Gratitude* written on it. It was my tribute to The Summit Project, the organization that honors Maine fallen heroes.

Carrying the stone of a fallen hero was not possible, so instead I had chosen a stone of my own and named it *Gratitude*. At that moment in time, standing at the summit, I was not only grateful for all the men and women who sacrificed everything so others might have a better life, I was thankful for so much more. I was grateful Shortcake invited me on her journey. I was thankful for the amazing man I married who helped us complete our trek. I was thankful for my God, who loves me and gently would remind me that all would be well even though I didn't always feel like it would be. I was grateful for all the friends, family, trail angels, fellow hikers, and strangers who encouraged us along the way. But most of all, I was grateful for the hero I called Dad, who I knew was looking down on us, smiling, knowing that we made it.

―――――

We could have stayed there for hours, but we still didn't have that kind of luxury. Katahdin is not a place one wants to be at night without proper gear. It wasn't even noon when we headed down, but as we enjoyed the summit and our success, the temperatures steadily dropped. We did not want to experience the whipping winds combined with low temps, so we left the mountain to herself.

We chose to descend by way of Abol Trail; it was quicker and less challenging than the way we came up. It would put us two miles from the car, but that's what we had Batman for. The hike down was quiet. We talked very little. Even if we would have felt chattier, the wind made it hard to hear. Lost in our own thoughts, we slowly made our way back to tree line. At one point I heard a loud *thud!* I turned around to see Batman sitting on the trail, legs out in front of him, stunned and not moving. My breath hung in my lungs, choked by my squeezing diaphragm as I momentarily panicked.

Realizing he had tumbled, I rushed to him. He shook off the dazed look that overtook his face and reassured me he was okay. Before he stood, I glanced down and saw the nub of a freshly cut tree about the size of my index finger sticking out of the trail a mere inch from where his tailbone had landed. *GRATITUDE* was all I could think. I hugged him tightly and helped him to his feet.

Thankfully, that was the only scare for the remainder of the hike, and at 3:47pm on October 20, 2017, we reached the trailhead and completed our thru-hike. And just like that, it was over.

BLACK BEAR TIP

Keep God in your heart, and He will remind you in dark times that all will be well as you hike toward your dreams and goals.

Sharon "Shortcake" Cassidy

Epilogue

*E*ver since I stepped foot on the Appalachian Trail in 2015, I have evolved faster than at any other time of my existence. My life is wonderful, without any major trials or tribulations other than what I guess you could call *normal* challenges.

I grew up in a lower-middle-class household with two loving parents and six siblings, where hard work and determination were taught and excuses were not accepted. Life was simple and without frills, yet we lacked nothing. The usual growing pains of youth existed. School was a challenge, trying to balance academics, sports, and friendships; many times failing at all three. Then the era of college brought on new hurdles to navigate. Finding my own way and—as a special friend likes to tease—earning my MRS degree as well as a BS degree took all the attention I had. The fun began as I started a new life with the love of my life, Bruce, known in the previous pages as Batman. Soon followed a career and kids. It wasn't a cheesy romance Christmas movie, but pretty darn close. Life truly couldn't get any better.

But it did. Fast forward through child raising, and with one simple text from a dear friend and fellow soon-to-be empty-nester, my world was rocked. You can read all about that in my first memoir, *Happy Hiking: Falling in Love on the Appalachian Trail*. Over the course of six months in 2015, my paradigm shifted. Sure, I still was the same gal. I was still madly in love with my hubby. And my kids were the reason for my existence. But as time separated me from my summit, I recognized how I had changed.

I couldn't see it at first. It wasn't until I finally recognized the conundrum that was happening to me. With the help and support of Bruce and our doctor, I realized I was suffering from depression. This ah-ha moment didn't occur until after my second hike, *Happy Hiking Take 2: On the Appalachian Trail with Shortcake.* The trail had changed me, yet when I returned home after my summit in 2015, I had just gone back to life as it was pre-hike, and my inner being was protesting. My spirit cried out for the new and improved me that developed on the trail. As I write this, I still don't know exactly what that is, other than I am not the same person now as I was before my Appalachian Trail adventures. Struggling with feelings I didn't understand, I escaped to the trail again, this time with Sharon, a.k.a. Shortcake, for my second go-around on the A.T.

For a host of reasons, it took me five years to commit to completing my first book and almost seven years to complete my second memoir. At first, I was disappointed in myself for not finishing them in a timely manner. But as I look back over my manuscript, tweaking here and there, I realize the end products of both may very well have been completely different if written right after each hike rather than allowing time to do its work on my thoughts.

The linear story would be intact, but I am sure the essence of the hike would have been totally different. Time has a way of healing most wounds. It's not really the time that is the healer but our own understanding of the situation and circumstances that does the healing. For me and others with a spiritual nature, we know that when we let God into our lives, He helps us to see what we can't see on our own. When we are in the midst of something—let's call that something pain—our emotions get in the way. But as we remove ourselves from that pain either by time, distance, or both, our emotions subside to reasoning, that which God wants us to see.

During my first hike, I complained all the time. I was one and done and never hiking again. I had a difficult time separating the great adventure from the current agony. I had to force myself to see the joy in the little things. I didn't do this on my own. God kept showing me, and as long as I was open to His creation, I could see it even amid all the yuck. If I would have written my book as soon as I unpacked, I would have been focused on the wrong story. It was over time and looking back at all the blessings I had encountered that I found the gifts the trail unlocked to me.

The same held true in completing this book. The story started out great: two best friends on a grand adventure. I strived so hard to keep the focus on Sharon since it was her debut hike. I wanted her to experience all she could without my interference. I did well for a while. But who was I fooling? That stopped when the honeymoon faded away and I allowed the yuck of the trail and my selfishness to seep in. When we finished the hike, I was so glad to be done. This is the first time I am admitting it. I couldn't take being together yet alone any longer.

Still suffering from post-trail depression of the first hike and not knowing that's what it was, losing my dad and all the family drama that goes along with that, and being lonely even though I was with my best friend for months on end, was all so much more than I could take. I needed off the trail asap. But things didn't improve. They got worse. It wasn't until I had help understanding what I was experiencing and getting my selfish eyes off myself that I began to feel a change. Slowly I began writing *Happy Hiking Take 2*. I would do a few days at a time then put it aside for weeks and sometimes months. These last two years, I dove right in to finish this epic story with new eyes and a new heart. Some days I am so ashamed of the feelings I had during the hike. I wrote the journey as I was feeling while it happened, but today I see the trip completely differently.

During our hike, my lips may have said, "This is about Shortcake," but my selfishness overtook too many moments and made it about me. I am so glad circumstances prevented me from writing this in a timely manner. As I have spent the last several months concentrating on completing this story, I have been able to see our hike for the amazing gift that it was. My in-the-moment notes I took while hiking may have sparked the content and were reminders of the yuck, but it was going through the thousands of photos and videos that brought back all the little things that reminded me of the joy. If only there was a scratch-and-sniff app to bring all the senses together. Except for the farts in the tent. We don't need reminders of that.

Time does heal if we let it. I could have remained irritated about those final days. Heck, I am sure I did many things that irritated Sharon. She even called them my *issues*. She was being polite. But life is too short to let pettiness interfere with a life well lived. It's time that has taught me that. Time spent away from painful situations. Time spent enjoying the little things. Time spent letting God show me His way of thinking and not mine. And time spent doing so many other things I would not have done if not for hiking the Appalachian Trail.

I was forty-nine when I did my first Appalachian Trail thru-hike and fifty-one the second time. It's now almost ten years since my first hike (my math). In the past ten years—let's call that A.T. time, about one third of my life (my math again)—I have learned and evolved more than the first two thirds of my life. The trail has taught me things about life that no lecture or conference ever could. The Appalachian Trail truly is more than a walk in the woods. If you know someone who has done such an adventure, raise your glass to them. It doesn't make them better than anyone else; but I can almost guarantee, it did make them better than when they first stepped foot on the trail.

Trail Language

A.T. – Appalachian Trail

ATC – Appalachian Trail Conservancy

AYCE – all you can eat buffet

Bald – an open area at high elevation

Bank Deposit – going poop

Bear Line – what you use to hang your food bag to keep it safe from animals

Blue Blazes – mark side trails or other trails that are not the Appalachian Trail

Blue Blazing – hiking alternate routes other than the white-blazed A.T.

Bubble – the hikers who are hiking around each other at any given point in time

Bushwhacking – hiking off trail to go around a hazard or for some other reason

Cathole – the hole you dig when you have to poop in the woods and there isn't a bathroom

Cairn – specially formed pile of rocks marking the trail

Camel-up – drinking water when there is a source because it's easier to carry it in you than on you

CDT – Continental Divide Trail

Flip-flop - hiking the trail in discontinuous sections

Ford – It's not a truck. It's crossing water without a bridge.

GORP – a hikers custom made trail mix

Half-gallon Challenge – eating a half-gallon of ice cream at the halfway point

Hiker Midnight – time for bed, usually when the sun goes down or earlier, because hiking is tiring

Hiking Poles – long, sturdy tools to assist hikers; help with stability

Hostel – usually shared accommodations at lower rates than hotels and motels

LASHER – long a** section hiker

Leapfrogging – passing the same hiker(s) randomly as you hike and then they pass you

LNT – Leave No Trace

Mail Drop/Bounce Box – Packages you mail to yourself or bounce ahead to your next stop

Naked Hiking Day – hiking naked on the summer solstice

Nero – a day with relatively few miles hiked

NOBO – hiking northbound

Pack – the item hikers use to carry all their gear on their back

PCT – Pacific Crest Trail

Pink Blazing – when male hikers chase female hikers, hoping to hook up

Post-holing – sinking into the snow while hiking

Privy – rustic bathroom/outhouse

PUDS – when the trail has what seems like Pointless Ups and Downs

Safety Meeting – smoke break of the wacky kind

Second Breakfast – comes soon after first breakfast because hikers get hungry

Section-Hiker – a hiker who pieces sections of the trail together over time

Shelters – usually three-sided structures on the trail for hikers to sleep in

SOBO – hiking southbound

Stealth – camping inconspicuously off trail, not at a designated campsite

Stove – small device that produces heat for cooking

Switchbacks – trail design to make inclines easier, seldom used in Maine

Terminus – the beginning or end of the trail

Thru-Hiker – a hiker who hikes a long trail continuously end to end

Trail Angel – someone who provides hikers with free food, services, or other acts of kindness

Trail-aversary – the anniversary of your long-distance hike completion

Trail Legs – when a hiker has developed strong legs and stamina

Trail Magic – unexpected serendipity gifts provided to hikers from trail angels

Trail Name – a nickname hikers use while hiking

Tramily – hikers who have become your trail family

Triple Crown – someone who has hiked the AT, PCT, & CDT

Turtling – when you need to go poop and you start to go before you make it to the bathroom

Water Filter – device used to purify drinking water from streams and ponds

Vitamin I – Ibuprofen

White Blaze – a white mark 2"×6" painted on trees to denote the A.T.

Yellow Blazing – following the road instead of the A.T.

Yogiing – being able to score food from someone without asking for it

Yo-yoing – Finishing a thru-hike, then turning around and completing it in the opposite direction

Zero day – a day without hiking

Bruce "Batman" Leonard

Emily "Black Bear" Leonard

More From The Author

Children's Books

Memoirs

Devotionals

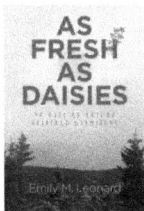

Coming 2026
Butterfly Kisses

Other

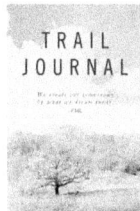 

WALKING HOME

Maine Outdoor
Film Festival
Award Winner
2018

Produced by
Ryan Leighton
&
Cody Mitchell

This photo is from chapter 32 and is my most popular print ordered. My photos were taken on hiking trips, most of them while I thru-hiked the Appalachian Trail. When I first started selling my prints, I wasn't too successful. They were just another picture in an already flooded market. At my shows, I began sharing the story behind each print. My sales increased. The photos, along with their stories, became personal for the buyer. While I don't always know who will purchase the item, I do have them in my heart.

The day I took this photo I was having a tough time. My hiking partner had been in a bad mood for several days and it was wearing on me. I just wanted the hike to be done. The trail didn't help since it was extra rooty and rocky. And to make things worse the weather wasn't so pleasant, and it was very windy. As I was having a pity party, I looked down and saw this cross on the trail. With the wind, I was amazed that the debris had remained that way for me to see. I knew in my heart Jesus was telling me all would be well.

This story sparked a fuller version that I published in my devotional *As Fresh As Daisies.* Each print comes with a color 4.5" x 5.5" note card with the full devotional. To purchase prints, go to my website EmilysEscapades.com or scan the code below.

Black Bear and Shortcake 2017

What's Next?

If you enjoyed reading this story,
please leave a review.

Amazon.com

Goodreads.com

Thank you,

Emily "Black Bear" Leonard